THE CASE FOR
DIVINE DESIGN

THE CASE FOR
DIVINE DESIGN
Cells, Complexity, and Creation

By Frank B. Salisbury

Computer-drawn illustrations
by Tami Allen Salisbury

CFI
Springville, Utah

ISBN 13: 978-1-55517-900-2
ISBN 10: 1-55517-900-2

Published by CFI, an imprint of Cedar Fort, Inc., 925 N. Main, Springville, UT, 84663
Distributed by Cedar Fort, Inc. www.cedarfort.com

LIBRARY OF CONGRESS CATALOGING-IN-PUBLICATION DATA

Salisbury, Frank B.
    The case for divine design / by Frank B. Salisbury ; computer drawn illustrations by Tami Allen Salisbury.
        p. cm.
    Includes bibliographical references and index.
    ISBN 1-55517-900-2 (pbk. : alk. paper)
    1. Creationism. 2. Creation. 3. Evolution (Biology)--Religious aspects--Christianity. I. Title.

    BS651.S3163 2006
    213--dc22

                        2006013646

Cover design by Nicole Williams
Cover design © 2006 by Lyle Mortimer
Printed in the United States of America

10 9 8 7 6 5 4 3 2 1

Printed on acid-free paper

DEDICATION

To my wife, Mary Thorpe Salisbury, who stood by me through the years that I prepared this book and who never wavered in her faith that it would some day see the light of day. And to all those who need to know something about how our world works and about the intelligent Creator who watches over us and our fellow organisms.

TABLE OF
CONTENTS

PREFACE

Our world is one of conflicting philosophies about many things. This book is concerned with two philosophies of Creation: Do we live in a no-God (*atheistic*) universe in which our world was the result of natural laws operating over vast time intervals, resulting in life, including even the brains that allow us to consider it? Or is there a Supreme Being, an Intelligent Creator, a God who exists and in some way was responsible for Creation—in my own philosophy—by guiding Creation through application of those natural laws?[1]

Philosophy is a broad term with many meanings in any dictionary. I like the German word *weltanschauung* (literally, *worldview*), sometimes used in our English language. It comes closer in its English and its German usage to what I mean by a worldview philosophy. *The American Heritage Dictionary* defines weltanschauung (vĕlt´än´shou´ŏong) as "a comprehensive worldview, especially from a specified standpoint." In German usage, it is a kind of universal way of looking at who we are, why we are here, and how the rest of our universe got here, based on intuition or scientific knowledge.[2]

A weltanschauung of an *Intelligent Creation* provides one good example:

a specific philosophy involving a role for God in Creation. The contrasting weltanschauung is that intelligence was *not* involved in how life and the universe came into being. In this book, I'll hold that science can neither prove nor disprove either weltanschauung. Yet, clearly, we must consider science in developing our personal views because science (especially biology) is giving us great insight into how our world functions. Actually, we'll see that *both* of these views are *consistent* with the findings of modern biology; hence, the findings of biology cannot *eliminate* either weltanschauung. Our views must of necessity be highly personal. I'm writing this book because my own weltanschauung includes an Intelligent Creator, God, who guided—engineered, actually—the Creation in which we find ourselves. I'll expand on these ideas in chapter 1.

This book is not an anti-evolutionary diatribe. Indeed, the case for evolution at some level is overwhelming as we'll see in chapter 2—but a conclusion, based on evolution, that Creation was atheistic (no-God) is not as conclusive as some think. My goal is to present both sides of each and every question, but of course my feelings about an Intelligent Creation will shine through.

In all chapters, I'll wonder if chance mutations are really sufficient for a no-God evolution in the grand sense, and I'll dutifully note that the vast majority of biologists are convinced that mutations are indeed a sufficient source of variability. I'll call your attention to the role of natural selection as a *conservative* mechanism in which the process functions primarily to weed out harmful mutations (the vast majority), but I'll leave open the possibility for a *progressive evolution*—the mainstream biologists' view and one supported by contemporary laboratory experiments with microorganisms. Still, I'll leave it up to you, and because science cannot settle the question, your *other* (spiritual?) reasons for accepting or rejecting an Intelligent Creation become very important. Such reasons play an important role in my worldview, as you'll see in chapter 1.

Chapters 3 is a brief look at modern cellular and molecular biology. This is information that we need to have in hand when we decide (or decide *not* to decide) on a personal weltanschauung. To me, what we have learned about life and how it works is beautiful to contemplate and more than worthy of an Intelligent Creation. I can't promise you final answers about God's existence, but I can promise to show you that life is wonderfully complex, far beyond what anyone imagined as recently as 1950. If you enjoy a beautiful mountain view, the music of surf rolling onto a sandy shore, the colorful stimulus of autumn, an early-morning walk in a city park, the face and form of a handsome or beautiful man or woman, the shape and perfume of a perfect rose, or the beauty of certain paintings, sculptures, or musical compositions, then I promise that you will be amazed at the beauty and intellectual satisfaction of beholding a living cell with its incredible complexities: its mitochondria, chloroplasts, ribosomes, genes, ATP-synthesizing rotary motors, and other spectacular but tiny structures.

I can promise that even if you already know all about these things, you can enjoy their beauty again. Life is truly something marvelous and beautiful and fun to contemplate. If a fine painting is worthy of its creator, life—regardless of how it got to be the way that it is—is certainly worthy of our appreciation and our appreciation of its Creator. I can't prove that God did it, but I'm convinced that his mind was behind it, and knowing he is there adds to my enjoyment of his wonderful Creation.

After taking a look at the fundamentals of modern cellular and molecular biology, we'll dive into the problem of getting appropriate sequences of amino acids in the protein enzymes that are the working molecules of life and the key to understanding life. I began to think about these matters about half a century ago as we learned about the role of amino-acid sequences in proteins and the nucleotide sequences in the nucleic acids that control those amino-acid sequences. Basic evolutionary theory (neo-Darwinism, as it has been called since the early twentieth century) says that the source of variability for natural selection to work upon consists ultimately of random changes in those sequences. We can wonder about the chances that suitable sequences will appear for natural selection to act upon, first to form the simplest organisms and then to lead to the evolution over vast time intervals of all the millions of species now on our planet. These chances can be expressed as numbers, and the numbers prove to be mind-boggling, to say the least. I see the numbers as a challenge to a no-God weltanschauung. I'll show you those numbers in chapter 4, which may well be the most significant chapter in this book.

That is not to say that only I became aware of these numbers! Virtually all the authors whose works I've read devote some discussion to them. After telling my own stories to provide some background in understanding the numbers and their implications, I'll tell you how others have grappled with them and what solutions they have proposed to the problems that the numbers present. I don't think that the proposed solutions really meet the challenges, but in one or two cases I can't *prove* that they don't. I'll explain why I *doubt* the proposed solutions, however, and then let you help me wonder what the ultimate solutions might be. One of those solutions could be that an Intelligent Creator applied creative intelligence to engineer the formation and development of living organisms, including us.

A critical part of understanding life is to understand how it started on our planet. I'll devote chapter 5 to the origin of life. I'll conclude that no one knows the answer—a conclusion shared by virtually everyone working in the field. There are some interesting stories to tell, and some of them allow us to probe in even greater depth the philosophies of how knowledge is gained and how answers to questions are often proposed as hypotheses, which I'll call "what-if" or "just-suppose" or "plausibility" stories. Such tales, many of which could even turn out to be true, are part of all evolutionary theory, but this approach is especially evident in studies of the possible origin of life on earth.

When it comes to the weltanschauung of Creation, or creation, biologists today are in a house divided, as we'll see in chapter 6. There are those who induce from the findings of modern biology that there is no God, and there are those who believe that those findings are completely compatible with an Intelligent Creation. Sometimes we read or hear in the media statements about how science and religion are coming together in our times, which must be the case in the minds of *some* scientists. But we'll see that concepts of evolution have profoundly influenced some biologists to reject a belief in God altogether. It is a red herring to suggest that knowledge of modern biology can be neutral in one's belief or nonbelief in an Intelligent Creator. Such an approach results from a failure to truly think about the implications of what we have learned, especially during the past half century.

There are those today, often referred to as *intelligent design creationists* (ID creationists), whose weltanschauung is the opposite of the biologists who have rejected a belief in God based on their understanding of modern biology. These modern creationists apply the ancient "argument from design" to claim that life's complexity is so high that it could *not* be the product of a neo-Darwinian natural selection; hence, by default, it can *only* be understood as the product of intelligent design. We'll meet an ID creationist, Michael Behe, in chapter 6, where we'll also take a look at what his critics have to say. I'll suggest that his arguments do *not* prove the existence of God—science is simply not capable of such proof—but that his critics do not really prove their case either. Behe's argument of *irreducible complexity* may not be proof of an intelligent designer, but it is certainly something to consider. And it includes some wonderful stories of life's complexity.

I draw my conclusions in chapter 7, in which I return to the idea that new genes come from changes in older genes, and in which I take an even closer look at the philosophy of just-suppose stories. I can't resist having a word to say about the faith of those who apparently find it essential to pay homage to evolutionary theory even when the topic they are discussing has nothing directly to do with evolution. I'll also show how Kenneth Miller reconciles his total acceptance of evolutionary processes (even to the point of vigorously contesting the ID creationists) with his belief in God—that reconciliation being based largely on some principles of quantum mechanics. Finally, I outline the choices we have to make in establishing a personal weltanschauung. Nothing I have to say in this book compels you to make your choice one way or the other. It is a personal matter, but you should know about modern biology as you consider the choices.

Appendix A is a summary of seven creationist viewpoints, plus the atheistic viewpoint. Appendix B presents some of William Paley's words. Appendix C summarizes some of the complexities of photosynthesis and cellular respiration (the most wonderful example of cellular life's complexity that I know). Appendix D gives some history of attitudes toward evolution and Creation in my Church with diametrically opposed attitudes existing among the members.

I like to think that this book is in the tradition of the title of a beautifully illustrated book (Meierhof, 1947) that I bought in Switzerland near the end of the 1940s—*Eyes up in the Garden of our Lord God!* The goal of that book was to build appreciation for nature's complexities—in my mind, God's creations. The primary goal of my book is the same.

Note on References

References are listed under the Sources section at the end of the book. In the text they are given in a standard scientific format (one of many) that includes the name of the senior author, the year of publication, and the page, when needed; if the page is not given, the reference is to the full publication.

For dates and other historical details, I made many forays into various electronic versions of the *Encyclopedia Britannica*. These are not referenced.

ACKNOWLEDGMENTS

Several people read my manuscript and made excellent suggestions. The following four friends made many detailed comments (the first two through several revisions): Richard Schmutz, Morris Cline, Michael Wessman, and Arthur Galston. Duane Crowther was especially helpful in recommending that I include summaries for each chapter, plus more headings throughout the text; he made other valuable suggestions as well. Others who read the manuscript and made more general suggestions include Wilford Hess, Daniel Peterson, the late Elvon (Bud) Jackson, Blake Salisbury, Steven S. Salisbury, and my wife, Mary T. Salisbury, who provided not only careful proofing and many suggestions but also the moral and emotional support that are so important for a project such as this. Robert Shapiro at New York University provided some excellent suggestions for the origin-of-life chapter.

I'm especially grateful to Tami Allen Salisbury, who applied her considerable computer skills to make five beautiful, original illustrations.

My thanks go out to the people at Cedar Fort who produced this book, especially Lee Nelson, Michael R. Morris, Christopher Wallace, and Nikki Williams.

1 GAINING KNOWLEDGE: BY SCIENCE AND BY FAITH

Did life happen with no directing intelligence, or is there a Creator God? Although science cannot answer these questions, science has uncovered an amazing amount of knowledge, especially during the last half century. We can and should use these findings to help build our personal philosophies. Thus, this book takes a look at biological complexity and how knowledge of this might influence one's personal philosophy, or weltanschauung—one's view of how the universe works. We'll need to see why most modern biologists are convinced that life's variety can be explained by evolution via the natural selection of random variability among living organisms. (The evidence is very strong.) And we'll see that such a process does not exclude God. But we need some philosophical considerations before getting into the nuts and bolts of modern life science.

Gaining Knowledge by Science

How do we find out how the universe works? Some things are intuitively true or self-evident (simple rules of arithmetic), and some other things are true by definition (the way our language works). But there are clearly many things about how the universe works that remain mysterious to us. Just what is life, for example? It turns out that the manifestations of living things are driven by events that occur at such a minuscule level that we could never discern them simply by applying our native intelligence.

By now we know that there are many things that we can't learn just by *thinking*—almost the only method used by the Greek philosophers. Indeed, there is only one way to gain knowledge that can be tested and totally accepted by others, and that is the method of *experience*. We all apply the method in our everyday lives, and at a sufficiently refined level, we call it *science*.

The method of experience

Although philosophers who analyze what we like to call the *scientific method* can fill books with the results of their analysis, we can summarize the method with a few, perhaps over-simplified steps:

1. A question is formulated about some aspect of nature, typically something that has been learned by gaining answers to some previous question. (Question: Why is grass green? It contains colored molecules called chlorophyll. What does chlorophyll do?)

2. To find the answer to the question, we first make a guess about the answer; that is, we formulate a hypothesis. (Hypothesis: Chlorophyll plays a role in photosynthesis.)

3. We test the hypothesis. We try to imagine an observable phenomenon that the hypothesis predicts, and then we see if the prediction turns out to be correct. (If chlorophyll plays a role in photosynthesis, and we can get rid of the chlorophyll—perhaps by treating the plant with the right chemical—there should be no photosynthesis.) If the prediction fails, then we say that the hypothesis is *falsified*. (If a plant devoid of chlorophyll still carried out photosynthesis, then this hypothesis would be falsified. But in this example, the plant does not photosynthesize without chlorophyll.) Of course, there are many complications, so a hypothesis may not be proved when one prediction comes true, but if the test fails, the hypothesis must usually be false. (Maybe the chemical changed some *other* part of the photosynthetic mechanism besides the chlorophyll.) Then we dream up another hypothesis or modify the first one.

We do all of this everyday. (Observing a functioning TV set, we hypothesize that pushing the button marked "power" turns the set on. We push the button. Either the set turns on, proving the hypothesis, or the set does not turn on. An example of a complication is if the TV was not plugged in. In this case, the hypothesis was not falsified because the set failed to turn on.)

4. The final step is almost unique to science: Results are published. In everyday life, we may tell others about our experiences, but we seldom explain those experiences to our peers at a special meeting, or write up our results for publication in books or journals. A scientist *must* pass on his results to others who are interested. If he does not publish, he perishes as a scientist and becomes just a hobbyist who studies nature for his own amusement. In science, the process goes on and on. Results published by one scientist or group of scientists stimulate their own thinking and/or that of others, who formulate and test new hypothesis.

The role of logic

The rules of logic were worked out by the ancient Greeks, especially Aristotle, who lived from 384 to 322 B.C. We speak of *deductive logic*, in which a major premise includes a minor premise and thus is *valid*, which is to say that the conclusion is logically implied by the premises:

> **Major Premise:** All bodies in the universe having mass obey the law of gravity.
> **Minor Premise:** The earth and moon are bodies in the universe having mass.
> **Conclusion:** Therefore, the earth and moon obey the law of gravity.

Note that, even though this syllogism is valid, we can't be positive that the conclusion is *true* because we can't verify that all bodies in the universe obey the law of gravity. In science, it is uncommon to find such valid inclusive premises as the primary one in this deductive syllogism. (I can't think of an example except in mathematics.) Thus it is seldom possible to find clear-cut examples of *deductive* logic. Instead, we mostly rely on *inductive logic*:

> **Major Premise:** The earth and moon are bodies in the universe that have mass.
> **Minor Premise:** The earth and moon obey the law of gravity.
> **Conclusion:** Therefore, all massive bodies in the universe obey the law of gravity.

Clearly, this syllogism is *not* valid because the primary premise does not include the qualifier "all bodies in the universe." We have not tested all bodies in the universe to see if they obey the law of gravity, nor could we. Nevertheless, by now, we have tested a relatively large *sample* of bodies in the universe that obey the law of gravity, leading to the *tentative* conclusion that *all* bodies must obey the law of gravity.[1] This hypothesis could be falsified if we find bodies that do not obey the law of gravity. At the moment, we feel confident that we won't find such exceptions, but in principle, we can never be absolutely sure. And that is the case with most scientific theories, including in biology. We have sampled much, and while we cannot, in principle, be certain of our conclusions, as long as the samples are large enough, we don't really expect the conclusions to change.

Faith in God

Why do many people believe in God? Nonbelievers like to say that people invent gods to answer questions that they could not otherwise answer, such as: How did the creation of the universe come about? Many ancient and some modern peoples have done just that. Consider the fantastic creation myths found in many cultures (see Shapiro, 1986, prologue and chapter 1).

The Nobel Prize winner Christian de Duve (2002, pp. 300–02), a cellular biologist, uses strong language to express his conviction that the Judeo-Christian God was a human creation many millennia ago:

> Anthropocentrism is also a keystone of many religions, especially those inspired by the Bible, which describes man as created *in the image of God*. No phrase could be more quintessentially—and arrogantly—anthropocentric than this excerpt from the Book of Genesis. . . . The God of the Bible resembles in many ways the ruthless kings of the time. He is domineering, vengeful, jealous, merciless. . . . The sentence from the Bible . . . should be reversed. It is man who created God in his own image.[2]

Yes, the early books of the Old Testament often describe God in such terms. Still, there may well have been good reasons to believe in a real God but with misunderstandings based on imperfect knowledge, knowledge often colored by the times. Thus, the authors of those ancient books may have painted their picture of God in the images of their times—an imperfect picture based at some level on a real God who had revealed himself to a few witnesses whose descriptions were distorted by the historians.

Actually, that is not so different from our current thoughts about God: incomplete and imperfect.

Most modern religions deny that they are based on myths devised to account for creation. They claim that the God of their religion *revealed* himself to its founders. If God really spoke to representatives of the human race about himself, and you had reason to believe it to be true, your acceptance of God would make much more sense than believing just because that faith provided answers to questions that you otherwise could not answer.

It is important to emphasize that we who believe that there is a Creator God typically base our faith on much more than the compatibility of biological knowledge with an Intelligent Creation. Such compatible knowledge can *confirm* our faith but does not inspire that belief in the first place. Although I can't speak for *all* believers, faith in God may not be what nonbelievers like to call *blind faith*, which De Duve (2002, pp. 293–94) describes as follows: "By definition, faith does not rest on rational grounds, even though attempts may be made to rationalize it *a posteriori*. It is based on the blind acceptance of authority, which itself claims to be enlightened by 'Revelation.' Not without reason is faith described as 'a gift from God,' not to be questioned."

Well, that is not my definition of faith. I don't believe in something that can't be proved because some authority tells me to believe. I see good reasons to believe in many theological and moral principles, and thus in God's existence. Then, by my own decisions, I extend that belief to things that are presently beyond my ability to prove making my faith "the substance of things hoped for, the evidence of things not seen" (Hebrews 11:1). Incidentally, that is what many who *reject* God also do, basing their faith on an atheistic account of creation according to many principles that can be proved, and despite many unproved aspects of the story.

Life is a test

It is reasonable to ask: If God speaks to some, why not to all? Most theologies, including mine, teach that an important purpose of our existence on earth is to undertake a personal search for God, or a personal challenge to live according to the concepts of right and wrong (morality) with which most of us seem to be born. This concept of life being a test has two important consequences: First, there can be no scientifically compelling proof of the existence of God because that would remove the need to search and to decide. Second, belief in God is indeed a personal matter. No one else can make the determination for you.

The role of testimony

The many claims that God has spoken to human beings differ greatly among different cultures. Let us assume, however, that God, for his own purposes, could reveal different aspects of himself to different cultures.[3] The *testimonies* of the Judeo-Christian scriptures are especially important to me. These provide evidence based on witness accounts—a kind of evidence that we rely on in many aspects of our lives. We can wonder if the witness is telling the truth, or even if the witnesses ever lived and wrote the accounts (because the Bible was assembled so long ago). Suffice it to say that there are scholars who reject the scriptural accounts of God's dealings with humans and those who accept them.[4] Two scriptural testimonies have always been highly impressive to me:

The first is the testimony of the Apostle Peter, in which he anticipates doubters and responds:

> For we have not followed cunningly devised fables, when we made known unto you the power and coming of our Lord Jesus Christ, but were eyewitnesses of his majesty. For he received from God the Father honour and glory, when there came such a voice to him from the excellent glory, This is my beloved Son, in whom I am well pleased. And this voice which came from heaven we heard, when we were with him in the holy mount. (2 Peter 1:16–18 King James translation)

Note that Peter uses the plural "we." Others were present, he says, so this is *almost* a multiple-witness testimony.

The second is the story of Saul, who became Paul. Luke records the story in Acts 9, 22, and 26; each account differs slightly from the others.

Saul is incensed by this new teaching of Jesus that seems to so contradict his Jewish heritage, and he obtains letters to the synagogues in Damascus to bring Christians back to Jerusalem as prisoners. But on the road to Damascus, he is struck by a blazing light and hears a voice saying: "Saul, Saul, why are you persecuting me?" The voice identifies itself as that of the resurrected Jesus and tells Saul to go into the city, where he will be told what to do. In Damascus, the Lord calls a man named Ananias to go "to the street called Straight and inquire at the house of Judas for a man named Saul from Tarsus." Knowing Saul's intentions, Ananias is reluctant, but the Lord tells him: "Go on your way, for this man is my chosen instrument to bear my name before the gentiles and their kings, as well as to the sons of Israel. Indeed, I myself will show him what he must suffer for the sake of my name." Saul, who was blind from his experience on the road, sees in his mind's eye Ananias coming to restore his sight. Ananias does as commanded and also baptizes Saul, who then preaches in Damascus that Jesus is the Son of God.

I find the story compelling, especially because of the multiple witnesses, particularly Ananias. Luke, in Acts 22, further records that the Lord appeared to Paul (renamed by then) in the temple in Jerusalem, and Paul himself bears a powerful testimony in his first letter to the Corinthians. Note that Paul says that he was writing while some of the primary witnesses were still alive—witnesses who could have refuted Paul if he had lied:

> For I delivered unto you first of all that which I also received, how that Christ died for our sins according to the scriptures; And that he was buried, and that he rose again the third day according to the scriptures: And he was seen of Cephas [Peter], then of the twelve: After that, he was seen of above five hundred brethren at once; of whom the greater part remain unto this present, but some are fallen asleep. After that, he was seen of James; then of all the apostles. And last of all he was seen of me also, as of one born out of due time.
> (1 Corinthians 15:3–8, King James translation)

Nowhere does Paul say that he became a Christian because doing so provided him with answers about the origin and complexity of his world and his universe. Paul testifies that he became a believer because of his personal *experiences* with the supernatural.

Personal experience

I suspect that we could all tell of experiences in our own lives when we were touched by the divine. I've heard enough of these accounts to suspect that anyone old enough to have gained sufficient experience in life might be able to tell one or more stories of this type. These personal experiences may *truly* touch only those who experience them, but they can be powerful moments in one's life. In my seventy-nine-plus years, such experiences have occurred so seldom that I can almost count them on one hand—and each was so personal that I am reluctant to share them. But I've decided to share one such experience, knowing that a nonbeliever can call it coincidence and reject it out of hand. It moved me deeply, and if it doesn't move you, maybe that's because you weren't there.

The experience occurred on the 24th of January, 1978; I had just finished an exhilarating day of skiing at Arapahoe Basin in Colorado. I drove over Loveland Pass (11,992 ft elevation) to a motel in Georgetown, where I waited for Nic Marinos, who was a visiting professor working with me at Utah State University. Nic was fascinated by the plants of the alpine tundra, which he had studied at Flinders University in Australia. We had devised an experiment to see if soil temperature, controlled independent of the air temperature, might have an effect on the growth of alpine plants. We had designed the equipment; now we needed the plants, and I knew where to get them. While at Colorado State University, my students and I had driven to Loveland Pass, going some distance from the parking area to hack blocks of soil out of the frozen ground. When thawed out in our growth chambers, the plants would grow and flower beautifully.

Nic, who was staying about 100 miles away, had called to say that he wouldn't be able to join me, for a reason I forget. I realized that I would be digging the plants alone, and I began to worry about what might happen if something should go wrong while I was out of sight of the road. If I were some way incapacitated, I could freeze to death. With such a thought in mind, I prayed aloud as I drove up that pass. At some point in my prayer, I asked: "Please arrange for a hitchhiker to help me dig the plants." As soon as the words were out of my mouth, I said, also out loud: "What a strange thing to say! I've never prayed for anything as specific as that before!" Immediately, the thought came into my mind, as clear as if words were spoken in the cab of that truck: "But you were inspired to ask for that blessing! Don't sell such inspiration short!"

The next day a blizzard hit. I was stuck all day in the motel and forgot about that prayer. The following day dawned clear and crisp, and I was soon on my way. As I approached the base of the pass, there was my hitchhiker! Amazed and almost struck dumb by the memory of my prayer, I gently slid to a halt, and he climbed into the cab. He was a ski instructor at Arapahoe, but his ride had taken him only to the first ski area. He was the only hitchhiker I saw on that trip of over a thousand miles in the dead of winter. I had about five minutes to tell him what he was soon going to be doing. He thought that was exciting, and before too long we had the blocks of frozen ground in the bed of the pickup. I dropped him off at Arapahoe and was so thrilled by what had happened that I broke into song. I also prayed again, this time a prayer of thanks.

Other kinds of witnesses

If my suspicions are correct, my story could bring to your mind some similar incident in your own life when you "felt the touch of God," even if you are not religious, or even if you are an agnostic or an atheist. Although I could be wrong, let me present a quotation from the book by Christian de Duve (2002, p. 308), in which he so vividly proclaimed his conviction that man created God in man's image. The quotation is an envoy (dedication or postscript) to his book; it comes close to being a testimony of the existence of a God:

> My whole life as a scientist has been permeated with the conviction that I was participating in a meaningful and revealing approach to reality. I have experienced the joy of learning, the almost voluptuous thrill of understanding, the rare flash of illumination, the austere satisfaction of observing the rules of the scientific game, based on intellectual rigor and integrity. I have shared these emotions and imperatives vicariously with other scientists. And I have also vibrated in different registers, in resonance with the poets, writers, artists, and musicians who have moved me by their works and performances. On exceptional occasions, I have felt close to something ineffable, utterly mysterious but real, at least to me, an entity that, for want of a better term, I call Ultimate Reality.

Living the life

There is one more reason why involved believers accept the existence of God: They make an honest effort, not always successful, to put into practice the moral teachings that go along with their religion and its teachings about God. It is not easy, and might even be impossible, to have a purely intellectual belief in God. As almost anyone who believes (or did believe) in God would tell you, belief is a spiritual experience; failure to follow the moral directives that go along with the teachings about God seems to "drive out the spirit" and weaken belief.

Yes, that statement implies that those who reject God do so because of failure to live the moral laws. However, often that isn't the case. There are moral agnostics and atheists who reject God on purely intellectual grounds. Charles Darwin, an agnostic, provides an excellent example. From all that is known about him, we can only conclude that he was an extremely moral person. Such was the testimony of many of his close associates, including his wife and children.

I hope I've made the point that belief in God can involve much more than "blind faith" in the teachings of one's youth (authority) or to feel comforted because the idea of God explains the mysteries of life and nature. Those things can play a part, but for me, there is much more, including a lifetime evaluating the teachings of my youth and much study of the mysteries of life and nature.

The Argument from Design

William Paley's *Natural Theology; or, Evidences of the Existence and Attributes of the Deity, collected from the Appearances of Nature*, published in 1802, and *A View of the Evidences of Christianity* (third edition published in 1795), were well known and greatly admired in the 1800s. Paley was an Anglican Priest who wrote a number of influential works on Christianity, ethics, and science. His *Natural Theology* was based on John Ray's *Wisdom of God Manifested in the Works of the Creation*, published in 1691 over a century before Paley's own work.[5] Both present the so-called *teleological* argument for the existence of God (that creation has purpose, and that its apparent design argues for a Designer). As is often related, Paley used the analogy of a watch. As the design apparent in the watch testifies of its creator, so the apparent intricate design of living organisms testifies of their Creator. (See Paley's argument in Appendix B.)

This is the "argument from design," which is not only alive and well today, but was taken for granted during Biblical times. For example, Paul writes: "For since the beginning of the world the invisible attributes of God, for example, his eternal power and divinity, have been plainly discernible through things which he has made and which are commonly seen and known" (Romans 1:20 Phillips translation; see 1:18–24.)

The argument from design can be stated as a hypothesis: The origin of the apparent design in nature is an Intelligent Creator God. From a scientific standpoint, however, this is a bad hypothesis. Science cannot study a supernatural Creator. Furthermore, the idea of an Intelligent Creation is *too inclusive*. It can be used to explain *everything* about life and the universe; hence, it cannot be falsified. To quote Kenneth Miller (1999, p. 92), a cellular biologist at Brown University: "There is no fossil, no intermediate form, no evidence of any sort that cannot be explained away by invoking intention, intelligent design." Miller (p. 134) also says: "It is the 'argument from design,' the oldest, the most compelling, and quite simply the best rhetorical weapon against evolution." He then elaborates on how Charles Darwin's natural selection "answered" the argument.

In logic, a *tautology* is a statement that is true because it provides for all logical possibilities. The Creator hypothesis is a good example of such a tautology: Whatever one encounters in nature, one can say that God designed it; there is no way to prove that he didn't.

Incidentally, we'll see that evolutionary theory also comes close to being a tautology. With the proper "just suppose" story, virtually every aspect of the living world can be explained by evolutionary theory.

We can state the argument from design as two syllogisms that help us to see why the argument is not a conclusive one:

>**Major Premise:** Complex objects can only be produced by *design*.
>
>**Minor Premise:** Living organisms are extremely complex objects.
>
>**Conclusion:** Therefore, living organisms must have been designed.

Or:

>**Major Premise:** An intelligent designer can design complex objects.
>
>**Minor Premise:** Living organisms are extremely complex objects.
>
>**Conclusion:** Therefore, living organisms must have been designed by an intelligent designer.

The first of these syllogisms is deductive and *valid*. But we don't know that the conclusion is *true* because we can't be sure that complexity can *only* be produced by *design*—and for that matter, we can't even define complexity (although I'll make some attempts later). The second syllogism is not valid because the conclusion is not derived from the premises. Just because a designer can make complex objects doesn't mean that they could not also be made in other ways.

To reiterate: the complexity of living organisms, which to many suggests design, is certainly *compatible* with an Intelligent Creation; that is, it does not falsify it, even as it fails to prove it scientifically. Although this all sounds very ambiguous, this book is meant to show that the evidence of complexity can certainly support one's personal philosophy if one has other personal reasons to believe in a Creator God. And from that individual standpoint, the beauty of Creation's complexity can strengthen one's belief.

What Kind of God?

There is a movement afoot that attempts to prove the argument from design scientifically: Intelligent design creationists assert that living organisms are so complex that no natural process could account for their origin. Thus, by default, there must have been an intelligent Designer. Some intelligent design creationists never even use the term "God" and refuse to describe their "Intelligent Designer."

As I see it, only three characteristics of God are important for an Intelligent Creation: creative intelligence, the power to create, and a motivation for doing so. These three characteristics define the God of this book. He must understand the laws of physics and chemistry needed to design life, he must be able to apply his knowledge to engineer life's Creation, and he must want to create.

The concept of "creative intelligence" is difficult to define. Suffice it to say that we humans and some other animals have it. Artists, writers, engineers are all able to intelligently create things. Knowing what we have to work with and the laws that govern how such things work, we can create something (a work of art, a bridge, a book, even a letter to a friend) that otherwise would not exist. Civilization is the cumulative product of such activity. There is precedent for intelligence in the universe, and we are it.

Beyond these considerations, any discussion of God's nature is in the realm of theology and essentially irrelevant to the main themes of this book. Who knows where God came from? We cannot know God's purposes, only that he must have desired to carry out an Intelligent Creation.

Many atheists reject God by assuming knowledge of what he would or would not do. If God is benevolent and loving, they wonder, why is there so much agony and pain in our world? In response, how can we know God's purposes? Traditionally, it has been suggested that pain and suffering are part of God's design, a consequence of our agency or free will, and a way for us to be tried and tested.

Can We Understand the Mechanisms of Creation?

How could God create the universe? Not understanding God, we cannot answer this question. The amazing thing is that we are approaching an understanding of how he *could* have done it. As I'll point out frequently, much of the evidence supporting evolution is in the form of plausible hypotheses: "It *could* have happened such and such a way." We can now say much the same about an Intelligent Creation: It *could* have occurred in ways about which we are presently learning. It is no longer necessary to retreat to the conclusion that creation must have been a colossal act of magic instead of applied intelligence. Rather, an Intelligent Creation required an omniscient and omnipotent God who, *knowing* all the laws of the universe, was *able* to apply those laws to matter and energy in creating life on Earth.

This view might be specific to my own theology. Many religions hold that God *created* and *controls* the laws of nature; they might take offense when I speak of a God who acts *within* the laws of nature. The question, however, is immaterial. If an all-powerful God created the laws of nature, the basic conclusion of this book remains the same. Our biology is consistent with an Intelligent Creation of life *and* with an evolution of life. (Incidentally, I'm not concerned here with the question of whether God created the whole universe—as are many other writers.[6])

There are other questions that are irrelevant to the theory of intelligent design, such as, "Is God male or female?" or "Is there one or more Gods?" (Following a monotheistic tradition, I'll use the singular, masculine form: *God, he,* or *him.*) Is God a spirit or a spirit with body? Miller (1999, p. 194) says: "By definition, a god is a nonmaterial being who transcends nature." That's *his* definition, and no doubt most theologians would accept it. My theology, however, requires a *material* Godhead, but again, the question is immaterial to the concept of an Intelligent Creation. I promise not to discuss or base my arguments on my own theology or that of my church. These arguments should stand on their own.

Evolution by Natural Selection

Half a century after William Paley, Charles Darwin and Alfred Russel Wallace presented the theory of natural selection. Most biologists today consider natural selection to be the answer to the argument from design. Natural selection is said to provide a mechanism whereby nature "designs" itself—a mechanism that allows biological complexity to arise without a designer.

Charles Darwin's cogitations

A fascinating introduction to the study of natural selection is to follow the life of Charles Darwin, who receives most of the credit for developing the concept. Unfortunately, space will permit only a brief overview in these pages.[7]

Charles Robert Darwin was born in 1809 in Shrewsbury, England, nearly 150 miles northwest of London. He spent a few years studying medicine at the University of Edinburgh, but decided that medicine was not for him. In the pivotal year of 1831, Darwin graduated from the University of Cambridge with a Bachelor of Arts degree in theology and embarked on the H. M. S. *Beagle*, which spent about four years exploring the coasts and nearby islands of South America before it circumnavigated the globe, returning to England in 1836 (see Darwin, 1860).

As Darwin studied the plants and animals he encountered during his time on land while the *Beagle* surveyed the coasts of South America, he began to question the generally accepted concept that all species were created individually by God and would never change. Other scientists were also questioning this concept. On the voyage, Darwin read Charles Lyell's *Principles of Geology*, published in 1830, which argued for *uniformitarianism*—the concept that geologic processes such as erosion and volcanism could, over vast expanses of time, account for the land forms that we see today. This was an alternative to *catastrophism*, which held that Earth's geology could be understood in terms of great catastrophes, such as the universal Noachian flood. Lyell's geology showed that the earth was at least many millions of years old, perhaps providing time for any one species to evolve into another.

A few scientists accepted the proposal of Jean-Baptiste Lamarck, published in 1802 and 1809 in France. Lamarck speculated that organisms changed as physical characters acquired during their life were passed to their offspring. For example, a giraffe's neck might grow longer as the animal reached for higher and higher leaves. This long neck would be passed to its offspring through the reproduction process. The idea is called the *inheritance of acquired characters*. Actually, Darwin's paternal grandfather, Erasmus, had published a similar suggestion in 1796, four years earlier than Lamarck.

Darwin (1860, pp. 393–94) records in his account of the *Beagle* voyage several evidences for changes in species over time. For example, he writes: "It is probable that the islands of the Cape de Verd group resemble, in all their physical conditions, far more closely the Galápagos Islands than these latter physically resemble the coast of America; yet the aboriginal inhabitants of the two groups are totally unlike; those of the Cape de Verd Islands bearing the impress of Africa, as the inhabitants of the Galápagos Archipelago are stamped with that of America." Wouldn't God create special island species to match their island environments? Or did the island species *evolve* from some of their mainland relatives that had found their way to the islands?

Upon returning from the voyage of the *Beagle* in 1836, Darwin lived in London, where he began to study the specimens he brought back from the voyage and to seriously contemplate the "species problem," as it was called. There were two important events in 1838: his marriage to his cousin, Emma Wedgwood, and his insight into the theory of natural selection as the mechanism of evolution. However, he did not publish his ideas for twenty years. In the meantime, he discussed his ideas with a group of close friends, including Charles Lyell; John Henslow, his old mentor and a botanist/clergyman at Cambridge; Joseph Hooker, another botanist; and a zoologist, Thomas H. Huxley, who became perhaps his strongest defender.

Alfred Russel Wallace's flash of insight

Darwin's agonies about publishing his natural-selection ideas, which he knew would be received with much antagonism, at least from the clergy, were brought to a head in June 1858. He received a manuscript from Alfred Russel Wallace, who had been collecting specimens (for sale back in England) in the Malay Archipelago and was thinking about the species problem—contemplations begun in 1847 if not earlier (Raby, 2001). Wallace's insight into the theory of natural selection was sudden, after remembering a book by Thomas Malthus first published in 1798 called *Principles of Population*. Malthus had described the potential of a population to expand exponentially, outgrowing its food supply. (Darwin related that his insight also came from Malthus.) Wallace and Darwin realized that this potential for an expanding population would lead to a "struggle for existence," with those best able to gain food and otherwise survive reproducing. In other words, "survival of the fittest."[8] Whereas Darwin sat on his ideas for twenty years, Wallace wrote his manuscript within a couple of days after the concept occurred to him, forming in his mind especially during a fever from malaria. Darwin and Wallace had corresponded briefly, and Wallace was aware that Darwin was interested in the species problem; hence, Wallace sent the paper to Darwin, requesting his opinion and asking Darwin to show the manuscript to Lyell.

The compromise at the Linnean Society

Receipt of Wallace's paper was a sharp blow to Darwin, who feared that he would lose credit for the discovery to the younger Wallace. Darwin's friends, particularly Hooker and Lyell, put together a couple of Darwin's writings (including a letter to the American botanist, Asa Grey), and presented them to the Linnean Society on July 1, 1858 along with Wallace's paper.[9] Darwin was not present at the meeting, having just buried an infant son, who had died of scarlet fever only a few days before.

Actually, there was very little response at the meeting, but Darwin, with the urging of his friends, went to work to shorten an "abstract," which consisted of almost 2000 pages. His shortened version was about 500 pages, which he had copied by a scrivener. *The Origin of Species by Means of Natural Selection or the Preservation of Favoured Races in the Struggle for Life* was published on November 22, 1859, and all 1250 copies were sold that day. Eventually, the book went through six editions (the last published in 1872), each with many additions and clarifications of the original. There are many fascinating details to the rest of the Darwin and Wallace story (Darwin lived until 1882, writing several books and doing original research, some even in the field of plant physiology, my own field), but it is important for our purposes only to have a clear understanding of the theory of natural selection.

Natural selection and the necessity for variability

Both Darwin and Wallace realized that, as we noted above, an over production of young in a population would lead to a struggle for existence and a survival of the fittest. But it is important to realize that this would only result in changed populations better suited to their environment (evolution) if there were sufficient *inherited variability* to continually create organisms that were indeed better adapted to their environment. That is, there must be a source of variety in populations such that *some* members of the population would have features that gave them an advantage in the struggle for existence. If evolution is to occur, this variability must include features that were not present in previous populations.

Natural selection certainly works if the variability produces *only* features that are *less* suited to their environments. Such handicapped organisms will be eliminated, and the population as a whole will remain adapted to the environment. In such a *conservative selection*, however, there will be no evolution leading to new species. Hence, it is valid to ask: Whence the variability? Lamarck had suggested that the variability came from the inheritance of acquired characters. Although Darwin struggled with the concept all of his life, he basically accepted that premise and even developed a theory, which he called *pangenesis*, in which changes in an organism's organs (a giraffe's neck, say) would be transmitted to the reproductive cells so the acquired features could be passed to the next generation. We now know that this is completely false. Countless studies have shown that acquired characters are not transmitted to the offspring.

Neo-Darwinism and the New Science of Genetics

With the development of the science of genetics during the first decades of the twentieth century, the answer appeared to be at hand. That answer is still the central idea of what is called neo-Darwinism. The source of variability is thought to be random mutations of the genetic material: the genes. Mutations are common in nature and have been intensively studied in the laboratory, where they can be induced by X-rays, ultraviolet light, or a host of different chemicals. One thing has always been perfectly clear: The vast majority of these mutations, rather than providing survival advantages to their possessors, are deleterious. In nature, they would be eliminated by natural selection. Biologists believe, however, that a few of these naturally occurring mutations *would* provide survival advantages and would be preserved by natural selection—leading to the evolution of species. Darwin (without understanding genetic mutations but using instead the notion of inheritance of acquired characters) was convinced that the mechanism would account for all of today's life forms, given some primeval organism, probably consisting of a single cell. And that cell might have been created by God. If Darwin believed that, he was a *deist*—someone who believes that God started life on its way but did not intervene in its evolution. Darwin never claimed to be an atheist. Instead, he said that he was an *agnostic*—a term invented by his close friend T. H. Huxley to describe Huxley's own feelings. Most of Darwin's friends, including Wallace, remained convinced that God had played some role in creation, even if it had only been to begin life and the process of evolution.

Returning to logic, we can state one part of the theory of evolution as a hypothesis: All organisms are related to each other by descent from a common ancestor. This hypothesis is a good one in that it makes predictions that can be tested and verified or falsified. As we'll see in the next chapter, most biologists feel confident that tests of the prediction have confirmed rather than falsified the hypothesis. That being the case, they get upset when some of us skeptics refer to evolution as a *theory* (instead of a *fact*), a term that in our everyday language seems to imply uncertainty.[10] Nevertheless, in a logical sense, failure to falsify the hypothesis does not make it true. Other tests could still falsify it. But let's examine the evidence.

Summary

1. The *scientific method* is a way of gaining knowledge by experience. It includes formulating questions, establishing hypotheses, and testing those hypotheses. We do this in our everyday lives, but in science, the results are published.

2. *Deduction* reasons from the general to the particular, drawing specific conclusions based on general statements. *Induction* reasons from particular facts (often a *sample* from nature) to general conclusions; it is logically invalid, but is often the only approach that can be used in science.

3. *Faith in God* may rest upon the testimony of witnesses (scripture), one's personal experiences, application of religious principles in one's life, and other insights including the beauties of nature.

4. If part of the *test of mortality* is to find God on one's own, then science will never be able to prove or disprove God's existence.

5. The *Argument from Design* holds that the complexity of life in particular and the universe in general testifies that nature must have had an Intelligent Creator because it is too complex to come into being any other way. The argument goes back to the beginnings of history (Old Testament writings), but William Paley formulated it nicely in 1802.

6. A God of Creation must have three attributes: the *knowledge* to carry out Creation, the *ability* to carry out Creation, and the *desire* to do so. God certainly has many other attributes, but these are the only ones that are essential to the discussions in this book.

7. While there is no reason for us to imagine that we could understand *the mechanisms of creation*, the amazing thing is that science has already discovered many principles (especially in the field of molecular biology) that *could* have been part of an Intelligent Creation.

8. Charles Darwin and Alfred Russel Wallace's *theory of natural selection* was presented at a meeting of the Linnean Society in July of 1858, and Darwin's book, *The Origin of Species*, was published a year later. There are many fascinating details in the story of these discoveries.

9. *Natural selection* notes that there is much variety in any population of organisms, that the ability of any species to reproduce exceeds the resources for survival of the species, and that, therefore, on average, those best suited for survival will survive and pass their characteristics on to the next generation.

10. Neo-Darwinism claims that *random changes* in genetic material are the primary and ultimate source of variation in populations. These *mutations* may be caused by such environmental factors as radiation or specific chemicals, or they may be the product of *chance* changes in the molecular structures of the genetic material with no discernable cause.

11. It is easy to observe that *most mutations are harmful* to survival of the individuals who are born with them. If natural selection serves *only* to eliminate these harmful mutations from a population, it is considered to be *conservative*. For *progressive evolution* to occur, some portion of the mutations must confer an increased fitness on their possessors.

2 MACRO EVIDENCES FOR EVOLUTION: A STRONG CASE

This was a difficult chapter to write. Not that the evidence for the evolutionary development of life on earth over a few billion years, or for Darwin's natural selection as now understood, is difficult to summarize or to present. My problem was to convey my *attitude* toward it in such a manner that the reader wouldn't get the wrong idea about what I think. I hope that you agree with me after reading this chapter that the evidence for evolution and for evolutionary theory is strong—although not quite conclusive in several respects.

As evolutionary theory predicts, all organisms are related, the fossil record is most impressive, and there is no doubt that natural selection acts in nature to change the genetic composition of populations over time. This is a text-book definition of evolution: changing gene frequencies in populations in response to environmental selection pressures. With a sufficient amount of new variations, organisms at one point in the history of Earth could be significantly different from organisms at another time in Earth's history, thanks to natural selection. Most modern biologists think that it is this process that accounts for the parade of life forms over Earth's history displayed in the fossil record. That such may well be true makes up part of my attitude toward the theory of evolution.

My belief also includes the idea that an Intelligent Creator, God, played a critical role in this process. I have no conclusion about what that role might have been. Did he engineer the first life on Earth and then let evolution take over, as the deists and others believe? Or did he intervene in other ways intelligently creating every species? My attitude is that we simply lack enough information to speculate at this time. It is not easy to sit on the fence and to suspend one's personal belief or conviction until more evidence is in, but that is what I try to do with regard to *how* creation occurred. Yet, for the personal, nonscientific reasons that I related in chapter 1, I believe that God *did* take part in an Intelligent Creation. I just don't know how.

This conviction has two highly important consequences for my attitude about creation: First, when I see the incredible complexity of living organisms, I am moved in a "spiritual" way, just as I am moved by anything beautiful and deeply touching—only more so. I know of no music, no painting or other work of art, nothing else on earth that compares in its beauty with the wonder of life in its myriad configurations, from the tiniest organisms to the human mind.

The second consequence of my belief in an Intelligent Creator is that I am naturally skeptical of the idea that life can be accounted for in all its detail *without* that Intelligent Creator. That is, my creationist leanings (even though I am not sure just where I stand along the spectrum of creationist beliefs as described in Appendix A) predispose me to be skeptical of the various lines of evidence presented in favor of creation without God. My goal in this chapter is to present the evidence for evolution as fairly as possible, and as completely as this brief chapter will allow. If there is reason to be skeptical of any line of evidence, I will present the reason for that skepticism—hopefully without sounding like a bitter anti-evolutionist, which I certainly am not.

The General and the Specific
Theories of Evolution

We have established that, using the scientific method, observations lead to questions about nature, hypotheses based on the questions are formulated and examined to see what might be predicted, and then tests are devised to test each hypothesis. Results of the tests lead to new questions and hypotheses, which infer predictions that can be tested, and so on, *ad*

infinitum. Along the way, observations, hypotheses, and results are published. The concept of evolution and neo-Darwinism uses this method.

For millennia, thinkers have observed similarities in the structures of
various organisms and attempted to classify them based on these similarities. Fossil of species that no longer existed had been observed in sedimentary rocks. Still, the supernatural explanation seemed sufficient: God had
made the species that way, or the devil had made the fossils to confuse us.
Although we can think of those statements as hypotheses, there is no way
to test the Creator or Satan hypotheses. Near the end of the eighteenth
century, however, and especially during the first half of the nineteenth century, some scientists had formulated what we might call the general theory
(I like to call it the grand theory) of evolution: All organisms are related to
each other by descent from ancient ancestors, but with modifications over
long periods of time. In short: Evolution happened.

In principle, this theory could be falsified by showing that organisms
are *not* related. On the other hand, every bit of evidence that supports the
idea that organisms *are* related fortifies the hypothesis, thought it does not
prove it, because God might have made them that way. Nevertheless, biologists have piled up evidence consistent with the idea that creation could
have happened without God. Some of these biologists have convinced
themselves on the basis of this evidence that there is no God; others have
not decided.

If evolution happened, *how* did it happen? Lamarck suggested that
change occurred via the inheritance of acquired characters. Enter Darwin
and Wallace, who suggested that it happened via natural selection. That's
the next really important hypothesis, the specific or particular theory of
evolution, we might say. In its modern form, variation is said to come via
genetic mutations, recombinations, and other mechanisms. Although
Darwin retreated to Lamarck's ideas (based on use and disuse, as he often
repeats in his book), the rest of his theory remains intact: potential for
surplus of young, the struggle for existence, and survival and reproduction
of the fittest. This theory can be tested, as we'll see.

Can the Creator hypothesis be applied to natural selection? Well, you
can formulate it just about any way you want, but you still won't be able to
test it. Did the Creator use natural selection in creation, perhaps intervening now and again to provide suitable variability (as some of us are tempted
to think)? Or was there a special Creation of every species (as many scientists during Darwin's time thought, and as some creationists still think)?

Since the Creator theory can't be tested, the sensible thing to do is to test the other theories by seeing how accumulating data fit the predictions. We'll see that the data fit very well, but never so perfectly that the concept of an Intelligent Creator is refuted. This is true especially because we can't say for sure what role such a Creator might have played. And some of us will remember the nonbiological reasons for believing in a Creator in the first place.

In his book, *Origins*, Robert Shapiro (1986) discusses various theories of how life originated, presenting evidence for and against the theories. To critically examine these theories, he uses the literary device of introducing the Skeptic, who appears now and then in the narrative to point out the weaknesses of the various theories. Inspired by this approach, I've decided to invent first a character called the Biologist, who will present the evidence as we know it. Then, crediting Robert Shapiro, I've invited his Skeptic to join me in this chapter. I liked the Skeptic's attitude in Shapiro's book; he should be a big help in mine. He is well acquainted with the principles of logic and scientific method, and he is reasonably well acquainted with our current knowledge about evolution, about as well informed as the Biologist, for that matter.

Let's face it; the Biologist and the Skeptic reside inside me. My Skeptic is not really Shapiro's Skeptic; he is my own, as is the Biologist. As I think about that, I realize that these two individuals inside of me are always debating over the theories of evolution and the evidence cited to support or question them. Because my belief in an Intelligent Creator does not include a belief in the exact role he took in creation, a creation that might well have involved neo-Darwinian evolution, neither my Biologist nor my Skeptic has been able to win the debate.

The Grand Theory of Evolution

The Biologist begins this discussion by referring to the paleontologist Niles Eldredge (2000, chapter 2), who reminds us that the first great prediction of evolutionary theory is that, if all organisms descended from some common ancestor (perhaps a bacterium), then all living things should be related. Does the evidence support this prediction?

Morphology and homologous structures

Traditionally, the Biologist says, this is the story of the familiar family trees of life forms seen in biology textbooks and other places. The trees were originally generated by the science of taxonomy (classification), aided by comparative morphology, which is the study of form—the structures of organisms. Ever since the grand theory of evolution began to be accepted, the goal has been to classify organisms in a manner thought to reflect their evolutionary descent. (Before that, the goal was to understand the Creator's *plan* in creation.)

For example, animals called primates have several anatomical (morphological) features in common: opposable digits on at least one pair of extremities (finger and thumb), the ability to walk upright, specific kinds of teeth, and certain brain features, especially brain size compared with body size, and a complex cerebral cortex.

The anatomist Richard Owen, Darwin's friend and later opponent (see Desmond & Moore, 1991), defined structures like the opposable digits found in different but apparently related organisms as *homologous*. Possession of such homologous structures suggests relatedness.

Actually, some features noted above exist in other animals, and not all primates have all of the features, but it is relatively easy to classify the higher primates into a group called *anthropoids*, which includes new-world monkeys, old-world monkeys, gibbons, orangutans, gorillas, chimpanzees, and humans. The homologous similarities clearly suggest that all members of this group are biologically related. Assuming this to be the case and using fossil evidence as well as morphological characteristics, zoologists attempt to create a family tree that expresses how these groups evolved from one or more common ancestors.

Next, we note that all anthropoids have features in common with other mammals—animals that have hair and suckle their young. Thus, it is assumed that all mammals had a common ancestor. Furthermore, all mammals have backbones or spinal columns, as do many nonmammals, including the many kinds of fish. These are grouped with the mammals to make up the *vertebrates*, who must have had a common ancestor. (Animals lacking backbones are *invertebrates*.) And so it goes. All organisms appear to be related, and putative evolutionary family trees can be constructed for virtually all groups of plants and animals. The Biologist notes that not everyone agrees on all the details of these family trees; indeed, many taxonomists make their living by making slight adjustments of these trees.

Vestigial organs

Another kind of morphological evidence concerns *vestigial organs*, such as the human appendix, that seem to have no current function (except perhaps a negative one), though they did have a function in ancestral organisms. This can be good evidence of relatedness and evolution, but the Skeptic notes that we do not always know for sure that such organs *really* have or had no function in their possessors. Human tonsils, for example, were once thought to be vestigial. They are now thought to perform a function in warding off infection by producing antibodies that help kill infective agents, although they may themselves become infected and require surgical removal. The Skeptic admits, however, that such organs, whether vestigial or not, provide strong evidence for relatedness.

The Biologist points out that developing embryos often have features that are lost before birth but that were typical of possible ancestors. For example, a developing human embryo (an embryo during its *ontogeny*) has, for a while, the vestiges of a tail, suggesting that humans evolved from animals with tails.[1] The Skeptic notes that embryologists have known for over a century that the evidence does not support the original theory: that developing embryos went through all the stages of their evolution.

The Biologist agrees but notes that all this has little to do with our modern knowledge of embryology, which shows that those species that most recently shared a common ancestor have a similar embryological development (Wolpert et al., 2002). Also, the characteristics of a group of animals that are shared by all members of the group appear earlier in their embryos than the more specialized characteristics. Evolutionists assume that these more general characteristics evolved earlier. Furthermore, all vertebrates do pass through a so-called *phylotypic stage* that is quite similar, albeit somewhat variable among the group. Typically, their embryos differ from each other most both before and after this stage. Thus, in the sense that development of an embryo provides insights into the evolutionary origin of the animal, ontogeny does recapitulate phylogeny.

Well, the Biologist says, Eldredge's "first great prediction of evolutionary theory" is certainly born out by the facts. Yes, replies the Skeptic, the facts of apparent relationships based on form are certainly what the general theory of evolution would predict, but does the fulfillment of this "great prediction" *prove* that evolution occurred by "natural means," without an Intelligent Creator? Of course not. It is quite possible to postulate that God followed a plan in creating living organisms, just as early biologists believed. Because we can't know the mind of God, we can wonder if an Intelligent Creator might have designed such things as vestigial organs and developmental stages in ontogeny for reasons unknown to us, or that these features might be byproducts of an Intelligent Creation that allows freedom for change (variability) and natural selection. With such possibilities, these features are not *proof* of a creation without God.

The skeptic calls our attention to the many special creations of humans: automobiles, airplanes, can openers, and so forth.[2] Consider automobiles: Someone who knows much about cars could no doubt construct a family tree from the first gasoline-powered vehicle to the present luxury sedans, trucks, SUVs, vans, buses, and racing cars. Because they all have wheels, engines, and other common features, the relatedness is clear. If we didn't know better, we could imagine that these cars evolved from that first gasoline-powered cart, the common ancestor, just like organisms are said to evolve. Yet no automobile can reproduce itself, and the evolution goes on in the minds of the engineers: the automotive intelligent creators. *Each* automobile is the product of special creation, a creation that takes place in a factory. Thus variability is produced by human intelligence, and survival and selection occur in the market place. Clearly, apparent relatedness does not *prove* descent from a common ancestor.

Analogous structures: parallel evolution

The Skeptic preempts the topic of so-called parallel evolution (or convergent evolution) before the Biologist brings it up because, he says, special creation or a directed evolution might explain the observations better than does a neo-Darwinian evolution with no God. Parallel evolution is said to occur when similar features appear in lines that otherwise seem to be unrelated. Richard Owen defined such structures as being *analogous* rather than homologous.

The eye provides a good example. A vertebrate eye, possessed by fish, birds, and mammals (including humans) has a lens that focuses light onto a retina. A cornea protects the lens, which changes its shape to correct for distance, meaning that the brain must interpret the signal it is receiving and, in turn, send signals that change the shape of the lens. There is an iris that opens or closes to admit more or less light through the pupil, and nerves to respond to the brightness of the light. Muscles around the eye change the direction that it is looking—up, down, or sideways. The eye is a marvelous structure. Many thoughtful people, including Charles Darwin, have long wondered how the processes of evolution could produce such a structure.

As if that were not enough, very similar eyes occur in the more complex mollusks, including squids and octopuses. The molluscan eye has a cornea, lens, iris, and retina, for example, and the signals sent by the retina must be received by a brain that is capable of reacting to them, forming a visual, mental image and responding to what is seen. Yet the line that led to the mollusks is thought to have split early in evolutionary history from the line that led to the vertebrates, long before the eye had evolved in either line (during the late Cambrian).

Thus, if the grand theory is true, the complex eye and a brain capable of handling the received images must have evolved *independently* in the two lines. The vertebrate eye and brain and the molluscan eye and brain are thus said to be *analogous* rather than *homologous*, and the Skeptic says that an Intelligent Creator could have designed the similar eyes in the two highly divergent lines, just as one automaker might copy the design of a special feature developed by a competitor.

The Biologist says he could cite many examples of convergent evolution. For example, he compares the several genera of cacti of the Western Hemisphere with the genus *Euphorbia* from Africa and Asia. Placed side by side, vegetative plants of the two groups appear very similar, but when they flower, it is clear that they have quite different flowers, and classification is based on floral characteristics. The two widely divergent lines, evolving in similar but distant environments, seem to converge in vegetative, analogous morphology.

The Biologist emphasizes that there is a vast amount of evidence for neo-Darwinian evolution, and most biologists find it totally convincing. If neo-Darwinism can account for so many features of life as we know it, then it must account for convergent evolution also. Sure, there are many steps involved in the evolution of a vertebrate or a molluscan eye, but the selection pressures toward such an eye are apparent. Given time and a source of variability, we can *expect* such an eye to appear. The most eminent biologists reaffirm the reality and the logic of parallel evolution. Richard Dawkins (1996, p. 139), for example, exults over how wonderful the process of natural selection is since it was capable of producing an eye of some kind "no fewer than forty times, and probably more than sixty times, independently in various parts of the animal kingdom."

Well, says the Skeptic, that may show how powerful evolution is, or it may show the workings of an Intelligent Creator. How can you know? The Creator might have set things up so that evolution would be capable of producing analogous organs, or he might have intervened in creation to produce them.

Speaking of family trees, the Skeptic says, at the bottom of the tree is life's origin, so the topic needs to be mentioned here. For more than sixty years, some scientists have tested ideas about how life might have originated by various processes, mostly at the molecular level. We will devote chapter 5 to this topic. Some brilliant workers in the field have done some impressive experiments and created some ingenious schemes, but all agree that the problem of the origin of life remains unsolved.

Molecular evidences

Recovering from his encounter with parallel evolution, the Biologist tells us that the strongest evidence for evolution (both relatedness and natural selection) may well be at the molecular level, but he agrees to postpone the topic until we have some background in molecular biology, which we'll introduce in the next chapter and return to in chapter 4.

An Ancient Earth: Time for Evolution

Both the grand theory of evolution and natural selection predict that Earth must be very old. Evolution takes *time*. Indeed, a huge body of evidence strongly indicates that the earth is billions of years old. The Biologist explains:

Uniformitarianism

First, there is the uniformitarian doctrine outlined by Charles Lyell during Darwin's time. It states that the same processes that we see going on today have shaped the earth from its beginning: Slow erosion of earth's surface produced sediments that collected in bodies of water (or shoreline and desert sands) and were eventually consolidated into sedimentary rocks; volcanoes and other forces produced igneous (once molten) rocks. Tremendous pressures caused *metamorphoses* (modification) of some sedimentary and igneous rocks. Slow shifting of the earth's crust brought some of these rocks to the surface, subjecting them to more erosion and more formation of sedimentary rocks.

Uniformitarianism does not insist that *everything* that took place in formation of the Earth was *gradual*; cataclysms are also evident in the geological record. It is now conceded by most scientists that a huge meteorite impact caused a cataclysm that destroyed the dinosaurs, for example.

In any event, the apparent combination of uniformitarian processes and known cataclysms clearly suggest time intervals in the earth's development of millions to billions of years.

We'll discuss the fossil record in a moment, the Biologist says, but note that some sedimentary rocks contain the remains of living organisms that accumulated over extremely long times. In northern Santa Barbara County, California, for example, there are beds of diatomaceous earth almost 500 meters (1500 ft) thick extending over 13 square kilometers (5 square miles). This material consists of opaline silica, the fossil shells of microscopic algae called *diatoms*, which are easy to see in the diatomaceous earth with almost any microscope. Eons of time were required to accumulate such a large amount of these tiny creatures. Limestones and dolomites consist mostly of calcium carbonates that are also the products of living organisms, and these rocks are hundreds to thousands of feet thick in many locations on our planet. Coal, natural gas, and probably petroleum also represent the remains of living organisms that must have lived over many eons to produce the quantities of these organic materials that exist. Furthermore, coal often occurs in layers separated by sedimentary rocks. The swamps that formed the coal, which contains many fossil plants, must have alternated with lakes or seas that accumulated sediments.

Finding ways to date the rocks has been a prime goal of geologists. The earliest method followed the uniformitarian assumption that the rates of erosion, sedimentation, and rock formation that we observe today are the key to understanding the amount of time that it took for ancient strata to form. This approach produced ages for sedimentary rocks in the millions to billions of years, but the dates were indeed based on assumptions, as creationists love to point out.

Flood geology

The Skeptic accepts the assignment, although his heart isn't in it, to note that *some* creationists have argued that a cataclysmic flood might account for sedimentary rocks (Morris & Whitcomb, 1964). It is really impossible, however, to apply such an explanation to all of Earth's geology. Why would a flood selectively put the more complex organisms, many of them ocean dwelling creatures, *only* in the upper strata where they are found today? Creationists say that the more advanced creatures could best escape the flood waters and thus survive the longest. Wouldn't there be a few exceptions, maybe some of Noah's fellow humans?

Furthermore, one can calculate that, if the quantities of fossil carbon (and diatoms) in the earth's crust are the remains of organisms all living together on the earth's surface at the time they were destroyed by a flood, there would not be room on Earth to contain them. The living flesh would amount to over a thousand tons per square meter of the earth's surface.[3] The calcium from organisms found in limestones and dolomites, as well as the silica in diatomaceous earth, *must* have been deposited gradually over long time intervals. The flood explanation for fossil carbon, limestones, and diatomaceous earth just doesn't work (Wise, 1998). Having said that, the Skeptic feels much better. In being skeptical, he was really agreeing with the Biologist, who picks up the dialogue.

Radioactive dating

The techniques of radioactive dating strongly support the theory of an ancient earth. Radioactive elements, such as uranium-238, decay into other elements, such as lead-207, at rates that are measurable and not at all affected by such factors as temperature and pressure. (In the case of $^{238}U \rightarrow {}^{207}Pb$, half of the uranium has decayed to lead after 703,800,000 years.) Radioactive dating assumes that when an igneous rock crystalized, the radioactive element was not in the presence of significant amounts of the elements to which it would eventually decay. After crystallization, the radioactive decay continued to take place, producing the product elements, trapped in the same crystal as the radioactive element. Measuring the proportion of original element to its decay product, we can calculate how long it has been since the crystal formed; the more of the decay product compared with the original element, the older the crystal must be.

This basic method with its refinements has been tested in numerous ways, and although there are assumptions in the techniques, the results compare well with the uniformitarian ages determined by the assumed times required for erosion, sedimentation, and rock formation. (In order to date a sedimentary stratum by radioactive dating, we must find an intrusion of igneous rock into the sedimentary rock and date the igneous rock by radioactive decay; this indicates that the stratum is older than the igneous rock that intruded into it.) It is the general conclusion that radioactive dating is by far the best approach to dating the earth's crust, and those dates strongly suggest that Earth has been around for about 4.65 billion years.[4]

Yes, some creationists present alternative ways to interpret the evidences for an ancient earth, the Skeptic admits. Personally, he finds their arguments to be extremely weak. In any case, he says, the age of the Earth is immaterial to the concept of intelligence in creation. Nothing about the ancient age of our world precludes a God working over the long times suggested by the evidence, or even intervening in creation more recently.

The Skeptic says that, logically, there seems to be only one way to account for a young earth. Two years before Darwin wrote his famous book, it was suggested that God might have created the earth to make it *look like* Creation took him a long time, although it really didn't. Phillip Henry Gosse wrote a book in 1857 titled *Omphalos: An Attempt to Untie the Geological Knot.* Gosse realized that, if God created Adam and Eve *de nova* from the dust of the Earth, but gave them navels implying that they had had a real birth, he could also create a garden with mature trees and their annual growth rings, even an Earth with strata containing fossils of animals that never existed. (*Omphalos* is the Greek word for *navel.*) If God is capable of *anything,* this argument is infallible. If God works within natural law (as the Skeptic believes he does), however, the laws of physics and chemistry might not permit such a fraud. In any case, such a possibility is for the Skeptic too much of a stretch and only of historical interest.[5] We have every reason to believe that the earth is extremely old, and there is no scientific reason to doubt it!

Following this *omphalos* train of thought, the Skeptic notes that the Creator hypothesis can be expanded and modified in various ways. Here are two extreme versions: A Creator capable of absolutely anything (even magic) carried out Creation, or an Intelligent Creator, working within the laws of physics and chemistry, was responsible for and took part in Creation. This is a theological matter, but only the second version makes any sense to the Skeptic. Even if a general Creator hypothesis cannot be tested, the limits suggested by the second version come close to eliminating an *omphalos* creation. We may not know *all* the laws of physics and chemistry, but the ones we do know seem to eliminate an *omphalos* creation—which is thus not so "logically infallible" after all.

The Fossil Record: Some Problems

The Biologist begins this discussion by quoting Niles Eldredge's (2000, p. 32) "grand prediction that flows from the simple thesis that all life has descended from a single common ancestor. There should be a record of the evolutionary history of life preserved in the geological record, and that record should reveal a general sequence of progression from smaller, simpler forms of life up through the larger, more complex forms of life over long periods of time." Eldredge then elaborates how this prediction is indeed verified by the fossils of organisms that lived in the past that we find in the earth's sedimentary rocks.

In general, the simplest fossils are contained in the most ancient strata. More complex organisms are nearly always found in strata that lie on top of the rocks that contain simpler fossils. Thus, paleontologists have been able to construct reasonable evolutionary "trees" showing how simple organisms could have evolved into more complex organisms.

Missing links

Traditionally, the Skeptic tells us, creationists have emphasized the gaps in these trees—the "missing links" at all levels of the organization of life. The Biologist explains that this was especially true during Darwin's time, and Darwin wrote an impressive chapter in *The Origin*, outlining why the fossil record had to be incomplete. The chances that an organism will become a fossil when it dies are obviously very small. It must be in, or fall into, a lake or sea that is depositing sediments on the bottom, and the organism must be covered with those sediments before it has time to completely decay or be eaten by a scavenger. In the vast majority of cases, uneaten flesh does decay, leaving only the skeleton or exoskeleton. Although some organisms might become fossils by being covered with blowing sand, which becomes sandstone, for the most part, fossils form only on the bottoms of bodies of water. So, there are far fewer fossils of land plants or animals, although some do fall into the water or special places like the La Brea Tar Pits, located in Hancock Park (Rancho La Brea), Los Angeles.

Furthermore, there are far fewer missing links now than there were in Darwin's time. Contemporary paleontologists can point out numerous examples of apparent intermediate fossil forms that have been discovered during the past century and a half. There was a time, for instance, when creationists could point to the whale as an example of an animal for which there were no postulated ancestors in the fossil record and even suggest that such fossils would never be found. As recently as 2001, however, fossils *were* found in Pakistan (and in other locations) that appear to bridge the gap between fossil land animals and whales (Gingerrich et al., 2001).

Continuous fossil sequences?

Furthermore, *some* fossil sequences are known in which there is quite clearly a continuous, gradual change in similar organisms through time (moving upward through the strata). For example, Miller (1999, pp. 44–48, 297) describes the continuity of two fossil sequences: a diatom called *Rhizosolenia* and the sequence leading to us humans.

Diatoms (microscopic, single-celled algae, as noted) were studied by measuring the height of a glass-like area of the cell wall and plotting it as a function of its location in the strata, assumed to be equivalent to a time beginning 3.3 million years ago and ending 1.7 million years ago (original data of D. Lazarus, 1986). Within the standard-error bars, there is a gradual shift in height, only slightly in one line but very distinctly splitting to another line (shorter heights) over a period of 100,000 to 200,000 years. Thus, the data even show formation of a new species (speciation) just as Darwin said the data should. This is an impressive example indeed.

Miller tells us that the human evolution example is almost equally impressive. Here he shows us a graph (drawn from Faulk, 1998) of cranial (brain) size of sixteen hominid fossils as a function of time before the present, beginning about 3 million years ago. Again, the change (increasing cranial size with time) seems rather continuous, Miller tells us: "a smooth transition from pre-human (*Australopithecus*) to human (*Homo*) forms." Still, the transition is nowhere near as continuous as that of the diatoms. Miller notes that cranial sizes below 600 cm^3 are usually assigned to the genus *Australopithecus* and those greater than 600 cm^3 to the genus *Homo*, the genus to which we humans belong.

Here the Skeptic seems excited to inform us that continuousness, or smooth transitions, are to a great extent in the eye of the beholder. In the case of the hominids, it might even be a matter of applying a deduction, based on some assumptions, to the data at hand. The major premise is that humans evolved like every other living organism, but this premise is itself an assumption. The minor premise (a prediction from the theory) is that things that evolve do so through a continuous chain of organisms, each differing slightly from its ancestors. Then, assuming that the fossil skulls are human ancestors, the conclusion is that they represent a continuous and smooth transition. The major premise is supported: Humans evolved like every other organism. The circular reasoning in this logic is clearly evident.

The Skeptic reminds us again that apparent relatedness does not necessarily mean genetic relatedness. Those hominid skulls were found at different places and in different situations (unlike the diatom example). It is assumed that they show a pattern of descent with modification because they tend to fit what is expected based on convictions about evolution, but there is no way even to be sure that any one of them (representing a population) descended from any other of them (also representing a population). The lines of descent must be assumed—and they continue to change with new discoveries. Relatedness is indeed often in the eye of the beholder.

Consider two recent finds of fossil skulls, the first in Toumai, Chad, in Central Africa. The subtitle of an article (Guterl, 2002) in Newsweek magazine reads: "Scientists find the oldest fossil of a human ancestor ever—a 7 million-year-old skull that is shaking up theories of human origins." This skull is said to represent a fossil of a human ancestor that lived close to the time when humans separated from apes. In my memory, almost every find reported during the past half century has "[shaken] up theories of human origins." Each find has required a new family tree.

The second skull was found in Dmanisi in the republic of Georgia. It is dated at about 1.75 million years old. The skull is thought to represent the first human ancestors that came out of Africa, but the brain size is only half that of *Homo erectus*, and those working in the field had predicted that only hominids with the larger brains would be able to migrate over the long distances and varied terrain.[6]

Exceptions to strata sequences

The Skeptic feels that it is his duty to note that creationists point out two other problems with the fossil record besides missing links, although he is personally not impressed by these "problems." First, there are a few exceptions to the rule that more complex fossils lie in strata above simpler fossils. Geologists have interpreted these situations as "overthrusts," in which movements in the earth's crust have pushed more ancient strata laterally so they end up on top of more recent ones. Although creationists have made much of these situations[7] (especially Chief Mountain north of Montana in Canada), the overthrust explanation fits detailed field observations very well. This creationist argument fails to be convincing.

The Cambrian "explosion"

Second, the Skeptic dutifully notes, paleontologists—as well as creationists—have long been aware of the *Cambrian explosion* of species

(Levinton, 1992; and Sepkoski, 1993). The Biologist picks up the story: The Cambrian period in geological history is dated at about 535 million years ago (about 11.5 percent of the estimated 4.65 billion-year age of the Earth), and the Cambrian strata contain fossils of most major groups of animals, but no fossils of multicellular animals appear in strata older than the Cambrian. Traces of multicelled animals were first found in strata about 580 to 560 million years old (possibly 600 million years old), but these signs of organized animal life before the Cambrian consist mostly of such traces as worm holes made by soft-bodied animals that would not leave fossils. These traces were first found in the late 1940s in Australia, but by now they have been found at various locations around the world. Of these, only *Cloudina* has a sort of skeleton that looks like a stack of ice-cream cones, about 3–4 cm long, made of secreted calcium carbonate. The "explosion" of the Cambrian was the appearance of numerous animals with hard parts that left fossils.

Paleontologists have puzzled over this situation since before the time of Darwin, at which time nothing was known of any fossils of life before the Cambrian. More recently, we have discovered fossils that appear to be identical to contemporary masses or mats of bacteria and cyanobacteria (blue-green algae), called *stromatolites*. The fossil mats go back about 3.5 billion years—in geological time, not very long after the estimated time when the earth cooled. About 2.2 billion years ago, cells with nuclei appeared (*eukaryotic* cells, which are described in chapter 3), and there is molecular evidence that there was a burst of evolution about a billion years ago that produced red and brown algae, diatoms and related algae, green algae, fungi, and some animals. Anyway, for something like three billion years, Earth was ruled by bacteria and single-celled eukaryotes, before the Cambrian "explosion" of life forms occurred.

The stromatolite fossils are quite convincing, but there have been claims of even older fossils dating back to 3.83 billion years before the present. These claims were based mostly on the ratio of the two most common stable carbon isotopes: carbon-12 and carbon-13. Because ^{12}C is slightly lighter than ^{13}C, it reacts slightly faster in the reactions of life, including photosynthesis. Thus, carbon from organisms has about 2–3 percent more ^{12}C relative to the CO_2 in the oceans. These skewed ratios were found in carbon from rocks in Greenland and a few other locations. During recent years, however, these earliest signs of life on Earth have been questioned (Simpson, 2003). For one thing, there is no way to be sure that no inorganic process could enrich the total carbon with[12] C. De Duve (2002, pp. 44–45; 314 n. 3) reviews the evidence and notes that "there are still uncertainties with respect to the earliest appearance of life on earth."

In any case, the stromatolite fossils must have been preceded by simpler forms of life, and we are left with the conclusion that life appeared on Earth relatively soon after its formation about 4.65 billion years ago. Taking into account those three billion years of only single-celled organisms on primitive earth, the "tree of life" had a very tall trunk consisting collectively of single-celled organisms—actually numerous strands representing the many kinds of single-celled organisms that must have appeared during that long interval. Then, not far from the top, branches of animal phyla suddenly appeared all around the trunk. Some of these phyla died out and are unknown in younger strata.[8] Green algae began to appear about the time of the Cambrian explosion, but land plants don't appear in the fossil record until about 408 to 438 million years ago.

Again, the Skeptic notes that creationists claim that this is a picture somewhat different from that presented in most biology text books.[9] Although paleontologists have provided various tentative—and reasonable—explanations, it is easy to see why creationists love to talk about this interesting situation. It is easy to imagine—but not to test scientifically—that an Intelligent Creator might account for this sudden appearance of varied life forms.

The Biologist tells us that in paleontological terms, "sudden" means within a few million years. Niles Eldredge (2000, chapter 3) also notes that the fossil record displays other examples of the "sudden" appearance of multiple new life forms. These events follow times of great extinctions (such as the one that caused the demise of the dinosaurs), and often occur during periods of dramatic climatic change (such as extensive glaciation or the after effects of an asteroid impact). Eldredge and a famous paleontologist friend, the late Stephen Jay Gould, suggested in 1972 that evolution occurred, at best, very slowly between these extinctions, followed by sudden bursts of new life forms (those "bursts" lasting "only" a few million years). The stable periods, which lasted many millions of years, might be examples of a conservative or stabilizing natural selection called *stasis*. Thus, the tree of life with its extremely tall trunk would have long vertical branches. Some of these branches died out while others "suddenly" formed many new branches. Eldredge and Gould called this process punctuated equilibria, and it is discussed pro and con by evolutionists. Sometimes it is misunderstood by creationists who say that evolutionists are in doubt about their own theories.

Lynn Margulis and Dorion Sagan (2002, pp. 83, 96) believe that an important source of variability is the acquiring of a new *genome* (full complement of genes in a nucleus) by an organism, which genome then interacts with the genome already present, and that this mechanism is, in the long run, much more important than the accumulation of small mutations. As to punctuated equilibria, they imply that the acquiring of genomes might be responsible for the "punctuations" (the times when many new species appear), and that the long periods of stasis are times when only natural selection of random mutations rules, mostly by eliminating all the bad mutations, which might be virtually *all* the mutations!

The Biologist and the Skeptic mostly agree on the bottom line: The fossil record, at least in broad outline and in spite of missing links and the Cambrian explosion, agrees in its main principles with our third "grand prediction of evolutionary theory," noted by Eldredge. At the same time, it does not disprove the concept of an Intelligent Creation, and some aspects of the fossil record might fit the predictions of such a creation better than those of an evolution in the absence of a Creator. A Creator, for example, could supply the necessary variability for the periods of rapid evolutionary change and for convergent evolution. The fossil record does argue conclusively against a sudden creation of all species in a short period of time (if one rejects *omphalos*).

Evidence for the Specific Theory of Evolution: Natural Selection

As with the "grand theory of evolution," we can also state the specific theory of evolution as a hypothesis: The mechanism of evolution is the natural selection of random mutations. This hypothesis is also a good one in that it suggests ways to test it. Most biologists think that the evidence supports the hypothesis by failing to falsify it. When it comes to the mechanism, however, most biologists are a little less certain that the hypothesis tells the whole story, although we won't go into all the complications here. Most biologists agree that, even if the hypothesis might have to be modified, it most probably will never be completely rejected.

Peppered moths and Darwin's finches

The Biologist says that there are many examples of natural selection at work in natural biotic communities. Peppered moths in England provide one frequently cited example. Before the industrial revolution, most peppered moths were light colored, matching the light-gray lichens that grew on the trunks of British trees. Smoke from many new factories covered the trunks with soot, the lichens died out, and dark-colored moths became much more common than the light ones. As pollution cleared, the moth population shifted again to light-colored moths. The explanation was that birds were eating the moths that least matched the trunks where the moths spent the day. The camouflaged moths were thus "selected" for survival and reproduction. In the 1950s, Bernard Kettlewell (1959; for recent summaries, see also Majerus, 1998; and Wells, 2000, chapter 7), a British physician and biologist, tested these ideas by releasing several dozen moths, mixtures of the light and the dark types, onto the black trees near industrial areas or onto the lichen-covered trees in unpolluted areas. Then he set out traps to capture the surviving moths, finding higher percentages of dark moths in the darkened-tree areas and more light-colored moths in the unpolluted areas.

Another example is provided by the finches studied by Darwin on the Galápagos Islands and by Peter and Rosemary Grant since 1973 (see Grant, 1991). The basic finding is that the beak and body size of one species increased during a drought, the better to break the larger and harder seeds produced by the drought.

The Skeptic notes that these stories are much less clear-cut than they appear to be in most modern biology textbooks, as creationists like to point out (Wells, 2000, chapter 8). For example, moths in their torpid daytime condition land wherever they can after being released; namely, on the trunks of the nearby trees, whereas in the wild they spend the day much higher in the trees and typically on the bottoms of small branches. Furthermore, detailed studies showed that the light-colored moths increased in number after pollution control but well before lichens had returned to the trees—even before the trees changed in appearance. And there were areas where the correlation between moth color and pollution was not clear. Natural selection must have been acting, but exactly how has still not been determined.

Regarding the finches on the Galápagos Islands, the bottom line is that average beak sizes returned to their previous values after the drought was broken. Over the years, there was a kind of cyclic natural selection, depending on weather conditions. When conditions were dry, beak and body sizes increased; when wet, they decreased, and these increases and decreases were shown to be inherited—not just caused by water or the lack of it. That is, natural selection adjusted the population to the environmental conditions, but the changes in beak and body size oscillated around a norm, not changing over time in a directional way that would clearly lead to new species.

The same was true for the peppered moths. Coloration seemed to be affected by pollution or the lack of it, and gene frequencies of the moth populations oscillated depending on the environment. Natural selection in these two cases, often said to be the best examples known to biology, only shifted the genetic composition of the populations to track the environment. To believe that these shifts would lead to evolution in the general sense requires an extrapolation well beyond what was actually observed. Moths of both colors were present at the beginning, as were finches with various sized beaks and bodies, so new mutations were not required.

It is natural selection alright, but creationists emphasize its limited effects while evolutionists emphasize that these examples really do show that the gene pools of populations can change in response to changing environments. Yes, we believe that evolution as a whole requires long time intervals, much longer than the lifetime of any evolutionist, making it difficult to observe evolution in nature. Nevertheless, on logical grounds, the Biologist grudgingly agrees with the Skeptic. Based on the small samples in these examples, compared with nature as a whole, it is not valid to induce a general law of nature. But then, the evolutionists could be right; their conclusion could be true even if these limited studies are not a completely valid demonstration of how species are formed in nature.

Geographical distribution

The Biologist notes that much modern study of natural selection concerns geographical distribution. Scientists study the way that new species may form as populations split into isolated groups, where mutations and natural selection can drive the isolated groups to differ from each other—often enough to allow a taxonomist to call them separate varieties or species. In such studies, and by now there must be hundreds of them, the investigator finds changes in the population as a function of location. Well, yes, says the Skeptic, but such studies are indirect. They don't demonstrate the process of natural selection; they just document situations where it seems highly reasonable that natural selection—or perhaps some other process that can influence gene pools—has been at work. The Biologist agrees, but notes that many examples are indeed impressive.

At this point, I must interrupt the Biologist and the Skeptic with a memory. One of my professors at the University of Utah, Angus Woodbury, was an authority on the distribution of rattlesnakes in the Great Basin and throughout the intermountain region. (I went with him once to the "snake pit" near Grantsville, where hundreds of rattlers hibernated under the rocks in a large field of boulders. I still remember the vivid dreams of caves of snakes that tormented my sleep during the night before the field trip.) Professor Woodbury told us how the snakes changed gradually in various features moving south from northern Utah along the western slope of the Wasatch mountains, around the southern tip of the range, and then northward along the eastern slopes of the Wasatch into the Uintah Basin. The specimens on the east of the range were different enough from those across the range to the west that they would normally be classified as two different species except that they seemed to be interbreeding all along their distribution range. Was this natural selection at work, or some other random change in the gene pool correlated with geographic distribution? It could be either or both.

The Biologist notes that the classic example, still one of the best, is the adaptive radiation of Darwin's finches, noted above, on the Galápagos Islands. Presumably fourteen species of finches descended from a common ancestor that long ago migrated (or was blown?) from the mainland to the islands. Here it is possible to see the circumstances that might have led to the natural selection. There is a woodpecker finch, which uses cactus spines to pry insect larvae and other food out of cavities in dead tree branches, a mangrove finch does the same on mangrove trees, a sharp-beaked ground finch, which perches on large sea birds, draws their blood, and drinks it, and others that remove ticks from tortoises and iguanas, live on bark (the vegetarian finch), and so on. In each case, the beak shape and size seem perfectly adapted to the finches' habits as though natural selection had acted in their evolution. It is a compelling story.

The Skeptic has no quarrel with studies such as these, or even with their conclusions. The evidence is good and the conclusions seem justified. But how far can we extrapolate? The Biologist is willing to go all the way to the grand theory; the Skeptic wonders if there might be limits to just how much mutations and natural selection can accomplish.

Microorganisms

The Biologist saved his biggest salvo for last. The story is widely repeated and highly impressive, as even the Skeptic must admit. It concerns the resistance that has appeared in many organisms (pests, from our viewpoint) against the chemicals that we have developed to eliminate them. There are numerous documented accounts of insects becoming resistant to insecticides, weeds becoming resistant to herbicides, fungi becoming resistant to fungicides, and especially various microorganisms becoming resistant to antibiotics. As you surely know, the situation with drug-resistant pathogenic bacteria and viruses, especially in hospitals, has almost reached crisis levels.

Even more impressive (but not nearly as well known) is the work going on in laboratories all over the world, in which improved enzymes are produced by random mutations and natural selection. Natural selection really does work. We'll return to these stories in chapter 4.

Problems with Natural Selection

Still, not everyone agrees that natural selection accounts for the evolution of all of the earth's organisms. Of the three problems mentioned below, the first has been argued since the time of Darwin and is implied in many discussions in this book. The second has received some attention from evolutionists and continues to be a challenge. The third is only a gut feeling of the Skeptic (and probably others, although he is not aware of discussions in the literature).

1. The problem of intermediate steps

Given ample time, the Skeptic could relate a long history of this problem and its discussion. As noted often in this book, the Skeptic says, natural selection only works if each stage in the evolution of a species is better adapted to its environment than the previous stage, so that the better adapted organisms tend to reproduce more than those members of the species that do not have the adaptation. As we'll note again in chapter 6, Darwin was well aware of this problem. He said in chapter 6 of *The Origin*: "If it could be demonstrated that any complex organ existed, which could not possibly have been formed by numerous, successive, slight modifications, my theory would absolutely break down. But I can find no such case."

Yet many creationists and other anti-evolutionists have described many situations in which it is difficult to imagine the intermediate steps in the evolution of some feature. The Skeptic tells how the evolution of flight provides an excellent and historically important example. If flight evolved by natural selection, the forelimbs of the precursors of birds (some kind of dinosaurs) must have become wings, presumably by small steps, as in the evolution of any feature. But can we really imagine small steps from fore-limbs to wings that would each have had selection value and been naturally selected over the precursor limbs by positively controlling the organism's survival)? And where are the fossils of those intermediate stages—the "missing links"?

The Biologist steps in to relate some of the many suggestions that have been made over the past century and a half to answer this question. There are "flying" squirrels, "flying" lizards, "flying" fish and many other organisms that manage to glide through the air, often from tree limb to the ground or to another tree limb. These "flying" (gliding, actually) creatures usually have some kind of membranous skin, or fins in the case of the fish, that allow them to catch the air and glide. Of course, the Biologist says, these may serve as models of the intermediate steps in the evolution of flight. He goes on to discuss the fossil birds and dinosaurs that have wings and feathers but other lizard-like features (*Archeopteryx*). Well, maybe, the Skeptic says, but some of us still see many complications that are neither solved by the fossil record nor "solved" by truly plausible stories. We'll just have to leave it at that, the Skeptic says.

Furthermore, he goes on to say, we'll encounter several other examples in this book. This problem is at the heart of the idea of irreducible complexity, which we'll discuss in chapter 6, and it certainly applies to the question of the origin of life (chapter 5).

2. Why do organisms live past the age of reproduction?

The end result of natural selection, the Skeptic says, is the ability to reproduce and pass on the genetic feature that was selected (by survival) in the first place. Once an organism has passed its genetic material on to the next generation, there is no reason for it to survive. So why do we (and other organisms) live for many years past the years during which we produce offspring?

The Biologist counters this argument with the idea that parents and even grandparents may be important in the survival and rearing of new members of the species, and if those new members have the genes to live long lives, they may be able to help their offspring survive. Evolutionists have proposed many arguments based on this principle.

Okay, the Skeptic says, but can such arguments account for the survival of organisms that carry highly maladaptive mutations that don't appear until *after* the age of reproduction? Huntington's disease in humans provides a good example. The disease is caused by a dominant gene, which causes uncontrolled movements, dementia, and finally death. These symptoms don't appear until the fifth or sixth decade of life, well after its carriers have had a chance to reproduce and pass the gene on to the next generation. Indeed, because the gene is dominant, statistically half the offspring of a person (male or female) with the gene will also carry it and eventually experience the terrible symptoms. Appearance of the gene has been traced back to as early as 1630, when it was brought by only a few individuals to both North and South America. Now it is carried by thousands of people (Klawans, 1983). Most are aware that they might have the gene (and now it is possible to detect it before symptoms appear), but they often marry and pass the gene on anyway, sometimes hoping that science will find a cure before their own or their children's symptoms appear.

The Skeptic has pointed out that the conservative function of natural selection is to rid populations of deleterious mutations, but what if those mutations do not manifest themselves until their carrier has passed them on to the next generation? The Biologist admits that this is a problem without an obvious answer.

3. Adaptations with little if any survival value

Can natural selection really account for the evolution of adaptations that have, at best, only minor survival or reproductive value? This is a subtle question, often no more than a gut feeling. The Skeptic has sometimes been reading along in some article when he encounters some adaptation that clearly provides only a minor advantage in the life of the organism. He wonders how such a feature could really make much difference in determining which organisms live to reproduce and which do not. And say that it does have some small survival advantage. Would that be enough for it to spread throughout a population, doing so while all those without the feature eventually die without passing it on?

Occasionally in the literature of evolution, an author will wonder about the selective value of music appreciation. That's about as good an example as any. During all those postulated years of human evolution on the African veld, it is doubtful that *Australopithecus* was exposed to music by Mozart or Stevie Wonder. So what advantage for survival resided in the mutations that produced the intricate structure of the inner ear with its ability to pick up the most delicate tones—especially of the functioning brain, which allows us to be enthralled by the rhythm and melody of *Clair de Lune?* (Okay, not all of us respond to the same kind of music, but love for some kind of music must be universally present in the human race—appreciation for specific kinds being to a great extent a matter of learning.)

The biologist scratches his head and begins to formulate a just-suppose story: Maybe some of those early humans learned to whistle a warning to others in the tribe when a predator or an enemy was approaching, and those who best responded to the sounds of the whistle were most likely to escape and survive. Having this ability to hear subtle sounds, and having a brain selected for emotions that led to love and fear and thus better survival, such adaptations (always based on mutations) allowed for *learning* to appreciate music—or something. Hence, the biologist feels quite certain that such minor adaptations *do* have survival value, enough to eventually spread from the individual with the right mutations throughout a population; we just don't know enough yet to tell the whole story, but some day we will know.

The Skeptic says that's okay for the Biologist to think, but the Skeptic's gut feeling *still* says that it's a problem. The Skeptic also notes that this is another good example of why the theory of evolution by natural selection of random mutations comes very close to being as much of a tautology as the Creator hypothesis. *Anything* good in an organism might have been put there by the Creator. Or it might have been the result of natural selection. If we try hard enough, we can probably devise a story to account for how natural selection could produce the feature.

Summary

1. The *general theory of evolution* holds that all living organisms evolved, over extremely long time intervals, from a common ancestor. The *specific theory of evolution* holds that the mechanism for this evolution was *natural selection* of random genetic changes.

2. The theories of both evolution and an Intelligent Creation are so broad that they can explain almost anything that is observed among living organisms. Since most features appear to be adaptive, it is easy to say that they must have been the product of natural selection. It is also easy to say

that God could have created any feature that is observed.

3. A primary evidence for the general theory is the structural relationships among organisms that allow the construction of *family trees* based on *homology* and classification schemes that will eventually show how *descent with modification* could account for all species.

4. *Vestigial organs* are easily explained by evolution and less easily by an Intelligent Creation.

5. There are many examples of *convergent* or *parallel evolution* in which similar (*analogous*) features appear in lines that diverged long before the structures developed (the vertebrate and the molluscan eyes). Evolutionists claim that these examples show the power of evolution; actually, they are easier to explain as examples of an Intelligent Creation.

6. Family trees can also be constructed on the basis of the similarity of *molecular structures* (especially proteins and nucleic acids). This is considered to be strong evidence for the general theory of evolution.

7. Study of sedimentary strata and inferences about how they had to be formed (*uniformitarianism*) has long suggested that the earth is ancient. *Radioactive dating* is a powerful means of dating the age of the earth, and it suggests that the earth is about *4.6 billion years old*.

8. Creationist *Flood Geology* completely fails to demonstrate that we live on a young earth: The *ordering of fossils* in the strata is not explained by flood geology, nor is the quantity of fossilized carbon (coal, limestones, and so forth) or *diatomaceous earth*, all of which clearly require extremely long periods for their deposition.

9. Creationists have tried to criticize the fossil record on several grounds: *Missing links* have always been a problem, but more and more of these intermediate stages in proposed evolutionary sequences are being reported.

10. Some *sequences in the fossil record* are especially striking (such as the diatoms that split into two species over a long time), but other such sequences may be more in the eye of the beholder (the record of human evolution).

11. Some *exceptions to the fossil record* are known, such as more ancient fossils lying on top of more recent fossils. But careful geologic study has revealed that these situations were caused by more ancient strata being pushed over more recent strata in the process of mountain building.

12. The *Cambrian "explosion"* (the sudden appearance of numerous species and groups of species in the most ancient strata that contain fossils

of multicellular animals) is indeed an interesting manifestation that has not been completely explained by modern paleontology.

13. *Natural selection appears in nature*, as illustrated by the peppered moths and Darwin's finches, but in those cases no new genes were necessary to account for the observations although gene pools apparently changed in response to selection pressures.

14. The *geographic distribution of related species* is in many cases exactly what one would expect if natural selection were working on gene pools in populations over extended time intervals.

15. *Natural selection and even new genes* can be demonstrated in microorganisms in the laboratory, as discussed in chapter 4.

16. Can natural selection really account for *intermediate stages* in evolution, features that appear *after the age of reproduction*, or *tiny adaptations* that apparently make little difference in an organism's ability to reproduce?

CHAPTER

3

MODERN CELLULAR AND MOLECULAR BIOLOGY: A CASE FOR DESIGN?

The task that I would *like* to accomplish in this chapter is an impossible one. It simply can't be done. I would like to bring you up to date on what is presently known about cellular and molecular biology. To really accomplish that task, I would have to write several books.[1]

The Cell Doctrine:
The Cell Is the Basic Unit of Life

Our understanding of cells is certainly as important to modern biology—to our understanding of life—as is the theory of natural selection. Again and again, however, authors quote Theodosius Dobzhansky (1973) who titled his article: "Nothing in biology makes sense except in the light of evolution."[2] Natural selection and the evolution that might result are said to form the great unifying doctrine of modern biology, but what could be more unifying than knowledge that all organisms consist of cells, and that the cells of all living things have very much in common in their apparent structure and biochemistry? The similarity of cell structure and function in all organisms is apparent, despite how much they differ.

I would love to tell the story of the development of the cell doctrine, but space simply will not allow it. Suffice it to say that the true understanding of the role of cells in life function was being developed, mostly in Continental Europe and especially in Germany, at the same time that Darwin was developing his ideas about evolution through natural selection (Harris, 1999).

The cell doctrine states, among other things, that cells originate only from the division of other cells, and that the cell is the basic unit of life. We might expand the original cell doctrine by noting that the unit of heredity is the gene, and that genes consist of DNA organized on chromosomes, though it is protein (enzymes) that account for virtually all cell functions.

Prokaryotic and Eukaryotic Cells

Study of those chromosomes has shown us that there are two fundamentally different kinds of cells: those in which the chromosomes are contained within a structure called the nucleus and those in which no nucleus can be detected, although there is usually a single chromosome. The cells with nuclei are called *eukaryotic cells* (yōōkar´ ē ōtic; means "true nucleus"), and those without organized nuclei are called *prokaryotic cells* (prō kar´ē ōtic; means "before a nucleus"). All multicellular animals, plants, fungi, and slime molds are eukaryotes, as are many single-celled algae and protozoa. Bacteria are prokaryotes, and relatively recent studies have examined a group of extremophiles—bacteria-like organisms that typically live in extreme conditions of temperature, salt concentration, and so forth. These are called Archaebacteria or simply Archaea, and studies of the DNA of Bacteria and Archaea have shown that these two groups are as different as Bacteria are from all the eukaryotes. Many biologists now speak of three great domains of life: Archaea, Bacteria, and Eukaryotes.

What about the viruses? Viruses are nucleic acids (DNA or RNA) surrounded with protein, and they are incapable of any of the manifestations of life until they enter a cell. They take over the machinery of the cell to replicate themselves, eventually bursting the cell and being released into the environment to enter other cells. Consisting only of nucleic acid and protein might make the viruses sound simple—they are anything but. Those nucleic acids and proteins are as complex and suited to their function as are those of the larger living organisms. And some viruses (bacteriophages) even *appear* complex.

But are viruses alive? They only exhibit that key manifestation of life (reproduction) when they are in proper living cells, so most biologists say they are only "alive" when in such cells. Does that mean that otherwise they are "dead"? That doesn't seem right, since they can become "alive" at any time after invading a cell. Personally, I would classify them as being part of "life," whether they are functioning or not. That is because they exhibit the *molecular* properties common to all obviously living organisms. Viruses are not cells, however.

Proteins: Cellular Machinery

Cells are incredibly complex machines. They carry out a vast number of chemical reactions, the sum total of which accounts for what we recognize as life function (and which we call metabolism). Almost all of this metabolism is under the control of the proteins we call enzymes, with a specific enzyme being responsible for each chemical reaction.

Enzymes are the key to understanding life, so it is essential that we have some understanding of just what proteins are. In one sense, proteins are rather simple: They consist of only twenty different kinds of *amino acids* hooked together to form long chains. We'll have to skip a detailed discussion of amino acids, noting that each amino acid has what is called a *carboxyl group* (-COOH), which is an acid, plus an *amino group* (-NH$_2$), which is a base. An acid donates a hydrogen ion (-COOH $\leftrightarrows$ -COO$^-$ + H$^+$), and a base accepts a hydrogen ion (-NH$_2$ + H$^+$ $\leftrightarrows$ -NH$_3$$^+$). The simplest amino acid (glycine) combines the carboxyl and amino groups with a single hydrogen atom; all other amino acids have a more complex molecular structure (denoted as R), attached where the hydrogen atom is in glycine. The amino acids in proteins are attached to each other with peptide bonds, which involve the carboxyl of one amino acid attaching to the amino of the next in the chain. Actually, even in proteins, the carboxyl can act as an acid and the amino can act as a base, all of which is highly important to an understanding of enzyme action.

As we will emphasize in the rest of this book, it is the sequence of amino acids in the protein chain that accounts for the specific function of the protein. Some of the R groups are acids; others are bases. Some R groups attract water molecules; others repel water molecules. The extent to which this occurs depends on the acidity (pH) of the milieu in which the protein finds itself and on other factors. One result is that the amino acid chain folds in highly specific ways that are determined by how the amino acids in the chain attract or repel each other. In principle, this seems simple enough, but in practice, molecular biologists can not yet predict exactly how an amino acid chain will fold, although it has been possible during the past few decades to determine the sequence of amino acids in any given protein and even to learn how they are folded. By August 2005, some 32,434 proteins had been sequenced (the sequence of amino acids determined), and their folded form visualized.[3] (As recently as the 1950s, it took ten years to sequence the 51 amino acids in bovine insulin, a relatively small protein that was the first to be sequenced.)

There are other complications, as you might expect, including the attachment of other molecules (many of which we recognize as vitamins) or mineral atoms. The end result is a protein with a specific function. Some proteins are structural, such as fingernails and hair or the storage protein in seeds, but the important proteins are enzymes.

How does an enzyme control a given reaction? To begin with, the reaction must be possible; that is, given enough time, the reaction would occur anyway. But this time could be tens to hundreds of years compared with the tiny fraction of a second required for the reaction in a cell. Hence, what the enzyme does is speed up a reaction that might otherwise be extremely slow. The reason the reaction might normally be slow is that it requires an input of energy to boost it over a so-called energy barrier. The enzyme greatly lowers this barrier so that the heat energy already present (the thermal activity of the surrounding molecules) is sufficient to drive the reaction in a very short time. This speeding of reactions is called *catalysis*; enzymes (*catalysts*) catalyze reactions. (Reactions are known in which a single enzyme molecule can catalyze thousands to millions of reactions per second.) The enzyme remains essentially intact after the reaction.

How does this work? The amino acid chain is configured by folding and other interactions such that it includes one or more *active sites*. The active site attaches to the *substrate* molecule, which then undergoes a reaction to produce a *product*, to use the terms used by biochemists.

An example is in order. The common household sugar, sucrose, consists of two simpler sugars: glucose and fructose. An enzyme, *sucrase*, or *invertase*, has an active site that exactly matches the configuration of the sucrose molecule. At any temperature above absolute zero, molecules are moving at rapid rates. (Each molecule in air is moving, on average, at the speed of sound, colliding with other molecules millions to billions of times per second.) In the cellular environment, millions of different molecules (most of them probably water) are colliding with the sucrase enzyme each second, striking at all sides at many velocities. When a sucrose molecule

Catalase: An important protein in cellular metabolism. Many metabolic steps in cells produce hydrogen peroxide (H_2O_2), which can be very damaging to cells. Thus, cells have the enzyme **catalase**, each molecule of which can break down millions of H_2O_2 molecules per second. The four active sites of the catalase that protects human red blood cells each has an atom of iron surrounded by a heme molecule, similar to part of hemoglobin, the red blood pigment.

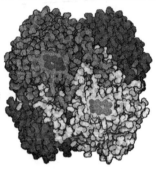

A 11-amino-acid Peptide; Typical of a Protein Back Bone (peptide bonds ■).

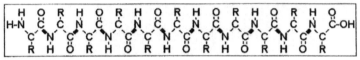

Formation of a Peptide Bond

Figure 3–1

A one-page guide to proteins. The boxes on the bottom show the generalized structure of amino acids, which combine by forming peptide bonds (vertical arrow, second box from bottom). Long chains of amino acids form the backbone of proteins (top box), such as the enzyme catalase (top right), which consists of four protein chains and a total of 2,108 amino acids. (#1QQW from the Protein Data Bank, drawing by David S. Goodsell, based on T. P. Ko et. al, 2000. *Acta Crystallogr.*, section D, p. 56)

collides with the active site of the sucrase molecule in just the right way (and this collision is strictly a matter of chance), it briefly attaches, and the sucrase bends slightly, putting stress on the sucrose (substrate), which then reacts with a molecule of water and splits into glucose and fructose (products).

To summarize: Life consists of enzymes in cells, the enzymes catalyze thousands of different reactions (each enzyme almost always catalyzing only a single reaction or reaction type), the total of which accounts for the functions of life. Each enzyme is able to do what it does because of its configuration. In many cases, those "vitamins" and/or minerals are part of the active site. The configuration, in turn, depends upon the sequence of amino acids that make up the protein or enzyme. We often refer to this sequence as *information,* just as we can refer to the sequence of letters in this sentence as being responsible for the information contained in the sentence. This is the real basis for the complexity that we call life; it is the "secret of life." Figure 3-1 on the preceding page summarizes the above discussion about proteins and what they do.

How Big Are Cells?

Before looking closely inside cells, let's consider the sizes of cells and the atoms and molecules (those enzymes) that constitute cells and are the actual players in the drama of life.

Begin with the meter (m), the standard of length in the International System of Units (*Le Système International d'Unités,* internationally called the *SI*). A tall basketball player can be 2 m (6' 6.74") tall. Divide the meter into 1000 equal parts to get millimeters, ten of which make a centimeter: ||||||||||| Now divide a millimeter into 1000 equal parts to get a micrometer (μm; formerly called a micron). Micrometers can describe the dimensions of cells as seen with light microscopes. But such instruments cannot resolve anything smaller than about 0.2 μm in diameter because that is half the wavelength of blue light, and anything smaller is simply too small to cast a shadow. The most powerful light microscopes magnify about 1000 to 2000 times (diameters). Lenses can be ground that magnify more, but only the blur is magnified, which is called *empty magnification,* so nothing new is revealed.

Bacteria are among the smallest cells. They may be a few micrometers long but are seldom wider than about 1.0 μm. Plant cells typically range from 10 to 100 μm in diameter. With a good hand lens, it is possible to see cells with a diameter of 100 μm (0.1 mm—one fifth the diameter of a period). The large pores in hardwoods are dead, water-conducting cells and are readily visible. Human cells are about 20 μm in diameter. A human body has about 75,000,000,000,000 (75 trillion) cells, and it would require about 10,000 of these to cover the head of a pin. (Our bodies each have more cells than the national debt in dollars.)

The next step down is to divide the micrometer into a thousand parts, called nanometers. The breakthrough in visualizing objects in the nanometer range came in 1933 with the invention of the electron microscope. Because beams of electrons (as in a television tube) have extremely short wavelengths (on the order of 0.005 nm), nanometer-sized objects can "cast a shadow of electrons" when focused on a view screen or a sheet of film. Electron beams are focused with electro magnets, but they cannot travel through air, so the source of the electrons, their path through the lenses and the specimen, and even the view screen or film must be in a vacuum. Tissue absorbs electron beams, causing it to heat and often to be destroyed, so microscopists use heavy-metal stains that coat the molecules that make up cell structures.

By the late 1940s, electron microscopes were in wide use by cell biologists, and the instruments are now taken for granted, although they are still very costly. The best instruments can resolve objects as small as 0.2 nm; hence, it is possible to view viruses, some molecules, and even atoms. (The limitation on resolution is not the wavelength of the electron beams but problems in focusing the beams to form an image.) Cell biologists still use light microscopes, but electron microscopes have revolutionized our knowledge of cells. For example, prokaryotic cells are so tiny that virtually nothing was known about their internal structures until the invention of electron microscopes. Viruses are invisible in light microscopes.

Eukaryotic Cells

Prokaryotic cells are highly organized and complex (Hoppert & Mayer, 1999). For example, Bacteria and Archaea are capable of many biochemical reactions that Eukaryotes cannot produce. Unfortunately, we must limit our discussion to a superficial description of typical eukaryotic cells, with some reference now and then to prokaryotic cells.

As noted above, eukaryotic cells are characterized by the presence of a nucleus. Outside of the nucleus is a watery matrix called *cytosol*. Several small bodies called *organelles* can be seen in the cytosol, and the cytosol and organelles are collectively called *cytoplasm*. Thus, cells inside their membranes consist of cytoplasm and a nucleus—sometimes more than one nucleus.

Membranes

The cytoplasm contains a highly complex system of membranes. As it turns out, all membranes are basically alike; they consist of two layers

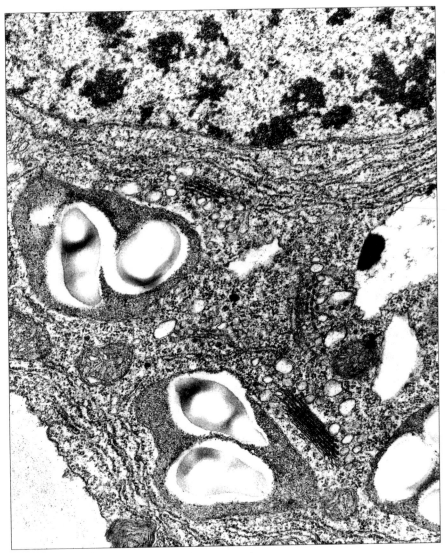

Figure 3-2A

A transmission electron micrograph of a thin section of a wheat-root cell. Compare figure 3-2B for identification of the various parts. (Courtesy of Wilford Hess, BYU Electron Optics Laboratory)

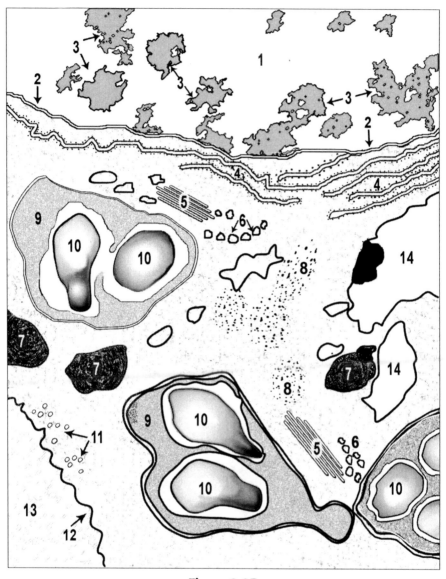

Figure 3-2B

Tracing of the electron micrograph of Figure 3–2A, identifying the various parts:

1. Nucleus
2. Nuclear Membrane
3. Chromatin
4. Endoplasmic reticulum.
5. Golgi Apparatus
6. Vesicles
7. Mitochondria
8. Ribosomes
9. Pro-plastids
10. Starch grains
11. Microtubules
12. Plasma membrane
13. Cell wall
14. Vacuoles

of *phospholipid* molecules, which have one *hydrophilic* end that is attracted to water molecules and another *hydrophobic* end that repels water molecules. The hydrophobic ends of the molecules attract each other, forming a membrane about 75 nm thick that consists of two layers, with the hydrophilic ends of the phospholipids on the outside of the membrane in contact with the surrounding water, and the hydrophobic ends in contact with each other. In properly prepared electron micrographs, cross-sections of membranes appear as two dark lines (the hydrophilic ends) separated by a lighter area (the hydrophobic ends). Thus membranes in electron micrographs can be referred to as *bilayers* (Figure 3-2).

But there is more to the membrane than its bilayer structure. If that is all there were, few things, including water molecules, could move in or out of cells. Life is highly dependent on specific molecules, ions, and such moving in and out of cells, or *not* moving in or out in other cases. This is accomplished thanks to highly specific proteins embedded in the bilayers. Each such protein has a sequence of amino acids that causes it to fold into a shape that allows the passage of some specific molecule or ion type through the membrane, and often in one direction but not the other.

The so-called potassium-ion channel provides a beautiful example. It was long a mystery how a potassium channel, which consists of four identical proteins arranged in a sort of teepee shape (the tip of the teepee pointing toward the inside of the cell) could exclude sodium ions (Na^+), which have the same charge as potassium ions (K^+) but are slightly smaller. The detailed protein structures were finally worked out by Roderick MacKinnon at the Rockefeller University in New York. I like the description by John Travis (2002) in *Science News*: "It turns out that the wide exterior opening of a [K^+] channel contains . . . a selectivity filter. Potassium ions, stripped of the water molecules that normally surround them . . . just fit inside this oxygen-lined tunnel structure [amino acids with exposed oxygen atoms]. . . . 'The potassium channel is organized to be a mimic of water,' says MacKinnon. 'The design is very simple and very beautiful.' Sodium ions are too small for a potassium channel's oxygen lining to effectively take the place of the ion's shell of water. As a result, the sodium ions generally remain outside the channel." Could such complexity come about by molecular natural selection as most biologists think? Perhaps, and perhaps not.

Membranes play critical roles in cells besides determining what goes in or comes out. Indeed, there is a system of membranes crisscrossing the cytoplasm called the *endoplasmic reticulum* or *ER*. These membranes, with

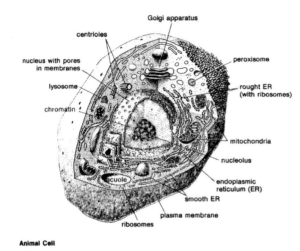

Figure 3-2C

Generalized drawings of an animal cell and a plant cell. The drawings are based on the appearance of cellular organelles in electron micrographs. (From Edward John Kormondy, *Biology: The Integrity of Organisms* [Belmont, Calif.: Wadsworth Publishing Co., 1977]; reprinted with permission of Brooks/Cole, a division of Thomson Learning: www.thomsonrights. com)

their special proteins, perform many functions in cells, including the synthesis of more membranes. The ER was unknown before the invention of the electron microscope.

Membranes also surround most of the structures in eukaryotic cells, including the mitochondria and chloroplasts, which we'll encounter below. Special membrane structures collectively called the *Golgi complex* (after Camillo Golgi, who observed them with a light microscope near the beginning of the twentieth century—see Harris, 1999) are known to process certain molecules and transport them to specific sites in a cell or to dump them outside of a cell.

Membranes surround *lysosomes*, which contain digestive enzymes that can digest cell contents when a cell dies. There are also membrane-bound *microbodies*, which play various roles in plant and animal cells. A structure highly specific to plant cells is the large, central *vacuole*, which is enclosed by a membrane with a special name: the *tonoplast*. A vacuole can occupy over 90 percent of the volume of a plant cell. Many newly formed plant cells (formed by cell division in the growing regions of stems and roots) have only small vacuoles, but growth of these cells occurs primarily as the vacuoles enlarge and coalesce into a single large vacuole. (Of course, cell growth after cell division also requires synthesis of all the molecules found in the mother cell.)

The vacuole contains many dissolved substances, and these solutes, more concentrated than the dilute solutions outside the cell, cause the cell to absorb water osmotically. Most animals need to be compact and highly mobile, but plants must expose a large amount of surface to sunlight and to soil, and the vacuoles provide volume based on water instead of cytoplasm. This volume can be spread into thin layers (most leaves) or thin tubes (most roots and evergreen needles) much more "cheaply" than if the entire plant body, like animal bodies, had to be made of cells containing only "expensive" cytoplasm and nuclei. Understanding the plant vacuole is critical to understanding plants.

The cytoskeleton

The cytoplasm of eukaryotic cells includes a system of fibers that collectively support the structure of the cells and thus is referred to as the *cytoskeleton*. These fibers do more than support cell form; they also account for cell movements. There are two primary kinds of fibers: *microtubules* and *actin filaments* (also called microfilaments). Microtubules are about 25 nm in diameter, while actin filaments are 5 to 7 nm in diameter. These fibers are neat little machines that can convert chemical bond energy into mechanical energy. Their protein subunits use chemical energy to form bridges that cause the tubule or filament to contract. In Eukaryotes, microtubules cause the beating of cilia and flagella and other cellular movements, while actin filaments are solely responsible for the flowing of cytoplasm around the periphery of living cells, a phenomenon called *cytoplasmic streaming*, which has been observed since the invention of the compound microscope. These filaments also account for ameboid motion and the contraction of muscle cells. Nuclear division (separation of the chromosomes) in animal cells depends on microtubules, while division of the cytoplasm requires actin filaments.

Ribosomes

In the cytoplasm around the nucleoid (prokaryotes) or nucleus (eukaryotes), there are minute bodies that are densely stained in electron micrographs. These are *ribosomes*, roughly circular and visible as black dots (Figure 3-2A). In prokaryotes, they are only 20 to 30 nm in diameter, which is about ten times smaller in diameter than the smallest objects visible in the light microscope. Cytoplasmic, eukaryotic ribosomes are somewhat larger—25 to 35 nm. Ribosomes prove to be extremely important and highly complex. It is the ribosomes that synthesize protein; ribosomes themselves each contain more than 50 different proteins in combination with several types of ribonucleic acid (RNA), all of which is essential to the synthesis of all proteins, including those in ribosomes. Ribosomes can occur free in the cytoplasm or embedded in the ER. There are thousands in each cell. We'll return to them later in this chapter.

Mitochondria and chloroplasts

Most eukaryotic cells have hundreds to thousands of small spheres, rods, or filaments, called *mitochondria*, which are about 0.5 to 1.0 μm in diameter—about the size of a bacterium. They consist of a double membrane system that encloses a fluid matrix. The outer membrane is smooth and permeable to many substances, but the inner one is folded or tubular in structure. These membranes are not formed by the ER; they have enzymes and even ribosomes (smaller than the ribosomes in the cytosol) and synthesize themselves at least partially under the control of their own DNA. Many enzymes are part of a mitochondrion, some embedded especially in the inner membranes and others suspended in the matrix.

Mitochondria can break down and oxidize all of the main cellular constituents—carbohydrates, fats, proteins, and nucleic acids. This breakdown is not a simple digestion, however, as it is in lysosomes. Through a highly complex system of about fifty reactions in a process called *cellular respiration*, the mitochondria can convert the chemical bond energy of the compounds that they oxidize into a form that can be used for all the energy-requiring activities of cells, such as synthesis of molecules such as protein, the transport of various molecules and ions through membranes, the contraction of microtubules and actin filaments (cell movements), and various other activities. The energy currency of the cell, formed in respiration and photosynthesis, is a compound called ATP (adenosine triphosphate; see appendix C). Because mitochondria are the only source of ATP in nonphotosynthesizing cells, they are often called the power houses of the cell.

Cellular respiration is not the only function of mitochondria. Many other chemical reactions are also carried out in these marvelous organelles. It has been estimated that over half of cell metabolism takes place in mitochondria.

The mitochondria are unique in many ways. They are passed from generation to generation via the egg cell but not the sperm cell that fertilizes it; that is, they are maternally inherited. These cellular power houses, to a great extent, act as agents unto themselves. They include their own DNA, RNA, ribosomes, and most of the enzymes needed to reproduce themselves, although they are dependent to a considerable extent upon proteins that are controlled by the nucleus.

Clearly, mitochondria resemble Bacteria in many ways, such as their size, nature of their chromosome, bacterial-type ribosomes, in-folded membrane system, and extensive metabolic talents. Because of these resemblances, many biologists believe that many eons ago some bacterium became incorporated into a eukaryotic cell, leading to today's mitochondria (see Margulis & Sagan, 2002).

Many plant cells contain *chloroplasts*, the green bodies responsible for *photosynthesis*, a fantastically complex process that involves numerous proteins, specific metal ions like iron, magnesium, molybdenum, copper, and chlorophyll molecules (Appendix C). Chloroplasts are much larger than mitochondria and are easily visible with light microscopes. Again, a double membrane system is crucial to their function, and it has also been suggested that an ancient photosynthesizing bacterium became incorporated into an ancient eukaryotic cell, leading to today's green plants.

The plant cell wall

The plant cell wall is a unique structure. Although prokaryotes have cell walls, prokaryotic walls are not closely related chemically to the cell walls of plants. (A few rare bacteria do produce cellulose.) Fungi cells have walls, but they also differ chemically from those of plants. A few green algae have walls similar to those of higher plants. Animals never have cell walls.

Plant cell walls are typically 1 to 3 μm thick, about as thick as a bacterium is in diameter. The wall consists of cellulose fibers embedded in a watery matrix. The cellulose is synthesized by enzymes in the cell membrane, which presses tightly against the wall. Indeed, a plant cell absorbs water by osmosis until the pressure inside the cell equals that in a culinary water system or a high-pressure bicycle tire. It is the wall that keeps the cell from bursting; cellulose fibers have the tensile strength of steel. It is this pressure in plant cells that gives the nonwoody parts of a plant their shape. A wilted plant has lost water. If a plant cell is growing, enzymes released from Golgi vesicles soften the bonds that hold the cellulose fibers together so that the wall can stretch as the cell continues to take up water. The cellulose fibers in the wall lie in layers of parallel fibers, with the fibers in the different layers arranged at angles to each other. There is space between the fibers allowing water and many dissolved substances to pass freely through the wall; it is the membrane inside that controls what goes into and out of plant cells, just as in animal cells and other cells that have no walls. As the wall matures in wood cells, it is hardened by impregnation with *lignin*.

Cell walls have many interesting features, including various pits and "carvings." Especially important are structures called *plasmodesmata*: pores that penetrate the wall from one cell to its neighbor. These pores are 30 to 100 nm in diameter, so they can only be visualized with the electron microscope. These tiny pores are important because they are penetrated by the cell membrane and by a minute strand of cytoplasm. This means that plant cells are not really individuals. The cytoplasms of virtually all the living cells in a plant are connected together, and dissolved substances, including large protein molecules, can pass from cell to cell through the plasmodesmata.

The nucleus and DNA

As suspected not long after Robert Brown, in 1830, observed the nuclei in many kinds of plant cells, the nucleus is truly the control center of the cell. During the last half of the twentieth century, we gained an amazing amount of knowledge about how this control is carried out.

First, we need a brief overview of the structure of a typical nucleus. The nuclei of all Eukaryotes are essentially alike. A double bilayer membrane, the *nuclear envelope*, encloses the nucleus (Figure 3-2). A thin space separates the two bilayers, and the envelope is penetrated by numerous pores, each 70 to 90 nm wide. Lining each pore is a ring of protein called the *annulus*, which controls the movement of large molecules of protein and RNA in and out of the nucleus. The nuclear envelope is itself a highly complex structure, yet it disappears each time the nucleus divides, reappearing after division is complete.

Inside the nucleus is a mass of *chromatin fibers*, which consist of DNA and two kinds of protein: histones and nonhistone chromosomal proteins. These proteins are critical in maintaining the DNA structures and in regulating which DNA molecules (genes) are active. During cell division, the *nucleoprotein* chromatin fibers condense into structures long recognized as *chromosomes*. The number of chromosomes varies in different organisms. Human cells have 46 chromosomes. These contain much more DNA than does a typical prokaryotic chromosome. If the human DNA in any one nucleus could be stretched out into one long strand, it would be about 1.8 meters long, although the nucleus itself is only about 6 μm in diameter. The total, stretched-out DNA in any human cell is as long as an average basketball player.

It is almost beyond our imagination to visualize how 1.8 m of DNA could be packed into each of the trillion-plus nuclei in a human body. Some other organisms have even more. A single cell of an amphibian such as a frog contains about 10 m of DNA.

Perhaps it might help to visualize this tight packing if we mentally enlarge everything a million times. Now the nucleus is 6 m in diameter (about the size of a really small house), but the DNA strands are only two millimeters thick, though they have a total length of about 1800 km (1100 miles).

Embedded among the chromatin fibers are one or more masses of small fibers and granules called the *nucleoli*. The nucleoli are a subpart of the chromatin, and their genes control the synthesis of the RNA of ribosomes. In a nucleolus, protein synthesized outside the nucleus is combined with the RNA made in the nucleolus to form two subparts of ribosomes, which then move through the pores in the nuclear envelope, out of the nucleus, into the cytoplasm, there uniting to form complete ribosomes.

The key to understanding how chromosomes in the nucleus control cell function—indeed, control life itself—is to understand the *deoxyribonucleic acid* (*DNA*), which makes up those long strands of chromatin fibers, and the closely related *ribonucleic acid (RNA)*, which is a key player in synthesis of protein.

The history of how we gained our understanding of DNA and RNA is fascinating, to say the least, but we must be satisfied with only a few summary sentences here. *Nucleic acid (DNA)* was isolated between 1869 and 1874 at the University of Tübingen in Germany. During the last of the nineteenth century and the first decades of the twentieth century, it became clear that heredity was controlled by genes on the chromosomes, and that chromosomes consisted of both protein and nucleic acid—that is, nucleoprotein. By the 1940s, some biologists were arguing about whether the genes were protein or DNA. Because, by then, it was clear that the role of a gene was to control the sequence of those twenty amino acids in proteins (enzymes), it was easy to argue that the genes might be protein, acting in some way as templates for the synthesis of more protein. After all, the nucleic acids were made up of only four kinds of molecules, called *nucleotides*. Because of their association with the chromosomes, they seemed to be important, but how could they be the genes that control protein synthesis?

Nevertheless, during the 1940s, evidence began to accumulate that the genes were indeed nucleic acids and not proteins. For one thing, electron micrographs showed that certain viruses left their protein on the outside of an infected cell, inserting only the nucleic acid, and for another thing, isolated DNA incorporated into certain bacterial cells changed the heredity of those cells.

Enter James D. Watson and Francis H. C. Crick. To make a long and most fascinating story very short, in 1953, at the Cavendish Laboratories in Cambridge, England, Watson and Crick determined the molecular structure of DNA, based on X-ray diffraction photos of high quality DNA crystals, the photos being made in the laboratory of Maurice Wilkins by Rosalind Franklin at Kings College, London (Watson, 1968; Maddox, 2002; Sayre, 1975).

The structure immediately suggested how genes might be duplicated as cells divide, maintaining the nucleotide sequence of the original DNA molecule. The key is the phenomenon of *complementary bonding*. DNA was long known to consist of four nucleotides (symbolized as A, T, G, and C), each one consisting of a phosphate group, a five-carbon sugar, and one of four molecules (as shown in Figure 3-3). Based on one of Franklin's photos, Watson and Crick guessed that each DNA molecule consisted of

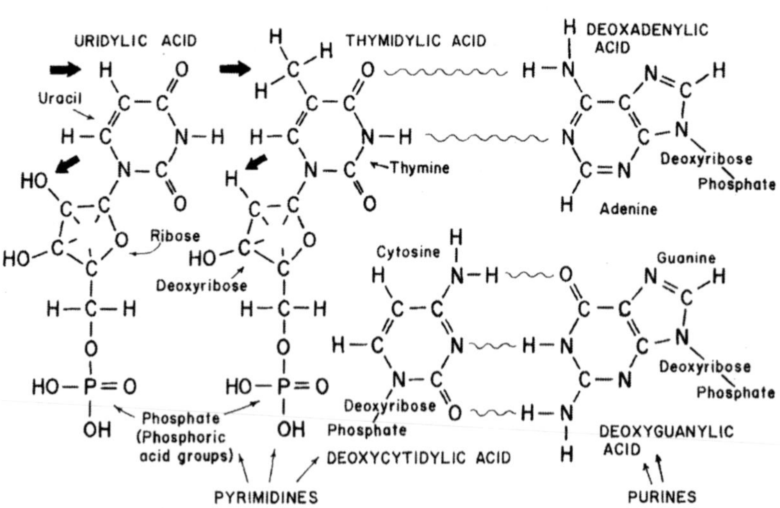

Figure 3–3

Molecular structures of two nucleotides (uridylic acid and thymidylic acid) that occur in RNA and DNA, respectively, plus the other three bases that occur in both DNA and RNA (adenine, cytosine, and guanine). The arrows point out the differences between uridylic acid and thymidylic acid: the side chain on the pyrimidine bases and the -OH on ribose compared with the -H on deoxyribose. Note that the purine bases consist of a six-membered and a five-membered ring, while the pyrimidine bases have only a six-membered ring. The wavy lines show how the complementary bonding works. (From F. B. Salisbury, 1965, p. 136; used by permission)

two strands, twisted to form the familiar *double helix* so often depicted in the current media. The key insight was that the molecular structures and sizes would only allow the two strands to be complements of each other. If an A existed at one point in the helix, only a T would fit across from it in the other strand, and a T would accommodate only an A. The G and C were likewise complementary to each other. If the two strands were to be separated and then new complementary strands formed along each of the separated strands, the result would be two helices that were identical to the original. It is not stretching things too far to say that, along with protein functions, such complementary bonding is the secret of life. The double helix is arguably the most important discovery of the twentieth century.

The detailed understanding that has developed from this initial observation (only a little over half a century ago) fills volumes and gives insights that seemed beyond hope to those of us who were students (or even professors) in 1953.

There are two parts to the story of cell function based on nucleic acids and proteins or enzymes: how genes pass their information (the sequences of nucleotides) from cell generation to generation and how this information is translated into suitable sequences of amino acids in proteins. Our summary here must be very superficial.

DNA reproduction

The reproduction of DNA (actually well before cell division occurs) is itself highly complex, yet it is currently understood in considerable detail. Specific enzymes are required to unwind the strands and to add the nucleotides to the newly forming double helices, and the process is complicated by the necessity of the addition of nucleotides going in one direction along one of the two strands and in the opposite direction, short segments at a time, along the other strand. A highly important detail concerns what it is that determines when DNA duplication will occur, and another detail involves special enzymes that correct mistakes that might be made in the process. Much molecular machinery is required for DNA (gene) duplication, but the machinery insures that the process is highly accurate, with far fewer "typographical errors" than in any comparable human process, such as printing of this book. It is important to realize that DNA has only two functions. One is to carry the sequence information from cell generation to generation and from parent to offspring; the other is to act as a template for mRNA and protein synthesis.

Protein synthesis

RNA, on the other hand, acts in various ways, almost all concerned with *translation* of the four-nucleotide DNA code into the twenty-amino-acid code of protein. This is accomplished with various kinds of RNA. (RNA differs from DNA only by the addition of one oxygen atom to the five-carbon sugar, and by a slight modification in the T nucleotide so that it becomes a nucleotide called U—which is still complementary to A. Yet these differences make complementary bonding of RNA much less stable, although we'll see that the bonding is still critical in translation.) We'll consider three critical RNA types (Figure 3-4 on the following page).

The first RNA to concern us is called *messenger-RNA* (*mRNA*) because

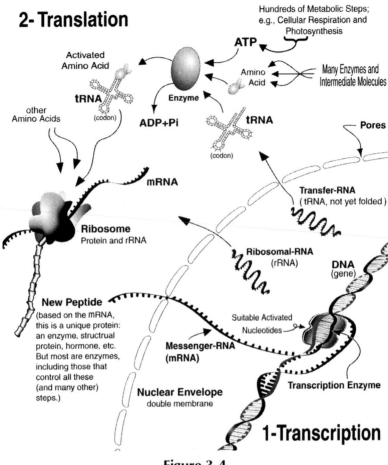

2- Translation

Hundreds of Metabolic Steps; e.g., Cellular Respiration and Photosynthesis

ATP

Activated Amino Acid

Amino Acid — Many Enzymes and Intermediate Molecules

tRNA

Enzyme

other Amino Acids

(codon)

ADP+Pi

tRNA

(codon)

Pores

mRNA

Transfer-RNA (tRNA, not yet folded)

Ribosome
Protein and rRNA

Ribosomal-RNA (rRNA)

DNA (gene)

New Peptide
(based on the mRNA, this is a unique protein: an enzyme, structrual protein, hormone, etc. But most are enzymes, including those that control all these (and many other) steps.)

Suitable Activated Nucleotides

Messenger-RNA (mRNA)

Transcription Enzyme

Nuclear Envelope
double membrane

1-Transcription

Figure 3-4

The roles of RNA in protein synthesis. The various molecules are not drawn to the same scale, and all molecules and the nuclear envelope are schematic and not truly realistic, except that the ribosome is known to have a complex shape much as shown, and the transfer-RNAs are pictured approximately as they are known to be. (The activated amino acid attaches to the end opposite to the codon, which complementarily bonds onto the messenger RNA chain within the ribosome). The ribosomal RNA is made within the nucleolus (complementarily bonded to DNA, as are mRNA and tRNA). The ribosome consists of about fifty-five proteins and three RNA molecules; the proteins configure the ribosome so that protein synthesis is possible. The proteins are synthesized in the cytoplasm (on ribosomes) and transported into the nucleolus, where they are combined with rRNA to form units, which then move back into the cytoplasm, where they are assembled into ribo-somes. Cellular life is indeed complex! (Drawing by Tami Allen Salisbury) it carries the message from the gene to the ribosomes where protein synthesis occurs. Only certain genes are active in any given cell, accounting for the differences in cell types in multicellular organisms. Which genes are activated depends on still more complex factors, some related to the protein that is associated with DNA in the chromosome. If a gene is activated, its helix is being separated into the two strands, and a strand of mRNA is being formed along one of the two strands (called the *sense strand*) by complementary bonding. This means that suitable nucleotides are available in the vicinity, and especially that suitable enzymes are present to catalyze the process.

Once the sequence of nucleotides in the DNA sense strand has been *transcribed* (copied) into a complementary sequence of a long strand of mRNA, that mRNA enters the cytoplasm and becomes associated at one end with a ribosome. Remember that the ribosome consists of over 50 proteins, plus *ribosomal RNA*. As it turns out, it is the *rRNA* that is the actual active site for protein synthesis. (The rRNA is our second kind of RNA.)

The next step involves *transfer RNAs* (*tRNAs*, our third RNA), which might as well be called translation-RNAs, because these molecules do the actual translation from the DNA nucleotide sequence to the protein amino acid sequence. There are many kinds of these molecules, but one part of each tRNA molecule is capable of becoming attached to a single kind of amino acid, and this is determined by specific enzymes (a different enzyme for each tRNA), which recognize (by configuration) both the amino acid and the particular tRNA. (To be recognized, each amino acid must first be activated by ATP in the presence of a specific enzyme.)

Translation is necessary to go from the four nucleotide nucleic acids to the twenty amino acid proteins. This occurs by taking three nucleotides at a time, a set of three being called a *codon*. Taking two nucleotides at a time, there are 4x4=16 possible combinations—not enough to account for twenty amino acids. Taking three nucleotides at a time, however, there are 4x4x4=64 possibilities—more than enough to do the job. Beginning in about 1960, it became possible, given any codon (AGU, ACU, and so forth), to learn what its role was. That knowledge constitutes what is known as the *genetic code*, and it proves to be *redundant*. That is, most of the amino acids are coded by more than one codon. Four codons play the role of *punctuation marks*; they start or stop transcription of a DNA strand.

(It is easy to think of the code as the sequence of nucleotides in DNA or even the sequence of amino acids in proteins, but the code is really a matter of matching each of the codons to the amino acid that it determines.)

Another part of a tRNA molecule (in addition to the part recognized by the enzyme) has three nucleotides exposed so that they can act as codons (or *anticodons*). By complementary bonding, they line up along the strand of mRNA at the ribosome. This is what insures that the proper sequence of amino acids will form—the sequence is ultimately determined by the sequence of nucleotides in DNA. The ribosome ties the amino acids together, forming peptide bonds between each two amino acids. Once the chain of amino acids is formed, it folds according to yet-to-be-understood mechanisms, making the final, functional protein.

There are hundreds to thousands of activated genes in any given cell at any given time, controlling the synthesis of hundreds to thousands of enzymes; the net result is the proper functioning of that cell. Much of this molecular machinery is concerned with making more of the same machinery—reproducing itself. Life is chemistry controlled by enzymes, which in turn are controlled by DNA.

The cell is a highly complex bit of molecular machinery. If this information is new to you, study Figure 3-4 and, if necessary, read the above paragraphs again. Charles Darwin would have been thrilled to know what we now know about this molecular machinery. If he had understood the complexity of these things, one wonders, would he still have arrived at the theory of natural selection? We'll never know. In any case, DNA and enzymes are clearly at the heart of the question of an Intelligent Creation. Can random mutations (changes in the nucleotide sequences of DNA) and natural selection really account for life's complexity? Although most biologists would answer yes, you are entitled to wonder as I do. There might well be a role for an Intelligent Creator.

The Mystery of Development

By now, it should be apparent that if life is to function, everything going on in cells and the organisms they constitute must be coordinated. We can think of this coordination as *programing*. At the cellular level, metabolism must be programmed so that some single process doesn't get out of synchronization with everything else that is going on.

At a higher level, multicellular organisms (eukaryotes) begin as a single cell, usually a fertilized egg cell. This cell then divides again and again. In a human being, this process produces 75 trillion cells. Along the way, the cells are specializing in just the right places and at just the right times. Some cells form a heart; others form the vascular system through which the heart will pump blood. Some cells become muscles, skin, or another one of more than two hundred different kinds of cells. Indeed, some cells even become neurons—cells that are capable of thinking about themselves. Clearly, in each cell type, only certain genes are active, making certain enzymes that account for what that cell is. The functions of all the cells are programmed in the DNA of a fertilized egg cell.

All of this is called *development*. Modern biology has made great strides in understanding how development works—how some genes control the activation of other genes and how some of these controlling genes are similar in widely different animals and plants. The programing leads to cell specialization, called *differentiation*. It is a large topic, and volumes have been written about it (such as Wolpert et al., 2002). Yet the basic programing of differentation remains a mystery—probably the most important mystery in biology—that just might be solved within the next decade or decades. All indications, however, are that understanding how development is programmed will *not* allow us to imagine that life is very simple, after all. Development of a mature, eukaryotic organism will most likely be one more layer of great complexity in life function.

Cell Division

To give you an idea of some of the complexities that are involved in development, we'll consider just one process that is universal in eukaryotic organisms: cell division. There won't be space to discuss the real complexities and subtleties of development in general and cell division in particular, but you'll see that cell division is a highly complex and programmed process.

Mitosis

The division of the nucleus, called mitosis, in eukaryotes is a most amazing phenomenon. The whole process is smooth and orderly, but for convenience cytologists have divided it into four main stages that include a number of substages. A fifth stage, called *interphase*, occurs when the chromosomes are not visible if the cell is programmed to divide. These events occur during cell division in all eukaryotes, so the process has been performed flawlessly countless trillions of trillions of times during all the billions of years that eukaryotes have lived on Earth.

There must be some kind of program, presumably a part of the genome (contained in the genes), that guides the replication of chromosomes successfully from cell generation to generation, *ad infinitum*, in each individual organism, as it develops from the fertilized egg—or even if it develops asexually.

Examine Figure 3-5 and compare the drawings with the caption and the description of mitosis that follows (and remember your biology class). We have already discussed the complex duplication of the DNA in the chromatin; this must be accompanied by duplication of the proteins that are associated with the DNA in the chromatin. All of this duplication occurs during interphase.

During much of interphase, the cell is going about all of its other

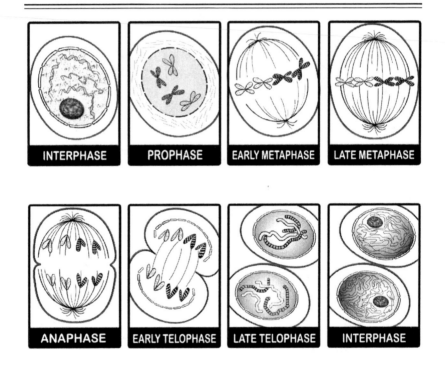

Figure 3-5

Mitosis: the process by which the nuclear material of a eukaryotic cell becomes divided in two. Two pairs of chromosomes are shown; they appear first at prophase and disappear at telophase, but there are also two pairs at telophase just before they disappear. Division of the cell (by formation of the cell plate in plant cells) is called cytokinesis; mitosis refers to separation of the chromosomes. (Computer drawing by Tami Allen Salisbury) business. Its DNA strands are not tightly coiled as they are in chromosomes; rather, they are unwound so that some genes can be transcribed to make mRNA and the consequent proteins. The cell is also generating ATP to power growth, which implies a great many metabolic reactions to make new plasma membrane, ER, ribosomes, and all the cellular organelles, including the mitochondria (and chloroplasts in plants) that generate the ATP.

If the cell is programmed to divide, it will also duplicate its chromatin during interphase. It is possible to study the duplication of chromatin by supplying the cells with radioactive nucleotides and noting when the nucleotides are incorporated into DNA. In many cells that have been studied, once the chromatin has been duplicated, mitosis will begin nine to twelve hours later.

The first steps of mitosis are collectively called *prophase*. As the strands of DNA and nucleoprotein begin to condense forming tight coils, the light microscope begins to reveal threads in the nucleus; these are the forming chromosomes. It is their early, threadlike appearance that gave the name to the process: *mitosis*, which comes from the Greek word for thread (mitos). Before long, if the cells have been stained with suitable aniline dyes (discovered in 1878), the light microscope reveals the chromosomes.

As the chromosomes are forming, three other important events are taking place: First, the nuclear envelope breaks up and finally disappears. Second, *poles* become apparent on opposite sides of the nucleus. In nearly all animal cells and mobile plant cells, there are a pair of barrel-shaped bodies called *centrioles*. During prophase, the centrioles divide, and the two new pairs migrate to opposite poles in the nucleus. Microtubules are attached to the centrioles, and these stretch and grow as the centrioles move. In most plant cells, there are no centrioles, but clear areas begin to appear at the poles. These clear areas are filled with microtubules that grow and stretch like centrioles. Third, the nucleolus disappears.

The next step is called *metaphase*. At the end of prophase, the chromosomes are fully formed and scattered throughout the area where the nucleus had been. The long DNA strands have been coiled and condensed until the chromosomes are clearly visible in the light microscope. During metaphase, these chromosomes line up on the plate where the cell will divide; they appear lined up along the cell equator. The microtubules form a *spindle* that stretches from pole to pole. Each chromosome appears as a body with four arms, all attached at a point called the *centromere*. The spindle microtubules attach to the centromeres of each chromosome.

During the next step, *anaphase*, the centromeres divide and begin to move toward opposite poles, apparently being pulled by the spindle fibers, although the real nature of this movement is still not understood. Each new centromere takes two of the chromosome arms, called *chromatids*, with it toward the opposite poles. These are the daughter chromosomes, and their number at each pole is the same as the number of chromosomes that first became visible, though each one contains only half of the chromatin that appeared at prophase. That chromatin will be duplicated during the coming interphase if the cell is programmed to divide again.

The final step is called *telophase*, and it effectively reverses the events that occurred during prophase. New nuclear envelopes begin to form around the collections of chromosomes at each pole. The nuclear envelopes form from the ER. The chromosomes begin to disappear as the tightly coiled strands of chromatin begin to unwind. Each new nucleus will soon have a nucleolus so that the new nuclei appear just the same as the original nucleus. This completes the process of mitosis.

Cytokinesis

A final event remains: the division of the cytoplasm. This is called *cytokinesis*, and it differs in plants and animals. In animals, the cell simply constricts around its equator as if someone had tied a string around it and pulled it tight. Actually, it is the microfilaments that are programmed to do the constricting. Of course, energy is required. Plants are more complicated because of their cell walls, which give a more rigid shape to the cells; simply constricting around the middle won't do. A new cell wall, called a *primary wall*, must be formed at the equator. The spindle fibers from mitosis begin to condense at the equator, forming a *cell plate*. Golgi bodies contribute cell-wall and membrane materials. The plate begins to form at the center of the cell and grows outward toward the edges, where it meets and unites with the existing membranes and walls. Each new daughter cell becomes completely surrounded with membrane and wall, although the wall may be penetrated with plasmodesmata. Cell growth occurs as the primary walls around the cell stretch, and usually this occurs only in one direction so that plant cells typically elongate along the axis of the stem or root.

Meiosis or Reduction Division

As cells divide by mitosis in multicellular eukaryotes, they are continually specializing (differentiating) to form the tissues and organs that will

Meiosis I

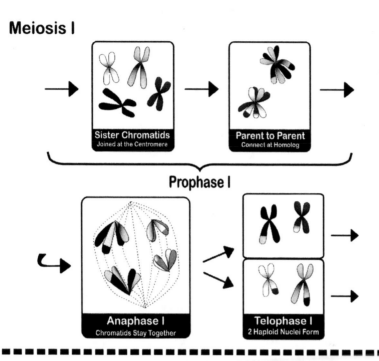

Meiosis II

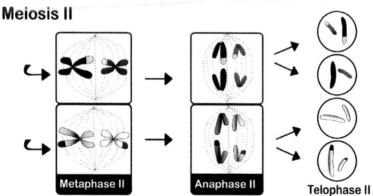

Figure 3-6

Meiosis: the process by which chromosome pairs are separated so that each of the final four cells has only half as many chromosomes as the initial cell. In sexually reproducing animals, all four cells become sperm cells in males, but only one of the four cells becomes an egg cell in females; the other three usually disappear. In plants, the four cells become spores, which will divide by mitosis and later form male and female gametes. (Computer drawing by Tami Allen Salisbury) constitute the mature organism. One aspect of the necessary programing is especially wonderful: If the organism will reproduce sexually, as virtually all eukaryotic, multicellular organisms do, some of the cells will form the primary sex organs that will produce *gametes* in animals or *spores* in plants. The cells that produce gametes or spores are programmed to perform the special kind of cell division called *meiosis* or reduction division, in which the daughter cells contain only half the number of chromosomes contained in the cells of the mature organism before meiosis. (Plant spores eventually produce gametes also.)

The two divisions of meiosis

Meiosis consists of two stages. The first stage produces two daughter cells from the beginning mother cell, and the second stage also produces two daughter cells each from the two cells produced in the first stage, so that the result of meiosis is always four cells (Figure 3-6). It is during the first stage that the reduction division occurs, and that first division resembles mitosis except for two important differences:

First, the chromosomes in each cell occur in *pairs*: one chromosome from the male parent and one from the female parent. During the first stage of meiosis, the pairs line up so that each member of a pair is opposite to its partner chromosome. This occurs in early prophase before the chromatin has completely condensed. At this point, the chromosomes intertwine with each other, and breaks occur and reform such that part of a chromosome from one parent might end up as part of the chromosome of the other parent, and visa versa. This series of events is called *crossing over*, and it means that two genes for two different characters that were originally on the same chromosome (say the chromosome from the mother), might, after crossing over, end up on different chromosomes (say one gene on the chromosome from the father and the other on the chromosome from the mother).

In crossing over, the chance that two genes on a single chromosome will separate from each other depends on how far apart they are from each other. The farther apart they are, the greater the chance that they will separate. Thus, in the early part of the twentieth century, geneticists applied this principle to *map* the chromosomes in various organisms. They would first determine by many crosses that two characters were located on the same chromosome; by seeing how often they separated from each other in these crosses, they could determine how far apart they were on that chromosome. Detailed maps were made for dozens to hundreds of characters on the chromosomes of the fruit fly, *drosophila*, for example. Other methods have now been developed to map chromosomes, and we have detailed maps even for human chromosomes (Ridley, 1999; Ridley, 2001—two separate authors). Our point here: Chromosomes are programmed to cross over during the first stage of meiosis.

Second, the reduction division takes place. Instead of the *chromatids* being separated during metaphase as in mitosis, the chromosome *pairs* are separated. One chromosome of a pair moves to one pole of the cell; the other chromosome moves to the other pole. This is totally random; the original chromosome from the father (now altered by crossovers), for example, might go to either pole. After the reduction division, if the mother cell had 46 chromosomes (as humans do), the two daughter cells after the first stage of meiosis will have 23 chromosomes each. Thanks to crossing over, these chromosomes will not have the same genetic composition as the original chromosomes in the mother cell.

There is a more-or-less normal telophase at this point, with new nuclei being formed and cytokinesis dividing the cytoplasm. The bottom line: Reproductive cells are programmed so that the two daughter cells after the first stage of meiosis have only half as many chromosomes as their mother cell had. All the proper enzymes to control these steps are in the right places at the right times.

The second stage of meiosis is very similar to a typical mitosis, except that the chromosomes after the first stage may or may not, depending on the species, have disappeared into thin chromatin strands as they do in mitosis. In either case, in the second stage of meiosis, the chromosomes again line up on the equatorial plate, and a spindle forms with spindle fibers attached to the centromeres, which then divide and move to opposite poles, taking the chromatids with them. Those chromatids had formed by duplication of the chromatin before the first stage of meiosis—during the interphase that preceded meiosis. The end result of meiosis is four cells, each with half as many chromosomes as their mother cell, with those chromosomes differing in genetic composition from those of the mother cell—all according to some kind of programming that we are far from understanding at this time.

In nearly all male animals, the four cells produced by meiosis further differentiate into *sperm cells* that often have flagella making them capable of swimming to unite with an *egg cell* of the same species. The four cells in female animals have a different fate. Typically, three of these cells do not develop further. The remaining cell differentiates into an egg cell, usually by absorbing nutrient material and becoming larger, in one case growing as large as an ostrich egg, which is, at one point, still only one cell. The sperm and the egg are the *gametes*.

Note how much programming is involved. Sperm cells were programmed to develop into the highly specialized cells that they have become, and the same is true of egg cells. They are further programmed to unite with each other, providing that they are members of the same or closely related species. After the two cells fuse together, their nuclei also fuse to form a new nucleus with the original number of chromosome pairs—the *fertilized egg* or *zygote*. In humans, each sperm cell and each egg cell has twenty-three unpaired chromosomes. After the sperm and the egg unite and fuse, there are twenty-three pairs, making a total of 46 chromosomes. Fusing of the male and female nuclei to produce the zygote is called *fertilization*.

Alternation of generations in plants

We could devote a chapter to an interesting complication found in plants. Here is a *very* brief outline of alternation of generations in plants: The zygote grows into a generation that will produce *spores* (called the *sporophyte generation*), and the spores grow into a generation that will produce *gametes* (the *gametophyte generation*). The relative importance of these two generations varies greatly throughout the plant kingdom.

The gametes of some simple algae unite to form a sporophyte (or zygote, with two sets of chromosomes), which immediately undergoes meiosis to produce spore cells that have only one set of chromosomes. These cells may divide many times before they again act as gametes, uniting to form a sporophyte.

The mosses have a dominant gametophyte generation (one set of chromosomes); namely, the green mats made up of tiny, leaf-like structures. When conditions are right, special structures form that produce gametes. The sperm cells *swim* to the egg cell, fertilize it, and it grows into a kind of lantern-shaped structure, the sporophyte (each cell with two sets of chromosomes). Meiosis occurs in these structures, producing spores that grow into the leafy mats.

Large fern fronds are sporophytes (two chromosome sets) that produce spores in small structures on the bottom surface of each frond. The spores develop into a small, often heart-shaped gametophyte, which eventually produces gametes that can unite to form a zygote.

Flowering plants are sporophytes that undergo meiosis in appropriate floral structures to produce pollen (which becomes a three-celled gametophyte) and an *embryo sac* (gametophyte) consisting of several cells, including one that is the egg; it will be fertilized by one of the *pollen* cells to produce a zygote, which grows into an embryonic plant in the seed. Note all the programing that must be involved, and wonder with me how this could come about by random mutations and natural selection—or how it could be *designed* by an Intelligent Creator.

Summary

1. The *Cell Doctrine* states in its simplest form that all living organisms consist of cells and that cells arise only by division of other cells. This concept is a great unifying concept for modern biology—at least as unifying as the general and specific theories of evolution.

2. Living organisms can be classified into two main groups: the *prokaryotes*, which have no organized nuclei or other organelles, and the *eukaryotes*, which do have nuclei and various cellular organelles. Beyond this grouping, biologists now speak of three great *domains* of life: the *Archae, Bacteria,* and the *Eukaryotes*, each with important subgroups.

3. *Proteins*, especially protein *enzymes*, constitute the basic machinery of cells. Proteins consist of *amino acids* attached to each other in long chains (often a few hundred amino acids in a chain) through *peptide bonds*.

4. *Enzymes catalyze* the reactions of *metabolism* by forming an *enzyme-substrate complex* with a *substrate molecule(s)* attached to an enzyme *active site*.

5. The catalyzed reaction is facilitated as the enzyme-substrate complex lowers the *energy barrier* that otherwise slows the reaction (sometimes greatly). A *product* or *products* are the result of the reaction—which can occur thousands of times per second for each enzyme molecule.

6. Most cells are in the *micrometer* (millionth of a meter) size range, while proteins and the molecules of metabolism are in the *nanometer* (billionth of a meter) size range. A human body consists of about 75 trillion cells.

7. Eukaryotic cells consist of the following constituents (plus some others that we did not discuss), and some of these also occur in prokaryotic cells.

A. All living cells are surrounded by *membranes*, which consist of a bilayer of molecules that are water-soluble on one end and lipid-soluble on the other, plus many complex proteins and structures made of proteins that control what moves in or out of cells.

B. A folded, membranous component of eukaryotic cells is the *endoplasmic reticulum* (*ER*), which performs many functions in cells. The *Golgi complex* consists of other membrane structures with special functions.

C. The semifluid material within eukaryotic cells (excluding the nucleus) is called *cytoplasm*. Other *organelles* including the nucleus are suspended within the cytoplasm.

D. Cells contain a *cytoskeleton*, which consists of fibers of *microtubules* and *actin filaments*; these are responsible for various cellular functions (for example, chromosome movements).

E. *Ribosomes* occur in both eukaryotic and prokaryotic cells (although they differ somewhat in these two cell types). They are responsible for *protein synthesis.*

F. *Mitochondria* are cellular organelles in virtually all eukaryotic cells; they are responsible for *cellular respiration*, a metabolic process that breaks down many kinds of molecules to produce (usually) carbon dioxide and water, plus *adenosine triphosphate* (*ATP*), which is the *energy currency* of cells. Oxygen is usually used in cellular respiration.

G. *Chloroplasts* are organelles confined to green plants; they are responsible for *photosynthesis,* in which water molecules are broken down, releasing oxygen, and the remaining hydrogen ions are combined with carbon dioxide through complex reactions to produce various molecules. ATP is also produced.

H. Plant cells may have large *vacuoles*, which often occupy much of the cells' volume.

I. *The plant cell wall* is unique to plants and a few other groups; animal cells do not have walls. The wall resists the pressure caused by osmotic intake of water (mostly into vacuoles), and these turgid cells give the soft parts of plants (their leaves) their nonwilted appearances.

J. The *nucleus* is a complex structure within eukaryotic cells. It consists of a double, porous membrane surrounding *nucleoplasm* in which is suspended *nucleoprotein*, consisting of *nucleic acids* and protein. There are also *nucleoli*, which synthesize ribosomes.

8. During cell division, the nucleoprotein condenses into *chromosomes*, and it is now known that the genetic material consists of the *DNA* portion of the nucleoprotein.

9. In 1953, J. D. Watson, F. H. C. Crick, M. Wilkins, and R. Franklin discovered that the DNA molecule is a *double helix*, and this structure makes it possible to understand how genetic *information* can be transferred from generation to generation.

10. Protein synthesis on ribosomes is facilitated by at least three kinds of *RNA:*

A. *Messenger RNA* (which is formed as it copies—*transcribes*—the *sequence* of *nucleotides* in DNA, carrying this *sequence information* to the ribosomes outside the nucleus).

B. *Transfer RNA* (which *translates* the mRNA *codons*—groups of three nucleotides of the *genetic code*—each to a specific amino acid, which becomes attached to the tRNA).

C. And finally, *ribosomal RNA* (which, with the protein portion of ribosomes, uses the information from the mRNA, via the tRNA molecules, to synthesize protein molecules, each with the correct sequence of amino acids as determined by the sequence of nucleotides in the DNA genes).

11. We can think of the events described above as following a *program.* Much of life function follows such programs, and the result is the process of *development* (such as the development of a mature human being from a fertilized egg cell).

12. A basic example of programming is the process of division of genetic material in eukaryotes: *mitosis.* This occurs as the nuclear membrane disappears, chromosomes appear from the nucleoprotein, line up on the cell equator, divide, with each half (each *chromatid*) moving to opposite poles of the cell, and a new nucleus forming around the chromosomes as they disappear back into nucleoprotein.

13. Cell division, or *cytokinesis*, occurs as membranes (and the wall in plants) separate the two newly formed nuclei.

14. In the process of *meiosis* or *reduction division*, another example of programming, a single cell undergoes two divisions, resulting in four

new cells, each with only half the number of chromosomes as the original *mother cell*. These cells with half the chromosomes become *gametes* (sperm and egg cells), or *spores* (in plants).

15. In plants, the spores go through a series of brief to extended developmental stages before becoming gametes; this is called *alternation of generations*.

16. Can all of this complexity be accounted for by "natural processes" without an Intelligent Creator?

4 THOSE PESKY SEQUENCES: WHAT ARE THE CHANCES?

The *sequences* of nucleotides in nucleic acids or of the amino acids in proteins form the basis of life function. This sentence contains *information*, based on its sequence of letters, because you, the reader, speak English and can understand what the sentence says. A protein contains information because its *sequence* of amino acids produces an active site, capable of catalyzing some critical reaction, or its amino acid sequence gives the protein structural or hormonal function. The nucleic acids contain information that determines protein information, either by the sequence of DNA nucleotides that will be translated to make proteins or by the sequence of RNA nucleotides that gives them the structural ability to act in protein synthesis.

The bottom line is that to account for the origin of life with or without an Intelligent Creator, you must account for those sequences. We'll talk about a few current theories of the origin of life in the next chapter; in this chapter, I'll try to give you an idea of just how much information is contained in the macro-molecules of life and how some scientists have tried to come to grips with the problems they pose.

Human Language As an Analogy to Macro-Molecular Information

The basic question concerns how the information in nucleic acids or proteins (their ability to *function* in ways that account for life) can come about. Will random changes and selection do the job? What role might creative intelligence have played in the origin of life and its multitude of organisms? First, we need some appreciation of just how much information resides in a functioning protein or nucleic acid.[1] One way to understand that is to consider the possible information in written language. For me, that is more fun than going directly to a discussion of enzyme complexity.[2]

It is important for you to understand how my language calculations (or protein and nucleic acid calculations) work. I've told these stories to various people, and often they ask if I have had a mathematician check my numbers. Well, it's true that I am not a mathematician, but we are only dealing with elementary math, mostly multiplication and division. However, we end up with some very big numbers. The number of possible combinations of amino acids or nucleotides is so great that the numbers go completely beyond any real comprehension.

Alphabets

We are going to talk about alphabets: the Roman alphabet used by English and many other languages, the amino-acid alphabet, and the nucleotide alphabet. Let's begin with a familiar example: the "numbers alphabet." There are ten "letters" in the numbers alphabet: 0 1 2 3 4 5 6 7 8 9. How many ways can these ten digits be combined? It depends on how many digits long the combination is. If there are two letters, then each one can combine with each of the others for a total of 100 combinations (starting with 00 and ending with 99). If there are three, we can combine them 1000 ways; four combine in 10,000 ways, and so on. We arrive at the power rule: *The number of combinations of letters in an alphabet is equal to the number of letters in the alphabet raised to the power of the number of letters in the combination.* So, with an alphabet of ten letters taken five at a time, the number of combinations is 10^5; that is, ten multiplied by itself five times, or $10 \times 10 \times 10 \times 10 \times 10 = 100,000 = 10^5$. (In this notation and example, the superscript is equal to the number of zeros.)

Shakespeare

Now let's contemplate the likelihood of creating a work of Shakespeare with random combinations and artificial selection. Such an exercise shows how numbers can become astronomical quickly. It also illustrates the importance of the origin of variations in a creation by mutations and natural selection. Although the alphabets are of different size, the Roman alphabet (my example uses 26 letters, a space, and 3 punctuation marks, making 30 "letters" in all) is a good analogy of the amino-acid alphabet (twenty amino acids), each letter in a sentence being analogous to each amino acid in a protein chain. The math is simple but laborious, so I decided to base this example on numbers that I worked out over thirty years ago (Salisbury, 1971). I found some mistakes in those figures, however, and had to do the calculation all over again anyway.

We have heard the analogy of monkeys pounding keyboards until they accidently manage to write a work of Shakespeare. Given enough time, we are told, anything is possible. Yeah sure! In my mental exercise, I decided to use computers instead of monkeys. There could be more or less than 30 letters in my alphabet, but 30 is an easy number to work with. The alphabet is:

A B C D E F G H I J K L M N O P Q R S T U V W X Y Z [space] : . "

Note that all the letters are in upper case; allowing lower case would double the letters to 52, for a total of 56. The goal was to write a 45-character sentence (*two* spaces after the colon):

"THIS ABOVE ALL: TO THINE OWN SELF BE TRUE."

How unique is that sentence? We've learned the power rule, so it is clear that the number of possible 45-character sentences in an alphabet of 30 letters equals 30 multiplied by itself 45 times, or $30^{45} = 2.954 \times 10^{66}$. That particular sentence is only *one* out of a possible 2.954×10^{66} 45-letter sentences that could be written with that alphabet. To convince you that it really is just multiplication, I took the time and multiplied the long way, as shown in Table 4–1.[3] Clearly, the invention of logarithms and then calculators and computers was a huge asset to scientists and engineers. (Incidentally, a grandson of mine wrote a program that checked my multiplications to be sure that each number was correct.)

Let's mentally try to write all of the forty-five-letter arrangements ("sentences") of our thirty letter alphabet. I imagined a computer that could write one billion arrangements per second. There are 31,556,962 seconds (s) in a Gregorian year (3.1557×10^7 s), so multiplying that number by a billion (10^9) and dividing the result into the number of arrangements gives us about 10^{50} years (more exactly, 9.360×10^{49} years). That was too long to wait, so I covered the Earth to a depth of 2 km with identical computers, each was one liter (1 L) in volume, and I programmed each one to work on a separate part of the arrangements so that no two computers ever wrote the same "sentence" (or *string* in computer language).[4] Now it only took about 10^{29} years to write all of the possible sentences. That was still too long, so I had no recourse but to cover 10^{20} planets (all the size of Earth) with my computers, again to a depth of 2 km. That reduced the required time to write all of the possible arrangements to a mere billion years (more precisely, 936,085,039 years).

The database

I've been trying to wrap my mind around the database generated by my 10^{41} imaginary computers, each of which produced 2.954×10^{16} different combinations of the 45 letters. First, where to store the database? At about 150 bytes to store each sentence, it would take about 100 million 100-gigabyte hard drives *per computer* to store the sentences. Then, how to search the database?

Let's imagine that it could be done. First, you would find our Shakespearean sentence only once on one of the hard drives. It might have been stored there during the first or the last second of the billion years or any time in between. You would also find every 45-letter sentence or sentence fragment ever written, or that ever could be written, in any language that could use my 30-letter alphabet, not to mention every sentence shorter than 45 letters, each with various other letters present in addition to the sentence, which could be embedded in any part of the 45-letter sequence.[5] Any sentence shorter than 45 letters will appear in many of the arrangements. If it is only 44 letters long, then it will occur in 60 of the arrangements (the one extra letter being at either the beginning or the end of the 44-letter sentence). A short sentence ("I love you" or "Jesus wept") would occur an astronomical number of times but would still be only a minute portion of the total arrangements. If the sentence were 22 letters or fewer long, it would occur twice or more in many of the 45-character arrangements. In short, everything the Bard ever wrote (translated into the 30-letter alphabet) would be included in 45-letter or shorter sentences, or fragments of sentences. So would everything you or I or anybody else ever wrote or could write.

Nevertheless, most of the 2.954×10^{66} possible arrangements would be meaningless in any language; they would have no information content.

Not only would the overwhelming portion of the arrangements be meaningless nonsense, but also a vast number would be only *nearly* correct, with, say, any one or two of the 30 characters at some incorrect location in the 45-character sequence. With such a chance for error, you can begin to grasp what a tiny portion of those possible 3×10^{66} arrangements would have any meaning, even though they would include all of the meaningful sentences or segments of sentences, in any language that could use that alphabet, up to and including those that are 45 characters long.

Clearly, sorting through a database of 3×10^{66} arrangements for appropriate sentences would have been a difficult way for Shakespeare to write his plays. It simply doesn't sound *plausible*. It is much more *plausible* that he used his *creative intelligence* to form the sentences that gave meaning to his dramas. We know that the intelligent method is plausible because that's how he wrote his plays. The analogy is far from perfect, but it illustrates how extremely mysterious to us creative intelligence remains—and on the other hand what a tremendous advantage creative intelligence provides over random changes and selection. We make mistakes and typographical errors, but our *intelligence* allows us to find and correct them. We can even devise spell checkers and grammar checkers to help with the job, though they differ in principle from random selection processes.

Language and creation

My language analogy was fun to create because of the "ah ha," boggled-mind feeling one gets when contemplating the vast number of meaningful strings that could be formed in any language using a thirty later alphabet to form meaningful sentences. With regard to the question of creation, we are really dealing with proteins and nucleic acids, not human language. Even the small molecule insulin, with fifty-one amino acids, is as complex as our Shakespearean sentence; that is, it would be almost equally difficult to generate insulin by random processes as to generate our sentence that way. Note further that *most* proteins have hundreds of amino acids. Table 4-2 gives some of the numbers for a twenty amino acid alphabet or a four nucleotide alphabet.

Originally, I devised ways to further boggle the mind with these huge numbers, but now that seems like overkill. Suffice it to say, the numbers are indeed huge, which should lead to the realization that obtaining sequences with meaningful information content by random changes (mutations) and natural selection is not easy. Indeed, anyone who has worried about the problem knows that.[6] I've seen various versions of the big numbers in virtually every book about creation that I've read, whether it was written by evolutionists or creationists.

I can think of three possible ways to beat the fantastic odds: getting there with small steps, active sites with only a few amino acids, and various amino acid sequences catalyzing a single reaction. Are these ways plausible?

Can We Beat the Odds with Small Steps?

With the first approach, instead of selecting only for the complete Shakespeare sentence, we could select any arrangement that had a letter in the right position. If we kept the first arrangement that randomly came up with one or more letters in the correct position and then kept rearranging the other letters, leaving the correct ones in place after each rearrangement, it would not take long to write the sentence. Going through each position one at a time would require at the very most only $30 \times 45 = 1350$ trials for our "be-true" sentence.

This is exactly what the evolutionist Richard Dawkins (1986, pp. 45–50) does in one of his books. He mentions the monkeys pounding typewriters to write Shakespeare analogy and quotes a line from Hamlet: "Methinks it is like a weasel." He correctly calculates the chances of getting the line by random rearrangements at $1/27^{28}$. (His alphabet has twenty-seven letters counting the space.) He calls this method single-step selection; in other words, the sentence must be correct to be selected. Another way, he says, is cumulative selection. His computer program rearranged the letters randomly but selected sentences that had letters in the right place as described above. Doing that, it only took forty-one to sixty-four generations (in different trials) to get his sentence. That's the way Darwinian selection works, Dawkins says.

Interestingly enough, Dawkins tells about cumulative selection right after noting that a hemoglobin molecule consists of four chains of amino acids. Dawkins considers one of those chains, which has 146 amino acids. He never tells us how cumulative selection could produce such a complex molecule, nor does he tell us that if only *one* of those amino acids, at position six in the chain, is valine instead of glutamic acid, the result is sickle-cell anemia, a hereditary disease that is harmful or fatal to its carrier. (There are, however, many other amino acid substitutions in various positions in hemoglobin that are innocuous.) Dawkins, although he mentions the molecular structure of hemoglobin, deals mostly in his theories with structural changes during evolution. He places his *faith* in the idea that his cumulative selection will also work at the molecular level. He thinks that this is plausible.

Minimum information content

It should be obvious, however, that such an approach is an even less perfect analogy than my computer-generated Shakespearean sentence. Consider the concept of *minimum information content*. Below some minimum (which would vary), the sentence makes no sense at all. True, we might get the sense of the sentence before all of the letters were in place, but we could not guess the sentence based on one or a few letters, so there would be no reason to select them. Some minimum number of letters coming randomly all at once in the right places would have to occur before we could guess the complete sentence.

So it must be with genes and their enzymes. Some minimum number of amino acids must be in the right places before there is an active site. That is, some minimum arrangement of amino acids must be essential to have any selective value at all. Most of Dawkins's computer-generated sentences have no selection value at all.

Applied cumulative selection

All this is not to say that cumulative selection can't play a critical role in molecular evolution. The power of cumulative selection is demonstrated almost daily in both industrial and academic laboratories around the world, for both practical and pure-knowledge purposes. The approach is to take an enzyme that already exists in all its complexity and mutate its gene one or two nucleotides at a time, randomly, in a million or so copies of the gene, put the mutated genes back into organisms (one gene per organism), allow the gene in each organism to produce the enzyme, and then screen for improved versions of the new enzymes.

Consider this example: Frances H. Arnold (1999) and her students (Gershenson, et al., 2000) at the California Institute of Technology are busily engaged in evolving improved enzymes.[7] They were initially interested in improving the heat tolerance of para-nitrobenzyl esterase because it breaks down the ester linkages in a group of compounds useful to organic chemists. The gene for the enzyme was first isolated from a bacterial culture of *Bacillus subtilis*. Then this strand of DNA was copied with the polymerase chain reaction (controlled by suitable enzymes), but just enough metal ions were added to the mixture to cause an average of one or two point mutations (changes of single nucleotides) in each new strand of DNA. The result was a mixture of a million or so genes, many with one or two mutations somewhere along the strand.

Each gene was then combined with a circular piece of double-stranded DNA called a *plasmid*, which has all the information that a bacterium needs to translate its DNA into a protein. Each plasmid, with a different mutated gene entered one bacterium. A dilute suspension of bacterial cells was plated on Petri dishes such that each bacterium was separate from the rest and formed its own colony. The medium in the dish contained a substrate that changed color if the new enzyme was functional, making screening easy. (Most mutations were *not* functional.) The screening also included tests at elevated temperatures to see if any new enzyme was more heat stable than its predecessor. This process was repeated for several generations.

The result was an enzyme that didn't unfold (destroying its activity) until the temperature reached 69.5 °C, an improvement of over 17 °C from the original enzyme. Because reactions go faster as temperatures are elevated, the new enzyme was ten times more effective at its optimum temperature than the original enzyme was at its optimum temperature.

Note that all of this was done blindly, with no knowledge of what was happening to the enzyme structure as heat stability increased, and with no knowledge of what *should* happen to increase heat stability. We don't yet know that much about how enzymes work. With help from another laboratory, however, the Caltech scientists were able to compare the amino acid sequences of the original and the final mutated enzymes, and also their three-dimensional structures; that is, they were able to determine what had happened during the mutation process. Only 13 of the amino acids were changed, but these were in two parts of the enzyme that were "floppy" in the original enzyme; new hydrogen bonds had made these segments of the protein chain more stable and thus resistant to the buffetings of surrounding molecules as the temperature increased. (Two other segments of the protein that were originally quite stable were also changed slightly, making them even more stable after the mutation process.)

So there we have it: cumulative selection of laboratory-induced mutations following the same principle that Dawkins used—change one or two amino acids at a time and select for improved enzyme activity. There is no reason to think that this couldn't or doesn't also happen in nature, especially with microorganisms that reproduce rapidly and have huge populations. (A trillion *E. coli* cells can fit in one cubic centimeter, the size of a thimble.)

Actually, as noted in chapter 2, there are numerous documented examples of organisms developing resistance to the chemicals that we have developed to eliminate them. Insects become resistant to insecticides, weeds become resistant to herbicides, fungi become resistant to fungicides, and various microorganisms become resistant to antibiotics. Indeed, drug-resistant pathogenic bacteria and viruses have become a serious problem. All of this might follow the same principles applied by Francis Arnold and her colleagues. Mutation and natural selection at the molecular level clearly occur in nature.

Still, remember that laboratory evolution must begin with a highly complex, fully functional enzyme. Arnold notes: "But if you want to create something really different, maybe even something totally new, nature doesn't offer much guidance as to how to go about it." That is, we just don't know the rules of protein folding and active sites, which is not to say that we won't ever know these rules or that an Intelligent Creator doesn't know them already. The question of the origin of complex enzymes remains. It is the question of the origin of life.

In any case, by the end of the twentieth century, human beings had progressed from such creations as fire and the wheel to the synthesis of many new and improved enzymes, and this process continues at full throttle in labs all over the world. As progress continues, we might learn the protein language so well that we will be able to create new enzymes from scratch for our own purposes. From what we know now, it is clear that it won't be easy, but it is surely within the grasp of an Intelligent Creator.

Can We Beat the Odds with Small Active Sites?

If we can't beat the odds by naturally selecting amino acids one at a time starting from scratch—and we surely can't!—how about reducing the odds by reducing the number of amino acids necessary to give the developing enzyme activity and thus selection value? Maybe only a few amino acids must be in the right places to make an active site, and all the other amino acids in a large protein are simply there for the ride. If this is the case, there would be a much higher probability that an active combination could appear by chance.

The problem was recognized by the radiologist and statistician Henry Quastler at the University of Illinois in 1964. Quastler discussed the problem in a small volume published just before his death. He went through many calculations similar to those presented here and concluded that, if life originated spontaneously, as he believed, there must be active sites on enzymes that are effective with only two to seven amino acids.

I took issue with Quastler's ideas by pointing out that, if only two amino acids were required for an active site, then most proteins would be covered with active sites. In addition, such small active sites could not account for the thousands of enzymes that are known to exist; there would be, at most, only $20 \times 20 = 400$ active sites (Salisbury, 1969). The vast majority of enzymes catalyze only one reaction; of the many combinations of amino acids on their surfaces, only one combination forms an active site that is effective in catalyzing only one chemical reaction. All of the other combinations are ineffective. Thus, the high specificity of known enzymes suggested that most amino-acid sequences were without catalytic activity. I proposed that at least 15 or 16 amino acids in a specified sequence would be required for activity.

By now, we know much more than was known in the late 1960s, and today's enzymes appear to be far more complex than we expected. But could they have been simpler and still functional during the earth's early stages? Some investigators think so. Indeed, some very small *peptides* (chains of amino acids, some too small to qualify as protein), and even single amino acids, have *some* catalytic activity, albeit slight.[8]

As far as I know, however, such enzymes with small active sites do not occur in today's organisms. As noted above, if only a few amino acids are needed for an active site, there can't be all that many active sites. In nature, however, there are tens to hundreds of thousands of active sites (functional enzymes, hormones, and structural proteins). To me, small active sites do not seem plausible in view of what is known about active sites in today's enzymes. Furthermore, I can't imagine life with a single enzyme; life as we know it depends on many interacting enzymes and other compounds. Let's consider three examples of enzymes that clearly have high levels of minimum information content. (See also the catalase molecule in Figure 3-1.)

Lysozyme: A protein with a high information content

Just before my 1969 *Nature* article was published, a relevant paper appeared in *Science*. The editor of *Nature* allowed me to add the following note during proof. Although the language is technical, the complexity of the enzyme being discussed should be obvious:

> I have just read an article (Chipman, D. M. and Sharon, N., *Science* 165, 454; 1969) that is highly relevant to this discussion. The action of lysozyme is now understood in terms of the structures of the enzyme and its substrates, the oligo or polysaccharides in bacterial cell walls. The roughly ellipsoidal enzyme has a deep cleft running up one side, into which six of the residues making up part of the substrate chain fit, resulting in a distortion that cleaves the chain. The substrate is stabilized in the cleft by 'a large number of hydrogen bonds and nonpolar interactions' (for example, three of the six residues are stabilized to the enzyme by six hydrogen bonds and over forty van der Waals contacts). Parts of the protein must move on formation of the complex. Clearly, such an intricate structure, involving so many amino acids in the enzyme chain, does not simplify the problem discussed here.

This was the first detailed analysis of enzyme-substrate binding. The lysozyme enzyme was obtained from egg whites, where it is responsible for egg-white sterility by breaking down the polysaccharides (chains of sugar molecules) of bacterial cell walls so that the bacteria burst and die. The protein consists of 135 amino acids, and it is interesting to note that the nineteen amino acids that form the active site are separated from each other singly or in four small clusters at various distances along the peptide backbone. When the chain folds, these amino acids come together to form the active site (Malacinski and Freifelder, 1998, pp. 81–82). Thus, the active site depends on the other amino acids in the chain folding in such a way that the active site forms. Although lysozyme is a small protein, it is a highly complex example of protein machinery. Furthermore, most enzymes have several hundred amino acids.

Histone IV in cows and peas

One way to see just how essential specific amino acid sequences are to an enzymes' ability to function is to compare the sequences of a given enzyme as it occurs in many different organisms. If an amino acid at a given position is not essential, a mutation that changes that amino acid at that position will have no positive nor negative selection value, so the change will tend to remain through coming generations. If, on the other hand, the mutation causes a significant decrease in the enzyme's activity, then the organism with that mutation will be less fit and will tend to be eliminated. Thus, evolutionists say that the necessary amino acids (those in the active site and those that help to configure the active site) are *conserved* through subsequent evolving generations (remaining the same in widely unrelated organisms that had a common ancestor), while amino acids that do not have such an essential role to play may vary from species to species.

In the late 1960s, James F. Bonner (my major professor at Caltech) collaborated in a project with Emil Smith (my former biochemistry lecturer at the University of Utah, who was by then Chairman of the Biochemistry Department at the University of California, Los Angeles). Bonner (1994; Salisbury, 1997) had become interested in the histone proteins that occur with DNA in the nuclei of eukaryotes, especially peas, his model organism. (The histones may control whether a gene is active or inactive.) Smith was interested in the histones of calves. Bonner's team had learned to purify the histones, discovering that there were only five of them. He and Smith agreed to study the amino acid sequence of histone IV, which is the smallest and easiest to isolate.

In those days, to determine the amino acid sequences, Smith needed two grams of pure histone. He isolated the calf histone from thymuses obtained at slaughterhouses. Bonner and his crew, however, had to germinate twenty-four *tons* of dried peas in barrels and manually separate the shoots from roots and cotyledons to obtain two grams of histone IV. The process took a full year. When the results were in, histone IV proved to be the most conserved protein known, and it remains such to this day. Histone IV has 102 amino acids in its chain, and only two of these differed between the calves and the peas—eukaryotic organisms that are about as unrelated as possible. Evolutionists must conclude that the essential nature of histone IV was established when cows and peas had a common ancestor.

Please note that the minimum information content of histone IV must include 100 amino acids. By our power rule, there are 20^{100} (10^{130}) possible combinations of 100 amino acids. Is there a plausible way to get the correct arrangement of amino acids in histone IV with tiny steps, each having selection value to the organism—before plants diverged from animals? It seems highly implausible to me, but I can't prove such a negative idea.

Cytochrome c: phylogeny and minimum information content

Another protein, *cytochrome c*, is less conserved than histone IV (Jukes, 1966, pp. 191–229).[9] Sugars and other molecules are broken down in all cells by the highly complex process of cellular respiration, which involves about fifty enzymatically controlled steps (Appendix C). In part of the process, hydrogen atoms and their electrons are removed from certain intermediate molecules and moved along a chain of about twenty enzymes in the *electron transport system*. Near the end of the chain, electrons (e) from hydrogen are passed from cytochrome b to cytochrome c^1, then to cytochrome c, and finally to cytochromes a and $a3$, where $4e$, $4H^+$, and O_2 combine to form $2H_2O$. Cytochrome c, then, is an enzyme, third from the end in this chain. It has been widely studied because it is relatively easy to isolate, and it is quite small, consisting in most organisms of only 104 amino acids.

All organisms, both prokaryotes and eukaryotes, contain cytochrome c molecules. As far as we can tell, all of those cytochrome c molecules perform equally well. Yet their amino acid sequences are not all the same. Sixty-nine of the 104 amino acids have been found to vary in different organisms. To determine this, the cytochromes c were extracted from 38 organisms, and the sequences of amino acids were determined for all these. There were mammals (human, chimpanzee, donkey, rabbit, and so on), other vertebrates (pigeon, Peking duck, rattlesnake, bullfrog, tuna, and so on), insects, lower "plants" (two yeasts and a mold), and higher plants (wheat, sunflower, pumpkin, and so on).

Cytochrome c from humans is identical to that found in the chimpanzee, and the cytochromes c from chicken and turkey are identical, but each of the others differed from all the rest. Thirty-five of the amino acids were identical at a given position in all thirty-eight organisms studied; that is, they were conserved. At twenty-three locations in the chains, either of two related amino acids could be found; at twelve locations, either of three amino acids. There were twenty-four locations where a considerable variety of amino acids could be found, but if a water-repelling amino acid, for example, occurred in one organism at such a location, then a water-repelling amino acid would occur in the other thirty-seven organisms at that same location. At five locations, apparently, any of the twenty possible amino acids could occur.

The significance of all this for evolutionists is that the organisms could be related to each other in an evolutionary tree with those having the greatest number of dissimilar amino acids being the farthest apart (Figure 4-1). The conclusion is that, because humans and chimpanzees have identical sequences, they must be closely related, while humans and higher plants must be distantly related, since they have the fewest sequences in common.

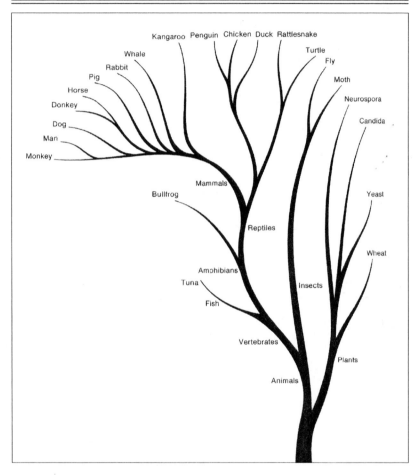

Figure 4-1

Evolutionary "tree" based on the degree of similarity in the cytochrome c molecules of several plants and animals. The greater the distance, following along the lines from one organism (at the tops of the "branches") to another, the larger the number of amino-acid differences in their cytochrome c molecules. For example, there are only two differences between a donkey and a pig, but fifty differences between a donkey and the fungus *Candida krusei*. (From Salisbury, 1976, p. 256; used by permission)

Stories such as this are compelling and are among the most impressive and plausible evidences that an evolutionist can produce, which is not to say that an Intelligent Creator could not have designed things that way.

There is another aspect to the cytochrome c story. Where did cytochrome c come from in the first place? We can apply the power rule to this information about cytochrome c. If all 104 amino acids were conserved, getting the right one by random mutation would have only one chance in 10^{135}. Only thirty-five of the amino acids were rigidly conserved, however, but the chance of getting even thirty-five amino acids in the right place is only one in $20^{35} = 10^{45.5}$. We could consider the other amino acids and calculate, among other things, the chance of getting the hydrophobic molecules in the right place. But even the $10^{45.5}$ number is a serious problem, as you'll recognize from our Shakespeare exercise. And what about the fifty enzymes of which cytochrome c is only one?

Yes, there are times when a small mutation can improve the function (in the next generation) of an enzyme that already exits (in bacteria, at least). A change in an amino acid here or there can improve the action of an active site, as we saw in the work of Frances Arnold. The problem is encountered when we wonder how the enzyme came to be in the first place.

I must digress and go on record with a problem that has been worrying me. In developing molecular phylogenies, the amino-acid sequences (or the nucleotide sequences) are determined from individuals within a given population, say yeast or wheat or human. Generally speaking, these sequences seem to be the *same for any member* of the species that is being sampled. The emphasis is on nonconserved amino acids, which are not conserved because they are innocuous and thus have no selection value. Yet mutations occur randomly in *individuals*, not simultaneously in all members of a population. If a mutation with no positive or negative selection value occurs in an individual, how does it end up in all members of the species way down the road of time? It seems plausible to imagine that there would be a hodgepodge of such innocuous mutations within a given protein and a given population. Of course there are differences, which is what makes identification through DNA possible, but there apparently was no such hodgepodge of differences in the populations sampled for the cytochrome c study, although I can't be sure of that.

The only plausible neo-Darwinian explanation that I can think of is that each modern species population is descended from a single individual, an individual that lived way back when that represents all the positive mutations in its genome; all others were eventually eliminated by natural selection. Now, of course, if an Intelligent Creator were to *design* things that way for some purpose unknown to us, that would also be a plausible explanation for what we observe.

Can We Beat the Odds with Multiple Active Sites Controlling One Reaction?

Our language analogy easily helps us understand this possible way out of the problems posed by the big numbers. Various combinations of letters (more or less than 45) may have *almost* the same information content as "THIS ABOVE ALL: TO THINE OWN SELF BE TRUE." "THE IMPORTANT THING IS TO BE TRUE TO YOURSELF." "IT IS MOST IMPORATNT NOT TO BE UNTRUE TO YOUR-SELF." "BEING TRUE TO YOURSELF IS CRITICAL ABOVE ALL ELSE." "DIES UEBER ALLES: DIR SELBST TREU SEIN." And so on. Those and many other more-or-less equivalent sentences, or their fragments, would all be present in that humongous database of ca. 3×10^{66} 45-letter strings. If there were a million such sentences or fragments, that reduces the odds to about 3×10^{60}—significant, but not really much help. The big problem is that we have no solid idea of how many such sentences there might be.

When it comes to the enzymes, there is the possibility that more than one amino acid sequence might catalyze a single reaction. Indeed, there is growing evidence that such is the case, and various authors have presented that possibility as a potential solution to the big numbers problem. If what is suggested turns out to be true, the language analogy may be imperfect indeed. It is difficult to imagine that a million different sentences might have the same meaning as Shakespeare's "be-true" sentence, still just a tiny fraction of possible sentences, but proteins could be different.

Stuart Kauffman (1995, pp. 139–44) describes some rather involved experiments carried out to search for drugs to kill specific viruses. Hexapeptides were synthesized. Such a peptide, consisting of six of the twenty amino acids, could come in 64,000,000 varieties (Table 4-2). A *library* (as it is called) of about 21 million of these hexapeptides was searched (with laboratory techniques) to locate particular hexapeptides bound to the bottom of a petri plate and representing the virus:

The results were startling and established a number of critical points:. . .nineteen second-key peptides were found. So the probability that two hexapeptides look enough alike to bind to the same antibody molecule is about one in a million. Finding molecular mimics is not incredibly hard. The ratio of needles to hay in the haystack is about one needle to a million straws. On average, these hexapeptides differed from the initial hexapeptide in three of the six amino-acid positions. One differed in all six positions! Thus molecules with similar shapes can be scattered far apart in protein space [all possible proteins]. . . .

This is stunning. The results suggest this: pick an arbitrary molecular shape, a dye, an epitope on a virus, a molecular groove in a receptor molecule. Make a library with 10 trillion random RNA sequences. One in a billion will bind to your site. One in a billion is a tiny needle in a large haystack. But the staggering thing to realize is that we can now generate and search, in parallel, among trillions of kinds of molecules *simultaneously* to fish out the molecules we want, the candidate drugs we seek. (Kauffman, 1995, pp. 139–44)

Kauffman's universal enzyme toolbox

Kauffman goes on to talk about "universal toolboxes [libraries of peptides] able to carry out essentially any desired [enzymatic or other] function. The diversity required to have a full toolbox may be on the order of 100 million to 100 billion polymers."

Humans have a repertoire of about 100 million different antibody molecules [all of which are proteins].. . .So 100 million skeleton keys are all it takes. There are only about 100 million effectively different shapes, even though there are hyper astronomical numbers of possible polymers and other molecules with these shapes.

A universal toolbox of about 100 million to 100 billion molecules should suffice to bind essentially any molecule whatsoever. . . . Binding is one thing. Catalysis is another. Yet we are led to a further amazing possibility: a finite collection of polymers may be able to function as a universal enzymatic toolbox. If so, a library of some 100 million or 100 trillion molecules might suffice for any catalytic task whatsoever. (Kauffman, 1995, pp. 139–44)

In his more recent book, Kauffman (2000, pp. 13–14) reviews the above material, adding the information that human antibodies can themselves catalyze certain reactions. He says: "Not surprisingly, similar molecules can have similar shapes. More surprisingly, very different molecules can have the same shape."

Are universal toolboxes the answer?

If all this is true, it certainly does weaken the big numbers argument. A trillion seems like a big number, but it is nothing compared to the size of "protein space" (all the possible proteins). That space is, of course, much larger than the 3×10^{66} strings of letters in the "be-true" sentence because it includes proteins of *any* length. If we put a maximum length of say 300 amino acids on the possible proteins, then there will be at least 20^{300} (10^{390}) different kinds of proteins. If all possible reactions can be catalyzed by at least, say, one in every trillion of those 10^{390} proteins, then *any* trillion (10^{12}) proteins chosen at random from the 10^{390} proteins in protein space might contain an enzyme effective in catalyzing any given reaction—and there are 10^{378} sets of one trillion proteins in that protein space!

Christian De Duve (2002, pp. 176–79), under the heading, "Mutations are rarely the limiting factor in evolution," says that: "Contrary to what is often assumed, evolution rarely has to wait very long for some favorable mutation to occur." He calculates that the chances of getting any given point mutation in a cell is about 99.9 percent after only thirty-four generations, which is one day for bacteria and a month for animal cells. He notes that point mutations may not be all that significant for evolution, but says: "It is therefore significant that all that we know of evolution in action tends to confirm the richness of the mutational field." This statement is followed by relating drug resistence stories. Asking if the bug intentionally produces the necessary mutations, he replies, "No, the mutations were always there in some individuals or happened frequently, but only exceptionally were they of any use under natural conditions." Like Kauffman, De Duve notes that "the immune system offers another example of the natural exploitation of genetic lavishness."

Of the three ways to avoid the implications of the big numbers, the third seems to me to be the most plausible. Dawkins's selection of one letter (or one amino acid) at a time simply won't get life going, although it might work well to improve a protein. The idea of just a few amino acids making up an active site also goes against our current understanding of enzyme activity. But if huge numbers of *different* proteins—say any random trillion of the proteins making up protein space—can catalyze *any* given metabolic reaction, then the origin of variety may not be as big of a problem as I have implied with my big numbers calculations.

Still, doesn't the speculation about Quastler's small active sites apply here as well? If a trillion random proteins taken from protein space contained all of the active sites needed for life to function, wouldn't we expect many instances of proteins with multiple active sites? According to Kauffman's cogitations, if any trillion random proteins from the total number of possible proteins contained the right combinations of amino acids for any active site, then there must be an astronomical number of combinations that could form an effective active site for any given reaction. If that were the case, it would be difficult to understand why the vast majority of proteins that have been studied have only *one* active site for *one* reaction as part of their structure. It seems that active sites are anything but common.

Right now, the universal enzyme toolbox is certainly speculation—a just suppose story—but it *seems* more plausible than the other stories. The word *seems* takes us right back to where the nineteenth century biologists were with their *feelings* about intermediates in the evolution of a wing or an eye. My *feeling* is that getting suitable proteins for selection to work with is still a very long shot, as I'll further illustrate with another example. Furthermore, an Intelligent Creator could always plausibly provide those proteins. Right now, however, in light of "universal toolboxes," we must conclude that creationists still can't *prove* the necessity for an Intelligent Creator, which is what I've been saying all along.

Acquiring Genomes: Can We Beat the Odds with Lateral DNA Transfer?

An important source of variability for evolution is the movement of genes, or even entire genomes, from one organism to another. A recent book by Lynn Margulis and Dorian Sagan (2002) advocates this approach. While the lateral transfer of genes or genomes might indeed account for important steps in evolution, such a mechanism does not help resolve the problems brought up in this chapter. Here, we are wondering about how the essential nucleotide and amino acid sequences came about in the first place. Mechanisms for acquiring genomes take place later, after the basic genes and genomes are in place.

One More Example of a Complex Protein: Reverse Transcriptase

On September 9, 2002, I visited the Protein Data Bank website organized by David S. Goodsell (www.rcsb.org). On that date, some 18,691 protein structures had been recorded in the database. The "Molecule of the Month" was *reverse transcriptase*, and there was a space-filling drawing of the structure of the enzyme that looked like a two-headed glob made up of sticky balls (atoms). The description of this enzyme's function is truly amazing. This version of reverse transcriptase comes from studying the HIV virus, which causes AIDS. HIV is a tiny virus with only a few genes. Its genes are in the form of RNA instead of DNA, and the host cell's machinery can create new proteins based only on DNA. This is where reverse transcriptase comes into play. In protein synthesis, you'll recall that the first step for the cell is to copy the nucleotide sequence of DNA with the nucleotide sequence of messenger-RNA. This special enzyme produces DNA molecules by copying the virus's RNA genes in the opposite direction: from RNA to DNA. Once the virus's genes have been duplicated as DNA and deposited in the cell, then the usual pathway can be followed to produce the enzymes needed to make many copies of the virus: DNA $\Rightarrow$ mRNA $\Rightarrow$ transfer RNA $\Rightarrow$ ribosomal RNA $\Rightarrow$ protein.

This process requires some fancy engineering. Recall that reproducing DNA is a complex process involving activated nucleotides (ATP, TTP, GTP, and CTP) and several enzymes. Reverse transcriptase manages to do the job all by itself. To do so, it must be intricately complex with a very high information content, which includes not only its shape but also the chemical (and electrical) properties of its active site There are two parts to the enzyme, but they are both encoded by the same RNA gene (transcribed to DNA). After they are made, one subunit is clipped in such a way that it can combine with the other, claw-shaped unit to form the complex piece of protein machinery that can carry out reverse transcription. As it turns out, this reverse transcription is so complex that there is a relatively high error rate, about one error in every 2000 nucleotide bases, and it further turns out that this is an *advantage* to the virus. Within a few months, it is able to mutate enough to become resistant to new drugs. The counterattack, so far, has been to apply a mixture of drugs (a "cocktail") in the hope that the virus cannot mutate fast enough to resist them all.

Return to Philosophy

Now back to philosophy. Could Kauffman's "universal toolbox" of a billion or trillion randomly created proteins include one that is capable of carrying out the function of reverse transcriptase? I surely don't know, but the incredible complexity of reverse transcriptase should make us wonder. Is it really plausible to think of that enzyme coming into existence by random chemical changes and selection? And remember, no RNA-based virus could exist without it.

Also, would we expect an Intelligent Creator to create such an enzyme so that a virus as terrible as HIV could exist? I won't say because I don't want to fall into the trap that often catches atheistic evolutionists, who say they know what a god would do.

Teleological evolution

An argument that is frequently brought up against statistical approaches like those in this chapter is that those calculations require a *teleological* evolution. In other words, evolution is working toward a particular enzyme and its amino-acid sequence, or evolution is moving toward a predetermined goal. Evolutionists like to say that such is not the case because evolution is never directed. Dawkins makes a statement to that effect after noting that his Shakespeare exercise is an imperfect analogy; he says it isn't fair to select for a sentence that is known beforehand because evolution doesn't work that way. It is often said that any Bridge hand is also highly improbable, but that any hand can be played. It is what it is because that is what it happened to be. Other random steps in evolution than those that occurred would have produced a different kind of life (maybe little green men), but life would nevertheless have been produced because life is what it happens to be.

It is not difficult, however, to defend teleological evolution, especially when we are thinking about the origin of life. How evolution could happen was postulated by the late Norman H. Horowitz (1945). Say that some mechanism had finally produced a simple living cell, but one that depended completely for its sustenance on the organic and other molecules that were present in the ancient seas. Such a cell would multiply until it filled its environment, but then there would be competition for the available organic molecules. Say that one of those necessary molecules began to run out, but that a mutation in one of those cells could occur, controlling the production of an enzyme that could convert an abundant molecule into the molecule that had become most limiting. Clearly, there would be a strong selection pressure for a cell with the new enzyme. It could multiply, while the more limited cells began to die out, until another molecule became limiting. Then there would be selection pressure for a cell with an enzyme that could produce the new limiting molecule from other molecules that were still abundant in the organic broth. This process might continue until the complex synthetic pathways so well known to biochemists were established. The organisms then living would have developed the metabolic pathways necessary to synthesize all that they needed from molecules that would *never* run out, like water, CO_2, and dissolved minerals. (That is, the organisms would have become like modern green algae or higher plants.) Here is Darwinian natural selection at the molecular level—and it is teleological. When a molecule became limiting, a purpose for mutation and natural selection was established: produce an enzyme with a specific ability to synthesize the limiting molecule from an available precursor.

There are many other examples of evolution toward a goal. Organisms interact chemically with each other in many ways, for example. Some plants produce chemicals that are deleterious to other plants, gaining some advantage in the competition for light, water, and nutrients. This sets a goal for the "victim" plants to evolve ways to overcome the effects of the deleterious chemicals. Also, plants evolve mechanisms to resist the animals that eat them: "As the defensive chemistry of the plants evolves, intensifies, and differentiates through time, the chemical adaptations of existing consumers of plants must evolve, if these consumers are not to become extinct." (Whittaker and Feeny, 1971) Biologists call this "coevolution," of which there are numerous examples. For instance, plants and their pollinators coevolve special features that are beneficial to each other. Of course, an Intelligent Creator could have designed such features, perhaps by guiding their evolution.

Actually, if life evolved, there must have been certain requirements for it to persist. Life on the earth's surface is difficult to imagine without the process of photosynthesis, for example, needed by plants to capture light energy to supply the biosphere (Vernadsky, 2006). Maybe there are various ways for photosynthesis to work, but I doubt that there is an *infinite* number of ways. If photosynthesis were to appear on earth, certain highly specific pigments and enzymes would probably be required. Here again is teleological evolution. Photosynthesis is such a complex system that it is difficult to imagine how enough of the necessary parts could come together at once to get any photosynthesis at all; there appears to be a minimum complexity to photosynthesis (see Appendix C).

And each time evolution must reach a goal, we face the big numbers again. Are random changes and selection a plausible way to reach sequence goals? To me, it doesn't seem plausible, but intervention by an Intelligent Creator is plausible enough.

Back to the origin-of-variability problem

Now that we have closely examined the information content of proteins in general and enzymes in particular—plus the complexity of their controlling genes—we are justified in wondering how there could *ever* be the needed mutations (sufficient variability) for the mechanisms of neo-Darwinism to function as evolutionists say that they do. Do new mutations *ever* confer a survival advantage on their possessors? The vast majority of *known* mutations are deleterious.

Most biologists seldom wonder about the origin of variability because they see so much variability in populations. They are convinced that evolution in the broad sense works, and they can't imagine how it could work without sufficient variability. Knowing that mutations can produce variability, they *assume* that the mutations will produce *enough* variability. Kenneth Miller (1999, p. 49) expresses it well: "Since mutations can duplicate, delete, invert, and rewrite any part of the genetic system in any organism, they can produce any change that evolution has documented." That is, since evolution works by mutations, then mutations must be capable of doing anything that evolution has done, proving that evolution works by mutations.

We don't know nearly enough about genes to know how to go about testing the hypothesis that random mutations are sufficient. *Development* is most likely the key, and we are just beginning to study the evolution of development. At the same time, what we have learned about the molecular biology of life strongly emphasizes the problem. In my opinion, what we now know about the complexity of genes, enzymes, and other cellular aspects of living things comes close to falsifying the hypothesis. Mutations and genetic recombinations may not provide sufficient variability in spite of what is often said, which, of course, does not prove that an Intelligent Creator provided the variability. There might be some other "natural" explanation.

We reviewed the evidence, suggesting that natural selection occurs in nature and concluded strongly that it did (chapter 2). Where did the genes come from in the examples that were given? They were already there in the dark and light peppered moths in England and in the finches on the Galápagos Islands with their large or small beaks. Evolution in those cases was clearly *conservative*, not *progressive*, causing the characteristics of populations to shift within their gene pools as environments changed.

The evidence relating to the evolution of resistance to pesticides or antibiotics is more impressive. New, advantageous genes apparently do originate frrom mutations. Still, when it comes to the origin of variability, we are left pretty much with only our *feelings*. I can easily imagine genes that are already present being modified in small ways by various kinds of mutations to improve an enzyme, but I still see a minimum complexity required for the effectiveness of some of the highly complex enzymes we've been talking about. How could they have originated in the first place? Could those *really* complex enzymes come from Kauffman's universal toolbox? To me, it doesn't sound plausible. And how could the complex pathways of interacting reactions have originated? This brings us back to the question of the origin of life, which we'll examine in the next chapter.

Summary

1. The *sequences* of nucleotides in nucleic acids or amino acids in proteins form the very basis of life function. These sequences may be thought of as *information*. Thus, if we are to account for the origin of life, we must account for the origin of sequence information.

2. Information in a *written sentence* is determined by the sequence of letters. Thus human language is an (imperfect) analogy for nucleotide and amino-acid sequences.

3. Consider various *alphabets*: numbers (10 "letters"), Roman (26 letters or more if punctuation or cases are considered), nucleotide (four letters), and amino acid (twenty letters).

4. If the information in nucleic acids or proteins is analogous to that of language, then *we can gain insight* into life by considering the amount of possible information (the number of possible sequences) in randomly generated sentences.

5. This number can be determined by the *power rule*, which states that the number of possible sequences is equal to the number of letters in the alphabet raised to the power of the number of letters in any given sentence (or *string*).

6. Applying the power rule to a 45-letter sentence constructed from a 30-letter alphabet, it is apparent that there are $30^{45} = 2.954 \times 10^{66}$ possible sequences, a *huge number* indeed.

7. We realize that, although these sequences would contain *every sentence or sentence fragment* that has been or ever could be written with that alphabet, the vast majority of these sequences would be meaningless in any conceivable language.

8. The conclusion implied (but not proved) by the analogy is that the possible *functional amino-acid sequences* (as enzyme catalysts for any conceivable metabolic reaction) must be only a tiny fraction of the total possible sequences ("protein space"); thus, the likelihood of their appearing through random processes is almost nonexistent.

9. By our *creative intelligence* we are able to produce meaningful sentences with various alphabets that we have learned, and an Intelligent Creator could, in some roughly analogous manner, produce functional enzymes and cellular organizations. In a logical sense, however, analogies are always imperfect.

10. *Various possible ways* have been presented *to sidestep the difficulties* brought up by the big numbers, and thus to account for the complex sequences by chance processes. So far, none of these possible ways is conclusive:

> A. If there is some *minimum sequence* below which no enzymatic function is possible, that sequence cannot be achieved by changing individual amino acids (letters) one at a time, selecting only the ones that are part of the final sequence (as Dawkins suggested). There is no selection value until the minimum sequence has been achieved.
>
> B. Starting with a functional enzyme, however, it is possible to *improve that enzyme* by changing only one amino acid at a time (actually, changing its controlling DNA). This is being done in laboratories all over the world.
>
> C. If the minimum sequence to produce an active site can be *very short* (as suggested by Quastler), the chances of getting it are much greater than the conclusions based on our calculation might suggest.
>
> D. Active sites based on *short sequences don't seem likely* in view of the complexity of known enzymes including lysozyme (the first enzyme to be understood), histone IV (highly conserved between peas and cows), cytochrome c

(much variability among organisms, but enough conserved to make its appearance by chance extremely unlikely), and reverse transcriptase (an amazingly complex enzyme of the HIV virus).

E. It is conceivable (as Kauffman suggests, supported by some evidence) that multiple sequences could function as the same active site making *universal enzyme toolboxes* possible. This would also greatly improve the chances of getting effective active sites through random processes. Current information about the complexities of presently understood enzymes makes this seem unlikely—but who knows?

F. *Lateral gene transfer* has been suggested to play an important role in evolution, but it offers no solution to the problem of the origin of suitable gene and enzyme sequences.

11. It has been countered that the analogies require a *teleological evolution* (evolution toward a goal), which may or may not be true. In any case, it is possible to find examples in which evolution toward a goal does appear to be the case.

12. In view of all of these considerations, the analogies of gene and protein complexity with language complexity *cannot serve as proof that creation could occur only with an Intelligent Creator*. Still, the analogies certainly provide insights into the magnitude of the problem and are compatible with an Intelligent Creation.

Table 4-1
Results of multiplying 30 by itself up to 45 times

x	30^x
1	30
2	900
3	27,000
4	810,000
5	24,300,000
6	729,000,000
7	21,870,000,000
8	656,100,000,000
9	19,683,000,000,000
10	590,490,000,000,000
11	17,714,700,000,000,000
12	531,441,000,000,000,000
13	15,943,230,000,000,000,000
14	478,296,900,000,000,000,000
15	14,348,907,000,000,000,000,000
16	430,467,210,000,000,000,000,000
17	12,914,016,300,000,000,000,000,000
18	387,420,489,000,000,000,000,000,000
19	11,622,614,670,000,000,000,000,000,000
20	348,678,440,100,000,000,000,000,000,000
21	0,460,353,203,000,000,000,000,000,000,000
22	313,810,596,090,000,000,000,000,000,000,000
23	9,414,317,882,700,000,000,000,000,000,000,000
24	282,429,536,481,000,000,000,000,000,000,000,000
25	8,472,886,094,430,000,000,000,000,000,000,000,000
26	254,186,582,832,900,000,000,000,000,000,000,000,000
27	7,625,597,484,987,000,000,000,000,000,000,000,000,000
28	228,767,924,549,610,000,000,000,000,000,000,000,000,000
29	6,863,037,736,488,300,000,000,000,000,000,000,000,000,000
30	205,891,132,094,649,000,000,000,000,000,000,000,000,000,000
31	6,176,733,962,839,470,000,000,000,000,000,000,000,000,000,000
32	185,302,018,885,184,100,000,000,000,000,000,000,000,000,000,000
33	5,559,060,566,555,523,000,000,000,000,000,000,000,000,000,000,000
34	166,771,816,996,665,690,000,000,000,000,000,000,000,000,000,000,000
35	5,003,154,509,899,970,700,000,000,000,000,000,000,000,000,000,000,000
36	150,094,635,296,999,121,000,000,000,000,000,000,000,000,000,000,000,000
37	4,502,839,058,909,973,630,000,000,000,000,000,000,000,000,000,000,000,000
38	135,085,171,767,299,208,900,000,000,000,000,000,000,000,000,000,000,000,000
39	4,052,555,153,018,976,267,000,000,000,000,000,000,000,000,000,000,000,000,000
40	12,157,665,459,056,928,010,000,000,000,000,000,000,000,000,000,000,000,000,000
41	3,647,299,637,717,078,640,300,000,000,000,000,000,000,000,000,000,000,000,000,000
42	109,418,989,131,512,359,209,000,000,000,000,000,000,000,000,000,000,000,000,000,000
43	3,282,569,673,945,370,776,270,000,000,000,000,000,000,000,000,000,000,000,000,000,000
44	98,477,090,218,361,123,288,100,000,000,000,000,000,000,000,000,000,000,000,000,000,000
45	2,954,312,706,550,833,698,643,000,000,000,000,000,000,000,000,000,000,000,000,000,000,000

	Table 4-2	
Results of multiplying 20 by itself 20 times or 4 by itself up to 50 times		

x	20^x
1	20
2	400
3	8,000
4	160,000
5	3,200,000
6	64,000,000
7	1,280,000,000
8	25,600,000,000
9	512,000,000,000
10	10,240,000,000,000
11	204,800,000,000,000
12	4,096,000,000,000,000
13	81,920,000,000,000,000
14	1,638,400,000,000,000,000
15	32,768,000,000,000,000,000
16	655,360,000,000,000,000,000
17	13,107,200,000,000,000,000,000
18	262,144,000,000,000,000,000,000
19	5,242,880,000,000,000,000,000,000
20	1,048,577,600,000,000,000,000,000,000

x	4^x
1	4
2	16
3	64
4	256
5	1,024
6	4,096
7	16,384
8	65,536
9	262,144
10	1,048,576
11	4,194,304
12	16,777,217
13	67,108,864
14	268,435,456
15	1,073,741,824
16	4,294,967,296
17	17,179,869,184
18	68,719,876,736
19	274,877,906,944
20	1,099,511,627,776
30	1.1529×10^{18}
40	1.2089×10^{24}
50	1.2676×10^{30}

5 THE ORIGIN OF LIFE: A RATHER WEAK CASE

The goal of the game we play in this chapter is to see if, through observation and experimentation, we can provide a *plausible explanation* for the spontaneous origin of life without reference to God. If we can, chalk up one more evidence for an atheistic theory of creation—knowing, of course, that such evidence doesn't *prove* such a creation, only that it is *plausible*. If we fail to provide a plausible story of an atheistic origin of life, chalk one up for an Intelligent Creation—knowing, of course, that laboratory failure at any point in time doesn't necessarily mean *ultimate* failure; such evidence might be forthcoming sometime in the future.

We'll conclude at the end of this chapter, along with virtually every scientist working in the field, that science has not (yet?) provided a truly plausible story explaining the origin of life without an Intelligent Creator. Still, it is fascinating to examine the lines of evidence that have been reported to support or reject current theories of the origin of life on Earth. The exercise provides yet another perspective of just how complex life really is, and why some scientists working in the field suggest that we may *never* have a fully plausible story, with all of the gaps filled, of how life could have originated spontaneously. These scientists are not saying that the lack of a plausible story proves the existence of God, only that what actually happened a few billion years ago might now be lost to us forever.

Spontaneous Generation

The story begins with the long-discredited theory of *spontaneous generation*. It's a fascinating story, and I'd love to tell it, but we'll have to settle for a couple of highlights plus the bottom line. From antiquity until only a couple of centuries ago, it was assumed by everyone that life could arise spontaneously in many ways, such as serpents and crocodiles from Egyptian mud and sunlight, mice from wheat wrapped in dirty underwear, and—after their discovery—microorganisms from a suitable broth (see Shapiro, 1999, pp. 82–86 from which the following summary is taken). It began to become obvious by the middle of the eighteenth century that most *macro*organisms were too complex to be generated spontaneously, but for at least a century, *micro*organisms were thought to be lumps of protoplasm, simple enough, perhaps, to appear spontaneously under the right conditions. Louis Pasteur, in 1862, published experiments in which he boiled his broths to kill the organisms that were present and then left them open to the air through curved tubes through which the diffusion of airborne spores seemed unlikely. The broths remained sterile, although organisms did appear if the broths were freely open to the air (without curved tubes). This settled the argument for most, and Pasteur was awarded 2,500 francs by the French Académie des Sciences for his work.

As late as 1877, Pasteur's experiments were still being challenged, however, and there were a few who continued to champion the idea of spontaneous generation until the early twentieth century, when it finally became clear that even the very simplest microorganisms were incredibly complex. For example, the bacterium *E. coli* has 4,639,221 nucleotides in its DNA, encoding 4,288 different proteins. (This book is encoded in binary code on my hard drive with only about 630,000 bits.) Indeed, Karl von Nägeli (1817–1891) held tenaciously to the idea of spontaneous generation, proclaiming: "To deny spontaneous generation is to proclaim a miracle." This really cuts to the heart of the matter. If life could not arise spontaneously, at least on the primitive earth, then it must have been created by God, which apparently was unacceptable to Nägeli.

Those who insist on an atheistic explanation of the origin of life claim that life *could* originate spontaneously, *if* conditions were suitable in the past (obviously different from conditions today), and *if* it could begin as something far simpler than even an *E. coli* bacterium and evolve afterward by some kind of molecular Darwinian natural selection.

Furthermore, based on interpretations of certain fossil evidence, life forms as advanced as cyanobacteria, which are biochemically highly advanced (especially in photosynthesis), probably existed on the earth as long ago as 3.55 billion years (Knoll, 2003; Simpson, 2003). Since the Earth is estimated to be about 4.65 billion years old, there may have been a period of perhaps 200–300 million years after it cooled for the appearance of life on our planet. Because such highly complex biochemical mechanisms as photosynthesis and cellular respiration are virtually identical in *all* organisms that possess them, these mechanisms must have appeared *before* organisms began to diverge into all the modern and fossil types that are known. That is, if life developed spontaneously, it had to happen in those 200–300 million years, which is a short time interval in geological terms.

The Soupy Seas

The story of the current theories for the origin of life properly begins with Aleksandr Ivanovich Oparin, who, in 1922, at a meeting of the Russian Botanical Society, first introduced his concept of life arising in a postulated ancient brew of organic compounds that formed on an earth much different from today. In Oparin's time, it was thought that the earth's atmosphere originally contained much hydrogen, methane, ammonia, and water vapor, along with much carbon dioxide, but *no* oxygen. Under these conditions, Oparin suggested, a great variety of organic (containing carbon) compounds would form. (J. B. S. Haldane in England made similar suggestions, published in 1929.) The prevailing notion was that the earliest forms of life synthesized all of the components needed for their existence from inorganic salts, water, and carbon dioxide, using light energy. Oparin suggested that the earliest life forms lived off of the organic molecules that were in that primordial soup. Although this suggestion was radical and generated much opposition, most of those now working in the field accept it.

The Miller-Urey experiment

In 1953, Stanley L. Miller was a graduate student in the laboratory of the Nobel Laureate, Harold C. Urey. Miller set up a closed glass apparatus in which he included some water and an atmosphere consisting of hydrogen (H_2), methane (CH_4), ammonia (NH_3), water vapor (H_2O), and electrical discharges simulating lightning—but *no* oxygen. The water was heated, and the vapor was condensed. After only a few days, the water began to darken, and after a week, the methane was gone and parts of the glassware were covered with *tar,* an insoluble material made of a network of carbon and other atoms connected together in an extended, irregular manner. About 15 percent of the material could be identified by chemical means. The two simplest amino acids, glycine and alanine, were present, as were other amino acids and various compounds, many of which do not occur in living organisms. The gummy tars always appear in similar quantities in similar experiments. Miller's results were published in 1953, the same year Watson and Crick published their discovery of the double helix of DNA.

Both the popular press and scientists interested in the origin of life were excited by these results, proclaiming that we were well on the way to understanding how life originated, and even creating life ourselves in the laboratory. Oparin (1968, 36) himself said: "Successes already presently attained by the use of these methods permit us to hope that the time is not far off when we will succeed in artificially reproducing the simplest forms of life."

Miller's experiment has been repeated and modified in many ways (even by high school students for science fairs); by now, there is a vast amount of literature on the many compounds that can be produced. The problem is that such experiments often go far afield of reasonable prebiotic conditions on Earth. For example, from fairly concentrated formaldehyde solutions, one can produce a mixture of sugars. But where on the prebiotic earth might one expect to find concentrated solutions of formaldehyde? Nevertheless, it is possible to produce in the laboratory under some *assumed* primeval conditions many of the compounds upon which our life form is based—the molecules of life in a prebiotic soup.

By 1995, however, most researchers agreed that the primitive atmosphere lacked significant hydrogen and contained some oxygen. Such an atmosphere would also lack methane and ammonia; hence, it was not like the one postulated for the Miller-Urey experiment (Horgan, 1991). Indeed, it now seems likely that hydrogen would have escaped into space, leaving mostly carbon dioxide and nitrogen, spewed out by volcanoes. Such an atmosphere might produce a greenhouse effect so powerful that temperatures would rise almost to the boiling point of water. Others, including Stanley Miller, long a professor at the University of California in San

Diego, continue to defend the hydrogen-atmosphere model of the primitive earth, even if it occurred only under local conditions, such as near to volcanoes. No one really knows.

Star dust

As it turns out, this setback was only temporary because other researchers have suggested other plausible sources of organic molecules on the primitive earth, and one possible source is outer space.

First, how do we know what we know? Astronomers could make little headway in understanding the cosmos if it were not for *spectroscopes* attached to their telescopes. For one thing, elements heated to high temperatures give off highly specific wavelengths (colors) of light. For example, sodium vapor emits the orange light produced by sodium vapor lamps, sometimes used in parking lots . Light reflecting off any substance or through any substance is affected by that substance, which is why, for example, leaves are typically green. The chlorophyll in them absorbs the blue and the red wavelengths but not the green. So the spectra from planetary atmospheres, stars, interstellar gas clouds, and other sources are studied intensely to learn which elements our universe consists of.

Thus, we have detected in spectra from the stars, using infrared and even radio wavelengths, a plethora of organic compounds in the stellar dust of our galaxy. There are plenty of compounds in space to form the postulated ocean broth. How do such compounds form in space? Current laboratory studies at the NASA Ames Astrochemistry Laboratory at Moffett Field, California, allow simple molecules to condense on extremely cold surfaces, which are then irradiated with ultraviolet light or treated in other ways. David Darling tells how "ethers, alcohols, ketones, and nitriles all form in this space-borne equivalent of Stanley Miller's prebiotic brewery."[1] Some of the products consisted of as many as 15 carbon atoms, and some spectra from space indicate the presence of even larger organic molecules. (The challenge is to match the observed spectra from space with those obtained in the laboratory, which is not always an easy task.)

Next question: How might these extra-terrestrial molecules get into Earth's primeval seas? We have samples of meteorites that contain many organic molecules, including the molecules of life. Based on radioactive dating, these meteorites are thought to be about 4.6 billion years old and are assumed to have existed from the time the earth formed from a cloud of interstellar material in which the young sun had begun to burn at its center. Indeed, analysis of these meteorites gives us some insight into what the composition of the soupy seas might actually have been. These substances, when they reached the earth, would dissolve or at least be suspended in the primeval seas. There would be no microorganisms to eat them as would happen today. Actually, these meteorites are still reaching Earth today. An estimated thirty tons of organic debris falls into Earth's atmosphere each day (Alper, 2002).

Another likely source of organic molecules is comets and their tails. Armand H. Delsemme (2001), now in his eighties, has studied comets for most of his life, summarizing what we knew by late 2001 in a most intriguing article, which I can only briefly outline here. One can argue that the forming Earth had no water. Temperatures would have been so high that water would have boiled off and escaped into space. Earth would have been as dry as its daughter, the moon (thought to have been born in a gigantic collision between Earth and an asteroid). Luna's gravity is not great enough to hold water against the intense heat from the sun (although ice has recently been reported to exist near the poles deep in craters where the sun never shines). Gradually, as the earth cooled, water accumulated on its surface from impacts with those deep-freeze snowballs called comets. Delsemme, based on then current thinking in the field, has provided an impressively detailed scenario of when and how this might have happened. From our perspective, two points are especially important, almost regardless of how it happened (and it may have happened differently; see Harder, 2002):

First, when the earth cooled enough, there would have been ample water from comets. Delsemme calculates that comets could have brought 5.8 times the water in our oceans, and 680 times the gas in our atmosphere! Where did the excess water and gas go? Probably, it was blasted back into space by the continuing bombardment of our young earth with asteroids and comets, each collision generating huge amounts of heat and throwing much earthly material back into space.

Second, those comets would have had, as spectra and recent space experiments show that they do now, large amounts of solid material besides ice, including many organic molecules, and some of those would have been the molecules of life. Delsemme says: "At Jupiter's orbital distance (and beyond), the temperature was so low that the dust grains never lost their frosty cover of water ice and organic volatiles, originally acquired in interstellar space. When they accreted into larger planetesimals, they formed the icy bodies that we now call comets." If all this is true, there may well have been many organic molecules in the primeval seas, even if they were not formed in some ancient version of the Miller-Urey experiment.

Down deep and dark

As if extraterrestrial sources of organics were not enough, there are current research projects that suggest various earthly sources. For example, according to Joe Alper (2002, 41) Geophysicist Friedemann Freund finds microscopic impurities trapped in magma from volcanoes, and some of these have the telltale infrared signatures of organics.

Origin-of-life researchers are most excited by the possibility that organics can be synthesized—and life might originate—near the deep-ocean, hydrothermal vents along the midoceanic ridges, where the great geological plates of the earth's surface are slowly moving apart. It seemed reasonable to expect that these ridges, often close to the hot magma below the earth's crust, would be ideal places to search for springs of boiling water gushing out of the ground. Ocean water might seep into cracks and pores until it met the infernal heat below, which would shoot it to the surface and out through the vents (Darling, 2001, pp. 20–23; Tunnicliffe, 1992).

Oceanographers went searching for these postulated vents, and in 1977, the first ones were sighted in the search lights of the submersible *Alvin*, some 2000 meters deep, off the Galápagos Islands. Since then, dozens of similar vents have been found along mid-oceanic ridges. Here were so-called *black smokers* shooting plumes of water at temperatures typically 200–300 °C, and sometimes as high as 400 °C, well above water's boiling point at the earth's surface (ca. 100 °C). They were "smokers" because when the hot water, loaded with dissolved minerals from the rocks below, hit the cold ocean water (typically only 4 °C), the minerals would precipitate out, forming a dark cloud of particles.

The big surprise was that these vents were populated with hundreds of living species, 95 percent of them unknown to science. There were tube worms three meters long, without mouth, gut or anus, along with crabs, clams, and mussels, most of them white. Where was their food supply? The environs of the vents were covered with carpets of microorganisms, which were also suspended in the surrounding water, forming dense blizzards around the vents.

But where do the microorganisms get their energy and raw materials? Mostly, they metabolize hydrogen sulfide (H_2S), which is poisonous to most of the organisms familiar to us (including us, even in relatively small amounts). The carbon source is dissolved carbon dioxide coming from inside the earth, as it must have done since the beginning of the earth. There are plenty of minerals dissolved in the waters. The microorganisms are not like those found at the earth's surface; rather, they are thermophiles (heat-lovers) or hyperthermophiles (extreme heat-lovers), and they are members of the Archaea, one of the three great *domains* of life along with the Bacteria and the Eukaryotes.

Similar extremeophiles were known from the hot springs of Yellowstone Park, and other places where microorganisms had been found growing at the boiling point, but some of the vent organisms are able to grow at temperatures well above 100 °C. That is, all the metabolic molecules in such organisms are able to function at temperatures that would immediately unfold the protein chains and especially the nucleic acids of organisms that grow at temperatures more amiable to us. Other extremeophiles grow in extreme acidity or alkalinity, saturated salt solutions like the Dead Sea or the Great Salt Lake, or even extreme cold or dryness.

The oceanographer Jack Corliss first saw the Galápagos vents from *Alvin*. He suggested that, if life could exist under those fantastic conditions, perhaps it could have originated there. Who needs a hydrogen atmosphere, lightning, ultraviolet radiation, and tidal pools to make the molecules of life when you have high temperatures for energy and plenty of minerals, ammonia, carbon dioxide, and probably other organics like methane added to the mix? So what if total darkness reigns? (Actually, recent news reports say that total darkness does not necessarily reign; rather, because of the high temperatures, there is a glow, perhaps enough to support photosynthesis.)

The Giant Leap

Clearly, there is much evidence that many organic molecules, including the molecules of life, *could* have existed on the earth in its primeval state. None of this is certain, but I'm willing to go along with it, except for one point that troubles me a bit: If organics are so common in space even now, why didn't we find them in our samples of lunar rock? Or in the Mars samples analyzed by the Viking I lander, which included a mass spectrometer specifically designed to detect organic molecules? Possibly organics are boiled away by the temperatures at Luna's surface. (We need to look for them in those icy craters.) And the Martian regolith appeared to be highly oxidizing, which might have destroyed organic molecules (Shapiro, 1999, chapter 9 and especially pp. 204–11; Sheehan and O'Meara, 2001, pp. 279–87). Future studies should provide some answers to these questions.

Now comes the key question: Does the presence of a primordial soup prove that life could originate in such a soup? This is often taken for granted (Achenbach, 2006). Yet, scientists working in the field are fully aware of the giant leap required to go from that soup to something as complex as the simplest living cell. Even a simple virus, which needs living cells to reproduce itself, is far too complex to have originated by chance in that soup. Some way, they say, life must have been far simpler than it is now, capable of reproduction with errors (so Darwinian selection could function), but at some kind of molecular level that, so far, has remained elusive.

In previous chapters, we've discussed the complexities of life. First and foremost, we must account for those pesky sequences of amino acids in proteins and nucleotides in nucleic acids. The sequences clearly have a minimum complexity—some minimum number of amino acids in specified places to form an active site to catalyze a given reaction. True, we don't know what that number is, and it surely varies for different enzymes.

Second, in life as we now know it, no single sequence of either amino acids or nucleotides can account for life function. Enzymes work in complex assemblages to carry out photosynthesis or cellular respiration—as well as protein synthesis, DNA duplication, membrane formation, and numerous other cellular processes. Could a single sequence—a replicator molecule— have accounted for life's beginning? I doubt it, but who knows?

Third, our life consists of protein assemblages protected in compartments—cells and cellular organelles. Enzymes, to function properly, must be protected from their environments. Even a "simple" prokaryotic cell contains subdivided compartments, such that many of its contents are protected from other contents that would interfere with their functions. Can random changes and selection account for all this? It seems doubtful to me.

Fourth is the mystery of development—the programming that leads to such events as cellular duplication and differentiation to form highly coordinated organ systems. Again, as far as we know, all this is a matter of gene and enzyme sequences, themselves minimally complex, forming foundations for the higher levels that also have characteristics of minimal complexity.

So, if one would explain the origin of life's complexities, one must

119

explain the origin of suitable sequences that control the thousands of enzy-matically controlled reactions going on in cells. (That sentence is possibly the most important sentence in this book.) Whatever your philosophy, sequence rules.

Today's world is a complex web of interacting sequences, and it is any-thing but obvious how such a web might have started. DNA, which only carries the message from generation to generation, cannot reproduce with-out a cadre of enzymes and precursors that have been "activated" by ATP. And those enzymes get their proper sequences from nucleotide sequences in DNA—with the help of RNA and enzymatic machinery. None of the complex molecules we know today is a step toward life; we need the whole shebang, including membranes, ATP, and many other things. Can we imagine a plausible, simple beginning?

RNA World

The origin of life is a chicken-and-egg problem. If DNA requires all that protein machinery to be reproduced, but proteins cannot reproduce themselves, which might have come first? In 1982, chemist Thomas R. Cech at the University of Colorado found that RNA, under some circumstan-ces, could act like a protein enzyme; he called such an RNA a *ribozyme*. For this insight and its supporting data, he and Yale biochemist Sidney Altman, who independently published his discovery in 1983, shared the 1989 Nobel Prize for Chemistry.

RNA: a self-replicating molecule?

The ability of RNA to act as an enzyme looked like a breakthrough for many origin-of-life researchers. Instead of worrying about whether DNA or protein came first, let's just suppose that it was the RNA that came first. Imagine that, with its enzymatic abilities, it could reproduce itself and maybe even build proteins from all those amino acids swimming around in the prebiotic soup. This situation could exist for several million years until many enzymes had formed, one of which could act like a reverse transcriptase, forming DNA on an RNA template, and then gradually the properties of DNA as the repository of genetic information was evolved by molecular selection. All the rest of the apparatus of DNA replication and protein synthesis might be accumulated, along with membranes and genetic programs. The first primeval cell could then appear. Perhaps sev-eral different kinds of primeval cells appeared, but one survived best and became the ancestor of all organisms living today. (The single ancestral cell is strongly implied by the unity of life today; the basic molecular biology of all living cells is the same. Either God created them that way, or they all evolved from a single cell.)

Walter Gilbert, who shared a Nobel Prize with Fred Sanger for developing methods to determine nucleotide sequences, suggested in 1986 that this postulated period in the earth's evolution, when RNA dominated everything, might be called the *RNA world*. Evidence that it is the RNA molecules in ribosomes that act as catalysts is considered by some to be strong evidence for the RNA world. Indeed, the RNA world, with its catchy title, took such a prominent place in discussions of the origin of life that Johnjoe McFadden (2000, p. 96) says the concept has almost become a dogma.[2]

Although Christian De Duve, who has written extensively in this field, is skeptical that the very beginning of life involved RNA, recognizing the associated serious problems, the RNA world intrigues him, and he leaves it in his postulated scenario for the development of life (1995; 2002, chapters 4 and 5). He imagines stages that might have led to that world, notably a kind of proto-metabolism involving randomly sequenced peptides that were not reproduced but that had some catalytic activity. (To save space and because RNA world is subject to many difficulties, we won't review the details of De Duve's proto-metabolism.)

In all of these speculations, the important time is when a molecule became self-replicating. De Duve says that would have been fairly early in the RNA world. In any case, self-replication with occasional mistakes might make Darwinian natural selection possible—and then anything is possible, proponents say. In chapter 4, we discussed Norman Horowitz's mechanism of molecular evolution, in which a postulated primitive cell or system depended on the molecules of the soupy sea for its sustenance. As any given molecule became scarce, there would have been selection pressure for an enzyme that could synthesize that molecule from available precursors in the primordial sea. Thus, metabolic pathways could evolve "backwards" from the necessary product through a chain of its precursors. There is, of course, a problem with this scenario: It requires that virtually all of the necessary molecules, or their precursors, be present in the soupy sea.

Beyond the RNA world

There are related matters to which we could devote many pages, even chapters. How did the first cell form if it followed some kind of self-replication metabolism in the prebiotic world? How did the developing machinery become isolated with a membrane, how did the genetic code develop, and did sulfur play an important role ("the Thioester World"). In short, how did prokaryotes and then eukaryotes come into being? Of the books I've read, Christian De Duve (2002, see his chapter 6) does the best job of speculating about how these things might have happened, and he recognizes that it is all speculation.

Discussion about the origin of cells might include the work of the late Sydney Fox, who headed the Institute for Molecular and Cellular Genetics at the University of Miami (excellent summary in Shapiro, 1986, chapter 8). For a quarter century and more, Fox advocated that proteins came first (rather than RNA). By certain manipulations with amino acids, he produced *proteinoid microspheres*, which he promoted as the one and only solution to the origin of life. These tiny spheres superficially resemble certain single-celled organisms both in size and appearance. We'll simply note that nowhere in Fox's proposals are there specific mechanisms to account for those all-important sequences.

Backing away from the RNA world

The real problem with the RNA world is that RNA is an extremely unlikely molecule for the primitive earth, and everyone knows it. To have an RNA world, we must have the four purine and pyrimidine bases: adenine, guanine, uracil, and cytosine. In his 1986 book, *Origins* (pp. 108, 186–87), Robert Shapiro tells about the late Cyril Ponnamperuma, who perhaps was the strongest proponent of life arising in a primordial soup. Ponnamperuma carried out numerous Miller-Urey-type experiments over several decades. At one point, he reported that he had detected the five bases used in DNA and RNA both in Miller-Urey mixtures and in a meteorite. Although the bases were present only at about two parts per million, he called his findings "almost an awesome result." Ponnamperuma assumed that it was sufficient for a substance to be present in *any* amount. We must note that he never observed *nucleosides* (bases with ribose or deoxyribose sugars), nor did he observe *nucleotides* (nucleosides + phosphate), which are necessary for the synthesis of RNA or DNA. Yet Ponnamperuma said: "Nobody doubts now that the components of nucleic acids can be made by a path that can be called natural.. . .There are inherent properties in the atoms and molecules which seem to direct the synthesis in the direction most favorable" for the molecules of life. In these statements of personal belief, he clearly resorted to the philosophy of *determinism*, Shapiro says; such statements are part of the "myth" based on the Miller-Urey experiments.

Ponnamperuma's approach and beliefs are typical of many origin-of-life researchers. If it is possible to produce the necessary precursors for RNA, say, in any experimental way remotely related to "natural conditions" (whatever they were), then that shows that RNA could have appeared in the prebiotic world, in sufficient quantities to lead to RNA world.

Shapiro (1999, chapter 6, especially pp. 102–20), in his more recent book, *Planetary Dreams*, outlines the approach in beautiful detail. I would love to review his discussion in some detail here, but if you're interested, you'll have to read Shapiro's book. Step by step, he examines the plausibility of getting first the pyrimidines, then the ribose (especially unlikely), attaching the phosphate to make the nucleotides, and finally hooking several together in a suitable sequence to create a functional ribozyme, which would then have to be reproduced to produce RNA world.

Shapiro's discussion touches on the real difficulty encountered in any soupy-sea scenario, whether or not it produces RNA or other minimally complex molecules of life. To get a molecule like RNA, the most optimistic proponent of a soupy-sea development must imagine several isolated situations, each ending with some of the precursors of RNA, which then combined in some way that didn't destroy them—or allow them to react with molecules other than the ones that lead to RNA—or allow them to become too dilute. Some puddle containing the unlikely ribose must drain into some bathtub full of the four RNA bases, and on and on. Aren't we stretching things a bit with these scenarios? It certainly looks like it, but one can always say that we just haven't dreamed up the acceptable scenarios yet.

In addition to the difficulty of imagining suitable situations, each different from the other, for generating so many essential precursors with Miller-Urey processes, there is the incredible difficulty of imagining even one such situation that had only the special reactants needed to get the essential precursors. All the sources of organic molecules so far imagined produce a great gemisch of compounds. Could peptides or RNA form in such a mixture? Even if today's common twenty amino acids were in the mixture, there would also be other amino acids, and many other compounds more likely to react with the amino acids than the amino acids would be to react with each other. Shapiro (2000) describes this situation beautifully in a paper based on a mixture of the compounds found in the Murchison meteorite.

To get our Shakespearian sentence in chapter 4, we limited ourselves to an alphabet of only thirty uppercase letters (because thirty was a nice number to work with). That's like limiting the gemisch to only the significant twenty amino acids—or the four RNA nucleotide bases. The real soupy sea would contain dozens of molecules. Shapiro says that it would be like trying for Shakespeare with both upper and lower case letters, all possible punctuation, and the Greek, Cyrillic, and Arabic alphabets thrown in for good measure. Make no mistake, the problems of getting any kind of RNA or protein barely touch the surface. The real challenge is to get the sequences so that the proteins or RNA will have enzymatic activity and be able to replicate at some point. If we skip over all the difficulties and just suppose that both RNA and proteins somehow form in the prebiotic soup, we are only at the beginning of the sequence problems of chapter 4.

Ribosome structure

Let's go one step above individual molecules and contemplate for a moment, the complexity of ribosomes. After all, it is the catalytic role of RNA in the ribosomes that led to the concept of RNA world. The structure and consequent function of the ribosome is now understood in exquisite detail.[3] In a perspective published in an issue of *Science*, Albert E. Dahlberg (2001) describes the fantastic complexity of these ribosomes (of which there are about 20,000 in a bacterial cell), noting that the key nucleotide sequences are the same in *all* organisms (they are *conserved*). The newly understood structures allow us to understand how a ribosome can distinguish the suitable tRNA molecules and match them up with the codons in the messenger RNA so that only the correct amino acids are placed in a growing peptide chain (see Figure 3-4). Because all of this occurs in all living organisms, it had to come into being before the postulated first ancestral cell—the cell from which all life sprang—and it must have worked well ever since. Then Dahlberg says that looking at a specific figure in one of the technical papers "is like uncovering an ancient drawing, depicting in exquisite detail a universal mechanism for one of the original steps in the evolution of life." Such faith! He seems to assume without question that all of this complexity could someway originate by molecular evolution in a primordial mixture before the ancestral cell came into being.

Looking for Answers: Contrasting Approaches

For the most part, these questions are obvious to all scientists working in the field, although some who are especially optimistic might tend to ignore them. Of course, no one can ignore the questions of sequences and reproduction, even if they might be put on the back burner for the time being. Those are questions that *must* be answered. Most scientists engaged with the topic have their favorite approaches, if not the full-blown answers that have evaded everyone. Let's take a look at some of the approaches. Although some of them tend to overlap, most of them are quite unique and intriguing.

Manfred Eigen's laboratory studies and speculations

Back in 1972, I went to a summer honors workshop for university students from Germany, held in Alpbach, Austria. I was invited to give a series of lectures and to discuss my *Nature* article. As I presented my doubts about the origin of minimal sequences, some of the students suggested that I should check on the work of Manfred Eigen, director of the Max Planck Institute for Biophysical Chemistry in Göttingen since 1964. So I did after procrastinating for thirty years. One of his books, *Steps towards Life. A Perspective on Evolution,* was published in Germany in 1987. An English translation appeared in 1992. The title seemed like Eigen might have found a solution to the origin of those minimally complex amino acid sequences. He certainly has some highly impressive credentials. Among his numerous scientific prizes and honors is a 1967 Nobel Prize for his research on extremely rapid chemical reactions.

Among other things, Eigen was inspired by the work of Sol Spiegelman, an American biochemist who, in the 1960s, carried out studies of laboratory RNA evolution (see the excellent summary by Shapiro, 1999, 99–102). Spiegelman isolated a single-stranded genome from an RNA virus, Q_β, which consisted of 4200 bases that are replicated within a bacterial host. Then he isolated the enzyme that could replicate the RNA in the presence of the four *activated* (phosphorylated) nucleotides, which could be purchased from a chemical supply house. With this system, he was able to study natural selection in the laboratory at the molecular level. (We saw some excellent examples of this in chapter 4, where we reviewed the work of Frances Arnold's group of researchers, who improve existing enzymes by letting them reproduce and mutate in bacteria.) Eigen expanded on

Spiegelman's experiments in his own laboratory, developing mathematical models and several important concepts.

So I read his book with care to see whether he could offer an answer to the problem of the origin of suitable amino acid or nucleotide sequences at life's beginning. In chapter 3 of his book, he outlined the seriousness of the problem, much as I did in chapter 4. He noted that a gene from the bacterium *E. coli* might have 1000 nucleotides, and he showed that there are $4^{1000} \approx 10^{602}$ possible arrangements of the nucleotides in a gene of that length. He calculated that the volume of a spherical universe with a diameter of ten billion light years, expressed as cubic angstroms, is "only" 10^{108} Å^3. (The angstrom is the smallest unit normally used by chemists: 1 Å = 0.1 nm.) It would thus require 10^{494} universes that size to include as many cubic Angstroms as there are possible nucleotide sequences in a gene 1000 nucleotides long. He concluded the chapter by noting that "the genes found today cannot have arisen randomly. . . . There must exist a process of optimization. . . . Even if there are several routes to optimal efficiency, mere trial and error cannot be one of them."

Eigen's chapter 4 is titled "How does information arise?" This is the key question. I have read and re-read the chapter (which is only three pages long) looking for his answer. Eigen states that "our task is to find. . .a natural law that leads to the origin of information." First, he talks about information in written language, noting that not all sequences of letters have an equal probability of occurring and containing information that is meaningful to one who speaks a certain language. For example, "e" is the most common letter in the English language, the occurrence of spaces determines the length of words, and a "q" is nearly always followed by a "u."

Having read this, I expected to learn of rules that determine which nucleotides must follow which nucleotides to provide biological information. No such rules appeared. Eigen wrote about the rules of thermodynamics including the concept of entropy, which can be thought of as a measure of nonrandomness. His discussion, however, seemed to lead nowhere toward accounting for those minimally complex but essential sequences. Eigen's bottom line was the Darwinian principle of natural selection, and he believes that the origin of variability in sequences is mutation. So we are back home. And small steps are implied at every turn. To my understanding, this chapter does not provide the "natural law that leads to the origin of information" in the first place. That natural law *can* improve the information, but it seems it cannot account for its origins.

Stuart Kauffman and complexity theory

In 1993, a book by Stuart A. Kauffman appeared. Its title seems to go right to the heart of the questions raised in this book: _The Origins of Order. Self-Organization and Selection in Evolution_. This book was followed, in 1995, by _At Home in the Universe_ and, in 2000, by _Investigations_. Kauffman tells us that he became intrigued with the origin of order in biological systems as early as 1965. During the early 1970s he became further intrigued with the manner in which elements within complex networks (not necessarily biological) interact with each other. Each element can respond to its neighbors by turning "on" or "off," depending on the status of the neighbors. The basis for these effects is Boolean logic, described by George Boole, the English inventor of an algebraic approach to mathematical logic.

Kauffman describes how these networks function and notes that, while a network can have a huge number of "states," certain rules limit those states to much smaller possible states. Hence, order can appear out of chaos—"order for free," he calls it. He also sees analogies of "order for free" in biological development in which, for example, a zygote can divide repeatedly to become a highly organized, multicellular organism. He calculates that even a large number of genes in a genome can produce only a limited number of cell types (perhaps 250 in a human, he says). The famous evolutionist, John Maynard Smith, notes on the cover of Kauffman's first book: "Given what we know about the way genes signal to one another, he [Kauffman] argues that complexity can arise more readily than one would expect. I am not sure he is right, but I am sure that we should take his ideas seriously." At the level of development (differentiation) and population kinetics, I would agree (see also Smith and Szathmáry, 1999).

Along with all of the other authors whose books on life's origin I've read, Kauffman devotes many pages to the big numbers, the difficulties with a naked gene consisting of either RNA or DNA, and the chicken and egg problem. In his own theories of the origin of life, he incorporates the idea of the soupy sea, visualizing a huge mixture of compounds, many of them peptides, interacting with each other. If you get enough peptides, he speculates, they will begin to catalyze each other's formation, and a complex but orderly metabolism will appear. Darwinian selection will eventually lead to life as we know it. Kauffman is adamant, however, in insisting that Darwinian selection alone won't get the job done. There must also be this "order for free" arising from the mixture. He summarizes his ideas most succinctly in this paragraph from *At Home in the Universe* (1995, pp. 47–48):

> I hold a renegade view: life is not shackled to the magic of template replication, but based on a deeper logic. I hope to persuade you that life is a natural property of complex chemical systems, that when the number of different kinds of molecules in a chemical soup passes a certain threshold, a self-sustaining network of reactions—an autocatalytic metabolism—will suddenly appear. Life emerged, I suggest, not simple, but complex and whole, and has remained complex and whole ever since—not because of a mysterious élan vital, but thanks to the simple, profound transformation of dead molecules into an organization by which each molecule's formation is catalyzed by some other molecules in the organization. The secret of life, the wellspring of reproduction, is not to be found in the beauty of Watson-Crick pairing, but in the achievement of collective catalytic closure. The roots are deeper than the double helix and are based in chemistry itself. So, in another sense, life—complex, whole, emergent—is simple after all, a natural outgrowth of the world in which we live.

In *Investigations* (2000, p. 10), he confirms that this belief is at the heart of his ideas: "In *At Home*, and also in this book, I explore a theory I believe has deep merit, one that asserts that, in complex chemical reaction systems, self-reproducing molecular systems form with high probability."

As Maynard Smith suggested, most researchers in the field have taken Kauffman's complexity theories seriously—but I haven't found any real converts. Consider these two examples of reactions to Kauffman. John-joe McFadden (2000, pp. 92–95) says the theory is "too rooted in this kind of digital simulation and takes little regard of *wet life*.. . .A second and more important objection to complexity theory, as a theory to explain the phenomenon of life, is that it is not relevant to the generation of ordered structures inside living cells." Robert Shapiro (1999, pp. 132–36) echoes these ideas, quoting from several authors who note that computer simulations are truly a long way from the real world. Shapiro summarizes his own thoughts by saying that he thinks "it very unlikely that enzymes would form spontaneously in a chaotic mixture." And further, with reference to a series of quotations from Kauffman's *At Home in the Universe*, Shapiro writes: "As written, the preceding statements are philosophy. They need to be demonstrated to enter the realm of science."

That is certainly my conclusion after studying Kauffman's last two books. I looked for an explanation of the origin of order of those sequences of amino acids and nucleotides, but I looked almost in vain. I say "almost" because Kauffman did make me aware of the concept of "universal enzyme toolboxes," which we discussed in chapter 4.

As I went over the final edit of this book, I encountered a one-page summary by Joel Achenbach (2006) of some current thoughts about the origin of life, printed in *The National Geographic*. Achenbach outlines some recent ideas of Harold Morowitz of George Mason University and Eric Smith of the Santa Fe Institute (where Kauffman was located when he wrote the books just noted). Morowitz and Smith propose a scheme involving just eleven small carbon molecules that would have been abundant in that prebiotic broth. These molecules are supposed to have been involved in the development of such molecules as amino acids, lipids, sugars, and eventually RNA, or something similar. "In other words, metabolism came first—before cells, before replication, before life as we commonly think of it."

This sounds very much like Kauffman's ideas. Achenbach goes on to talk about molecular evolution as though it were a new idea: "Some types of molecular chains outcompeted other molecular chains for the planet's resources, and gradually they led to the kind of molecules that life depends upon." Actually, as we've seen, such ideas go back at least to Norman Horowitz's paper of 1945. Clearly, some of the early suggestions are still alive and well.

Achenbach goes on to discuss a recent book by Robert Hazen titled *Gen·ne·sis*, which further elaborates on the idea of "emergence" outlined by Kauffman. Hazen says many theories of the origin of life depend upon "emergence." Achenbach ends his summary by saying, "All of this is sure to be a matter of contentious debate for a long time." That's for sure.

Günter Wächtershäuser: complexity and fool's gold

Another individual whose speculations about the origin of life seem to fit in the complexity category, but which also relate to my next topic, is Günter Wächtershäuser. He obtained a doctoral degree in organic chemistry but works as a patent attorney in Munich, Germany. He has long nurtured an interest in the problem of the origin of life, and in 1988, he proposed a theory that caught the attention, and sometimes the lavish praise, of others working in the field. For example, Leslie Orgel, of the

Salk Institute, is one of the most profound thinkers in the field, and he told Shapiro (1999, p. 136) that Wächtershäuser's proposal was "the most important finding in the origin of life in the last half century."

Just what is this revolutionary theory? It returns to the deep-ocean vents. Wächtershäuser suggested that the chemistry that led to the origin of life took place at these vents. He is not just talking about producing compounds for the broth, however; he suggests that the earliest signs of life were a series of chemical reactions (perhaps similar to Kauffman's theory), catalyzed by iron-sulfide (pyrite, or fool's gold) and nickle-sulfide crystals. These crystals have a positive surface charge and thus would attract negatively charged organic molecules. Other heavy-metal sulfides may also have taken part, he speculates. The breakdown of hydrogen sulfide (H_2S) was the energy source, as it still is at those deep-sea vents. Being even more specific, Wächtershäuser postulates that the reactions were probably related to the modern citric acid cycle; instead of CO_2 being a *product* of the cycle, energy *input* (from H_2S) caused the cycle to run backward so that CO_2 was a *substrate*, and the products were organic molecules such as succinic acid, from which long-chain organic acids (as in membranes) can be built up. Under the postulated conditions, all this would occur *without* the need for protein enzymes—just the metal-sulfide catalysts.

Contrary to Kauffman's speculations, Wächtershäuser's (2000) ideas are specific enough to be tested in the laboratory. For example, key compounds in this cycle are acetic acid (the acid in vinegar) and pyruvic acid, and Wächtershäuser says that these compounds might be synthesized in the presence of the sulfides at the extremely high pressures and temperatures around deep-sea vents. This would indeed be "life as we don't know it," because in life as we do know it, the reactions of metabolism are catalyzed by enzymes rather than pyrite and its relatives. Eventually, Wächtershäuser said, this strange metabolism would lead to proteins and hence to enzymes, with DNA, RNA, and even membranes following somewhere down the line. To test these ideas, scientists should set up the conditions in the laboratory and see what happens—or continue to study the deep-sea vents to see if the proposed chemistry still prevails there.

Actually, it is not easy to carry out such studies in the laboratory; it can be dangerous to work with extremely high pressures and temperatures, not to mention such gases as carbon monoxide (CO). Visiting the vents to study their chemistry is also a daunting challenge. Nevertheless, it has been possible, in slightly modified laboratory studies with high pressures and temperatures, and with plausible starting compounds including the sulfide crystals, to synthesize acetic acid, pyruvic acid, some amino acids, and even dipeptides (two amino acids connected by peptide bonds) when amino acids were supplied (Huber and Wächtershäuser, 1998). Many commentators see these results as strong support for Wächtershäuser's theories.

Although we won't pursue the specifics of Wächtershäuser's ideas in detail here, just as I'm polishing these paragraphs, two other origin-of-life researchers have expanded on those ideas: William Martin in Düsseldorf, Germany, and Michael J. Russell in Glasgow, Scotland. These scientists note that those black smokers build up mineral chimneys, sometimes meters high within just months, and the material that these chimneys are made of consists of iron sulfide in a porous form that includes water-containing "cells" in which the early steps of metabolism might have taken place (see Morgan, 2003). Indeed, the walls of these compartments might have acted as the first "cellular membranes," and ion concentration differences might have provided voltage differences (600 millivolts) between the inside and outside of the compartments, which might have driven some of the chemical reactions. Martin's article says that, at some point, these rock-cradled life-forms must have "invented the biochemistry required to produce their own membranes" and escape from their rocky compartments as full-fledged archaebacteria or eubacteria. Interesting terminology, and certainly not the only place it is encountered in the origin-of-life literature. "Invented," of course, means random mutations and other changes that have selection potential.

All of this speculation is well and good, incorporating some unique ideas about how compounds might form at those deep, hot vents, and with some stretch of the imagination, it is even possible to think of proteins being formed down there. There are many problems, such as instability of pyruvic acid and other necessary compounds, but perhaps with these theories, the answers to these problems will be found before long.

Nowhere in my studies of Wächtershäuser's ideas (or those of Martin and Russell), however, have I encountered any suggestion about the origin of sequences. Chapter 4 should have made it clear that, even with the "universal enzyme toolboxes," sequence still rules. Hence, even if Wächtershäuser's concrete suggestions turn out to be right, it is still a mighty distant leap to proteins as we know them, with their active sites, and another leap to organized cells.

A. Graham Cairns-Smith and clay life

Günter Wächtershäuser is not the only researcher to suggest that minerals might have acted as catalysts in a prebiotic world's chemistry. For example, a recent article (Hazen, 2001) outlines the evidence that such minerals as calcite might attract organic molecules. Indeed, the surfaces of such minerals might attract the L form of amino acids more than the D form, accounting for why only L amino acids (and D sugars) are found in nature (with just a few exceptions).

However, the scientist who has taken the idea of clay (mineral) catalysts to its limit—namely, that the earliest life *was* a clay—is A. Graham Cairns-Smith (1985), a chemist at the University of Glasgow, Scotland. Cairns-Smith has an interesting book called *Seven Clues to the Origin of Life: A Scientific Detective Story*. In it, step by step, he makes his case for clay life. Only genetic information can evolve, he writes, but DNA and its duplication machinery are too complex to be accounted for. (Like the other authors, Cairns-Smith first shoots down other theories to make room for his own.) We need a "scaffolding" to lead to life as we know it, he says— some simpler form upon which our kind of life could develop. Clay minerals, based on silica, are quite active chemically, and they are everywhere; they might have been the scaffolding. By now clay crystal structures and the reactions that they undergo (in soil) are well understood, as Cairns-Smith points out in considerable detail. Clays can reproduce (as all crystals do), even passing small imperfections onto the next "generation"; in other words, they exhibit aspects of "heredity." Selection would favor the clays that reproduced best. Finally, clay surfaces have electric charge (negative) and thus can attract polar organic molecules. On the surface, reactions of the molecules of life would occur, and those molecules would gradually become incorporated into the clay life until the clays themselves were no longer necessary, and life as we know it had emerged.

It is an interesting theory. Like Wächtershäuser's ideas, it is specific enough to be tested in various ways, including looking for signs of clay life in nature. Unlike Wächtershäuser's ideas, however, Cairns-Smith's theories have not caught the attention of other researchers, so they have not been examined critically. Shapiro (1986, chapter 8) discusses Cairn-Smith's ideas positivly, but that is about the only such discussion that I have encountered.

As I followed Cairns-Smith's arguments, I was impressed with his style of writing, his ingenuity, and the logic of his arguments based on our understanding of life and clays. I could accept most of his account until the final chapter. Here, I hoped to learn just how organic molecules got together on the clays. I never did. At that point, Cairn-Smith had hardly any valid speculations, and a huge leap of faith is still required.

And of course, that being the case, there are no suggestions about those all important *sequences*. Except for Kauffman's "universal enzyme tool boxes," no one seems even to have a good suggestion about how it might have happened.

A Brief Look at Quantum Mechanics

The science of quantum mechanics plays a role in the origin-of-life question. I mentioned to a few friends that I was writing a section on quantum mechanics. Without exception, these nonscientist friends said, "What's that?"

Quantum mechanics is one of the great discoveries of the twentieth century, right up there with relativity, the double helix, quasars, plate tectonics, and other powerful insights into how our universe functions. It provides an incredible (and that means almost unbelievable) view of how things work at the level of subatomic particles and also atoms and molecules. Yet, while most of us have at least some knowledge about most of the other discoveries, quantum mechanics is unappreciated by nearly everyone except those who have been exposed to a lot of physics. Most biologists, including me, are among those who do not (did not, anyway) appreciate quantum mechanics.

Oh, we biologists apply a small portion of quantum theory in our discussions of photosynthesis and related processes. We know that radiation (including visible light) not only travels through space with the characteristics of waves, but it also consists of discrete "particles of energy." It is strange indeed to try to imagine particles that are at the same time waves, but that is just the beginning of the strangeness of quantum mechanics.

Now and again in my career I've been exposed to some of that other strangeness, but it was indeed so strange that I tended to ignore it. For example, quantum mechanics tells us that the more we know about the velocity of a photon (or an electron or even an atom or molecule), the less we know about its location, and vice versa.

How difficult it can be to accept the implications of experiments that led to quantum mechanics is illustrated by some of the early history.

In Germany in 1900, Max Planck did some experiments on radiation that he could only explain mathematically by assuming that radiant energy (which includes light) occurred in "packets" that could not be subdivided; these he called *quanta*. He was not happy with his result and spent a few years trying to explain it (mathematically) some other way. But one of the five "miraculous" papers written by Albert Einstein in 1905 while he was still a clerk in the Swiss patent office was concerned with the photoelectric effect. The paper showed convincingly that light does indeed occur in energy packets, which we now call *photons*, and yet light also has a wave nature. Some simple equations relate the photon energy to wave length (or to frequency) of radiant energy.

These critical studies of Planck and Einstein started development of the science of quantum mechanics. (Einstein received a Nobel prize for his photoelectric paper; his special relativity paper published in the same year was ignored by the Nobel committee!)

But as quantum mechanics continued to develop, especially by Niels Bohr in Copenhagen, various unexpected things began to pop up. For one thing, it appeared that events at the atomic level could be completely random and thus unpredictable. For example, it is impossible to predict when any given atom of a radioactive substance will itself decay by giving off radiation. Einstein was not happy with this apparent lack of total order in the universe. He made the famous statement: "God does not play dice."

Although he was involved in other things at least until the late 1920s (for example, development of *special relativity*), Einstein spent much of his time trying to apply classical physics to the experiments of quantum mechanics (Bolles, 2004; Crease and Mann, 1986). He contended with Bohr and others at scientific meetings and in scientific papers, some of which were written with collaborators. But always, Bohr and others found weaknesses in Einstein's arguments, and Einstein was never able to bring quantum mechanics into line with classical physics.

By now, the concepts of quantum mechanics have been tested in thousands of laboratories, and the results continue to support the science. Detailed mathematics describe these experimental results. As a matter of fact, some aspects of quantum mechanics are applied in our computers and other devices, which would not work without these principles. Thousands of experiments in hundreds to thousands of laboratories support the principles of quantum mechanics. Only a very few dissenters remain.

Johnjoe McFadden:
quantum mechanics and the origin of life

A few theorists refer to quantum phenomena in their discussions of life's origin, but these references are rather superficial except for the ruminations of Johnjoe McFadden (2000), a reader in molecular microbiology at the University of Surrey, England. Quantum mechanics is for him the end-all and be-all of how life on Earth might have started and then evolved.

McFadden's book was my first semi-in-depth look at quantum mechanics—beyond the quanta and the photons—and the _uncertainty principle_, which even biologists have at least heard of—albeit with little real understanding of what it actually is, as we'll see in chapter 7.

Quantum mechanics requires high-level mathematics that takes years to master, so I'm not going to be able to explain it to you properly in a few pages. I've studied McFadden's chapters as thoroughly as I can, as well as several other descriptions of quantum mechanics, and I'll try to present a summary of McFadden's ideas, which obviously will be superficial. If the ideas of quantum mechanics catch your interest, I would suggest that you study McFadden's book as well as going to other sources (for example, Liboff, 2002; Hey and Walters, 2003; Tegmark and Wheeler, 2001; Crease and Mann, 1986; Darling, 2005; and _Encyclopædia Britannica_, which has an appropriately long and detailed article on quantum mechanics).

A basic experiment of quantum mechanics is to pass a beam of light through two vertical slits that are very close together. Although we won't examine this experiment in detail, suffice it to note that the beam of light through the two slits produces a row of vertical bands of light alternating with darkness on a screen, as Thomas Young had discovered in 1801. If there is only one slit, only one band of light (diffuse at its edges) appears on the screen. Experimenters reduced the energy in the beam of light until the "beam" consisted of only one particle (photon or electron, atom, or molecule, as it turns out). It would certainly seem that a single particle, say an electron, could pass through only one of the slits, arriving where the band of light was when the beam consisted of many particles. But that was not the result. The single electron struck the screen in places that strongly implied that it was passing through both slits at once! That is, the photon could exist in both slits at once: two places at one time!

The next step was to use some kind of measuring device, which worked better with electrons than with photons, to see which slit the electron passed through. When that was done, it was always seen that the electron went through either one slit or the other but never through both, and where the electron fell on the screen was consistent with the idea that it passed through only one slit.

The conclusion was that a photon, electron, or even a large molecule can only be in two places at the same time when it has not been measured! Needless to say, the situation gets complicated at this point. Niels Bohr and others developed concepts and a vocabulary to account for the implications of this experiment. When the particle has not been measured (and any kind of interaction with the environment is a "measurement"), it was said to be *coherent* and in a *superposition*. Being in a superposition means being in *all of its possible states at once*. That is, the electron could go through either slit, so it could be in two possible "states" as far as going through the slits is concerned—going through both slits at once. Measurement *causes the wave function to collapse*, meaning that measurement causes the coherent particle to become *incoherent* and exist in only one of its possible states.

With these ideas in mind (and as you can imagine, there are many aspects of these ideas that we have no space to discuss), McFadden, like de Duve, accepts the notion of a prebiotic soup despite expressing some misgivings. Then he relates studies with a thirty-two-amino-acid peptide that can catalyze its own formation provided it is given two parts of itself—the parts already "activated" and ready to be hooked together. Of course McFadden realizes that this is a completely arbitrary example—a sort of thought experiment for which Einstein was famous.

McFadden then imagines that a peptide molecule consisting of thirty-two amino acids in *any* sequence becomes totally isolated from all similar molecules. This might occur in a nanotube or something similar. In such a state and in the language of quantum mechanics, the molecule is *coherent* because it has not been *measured*; it exists in a *superposition* of all its possible states. And because it consists of thirty-two of the twenty amino acids, it can exist in $20^{32} = 10^{41}$ different states (that is, amino-acid combinations). At least one of those combinations has the ability to reproduce itself.

At some time in earth's early history, the molecule does interact with its surroundings and hence is "measured," which causes it to *collapse out of its superposition* into *one* of its 10^{41} possible states. Because life on our planet exists, that one molecule on our planet must have been the peptide that could reproduce itself! What about all the other peptides? There are various possible explanations. According to the unprovable theory of parallel universes—an infinite number of them—each of the other possible amino-acid combinations crashed out into another parallel universe (Tegmark, 2003). If this theory is true, life might exist only on our planet in our universe.

McFadden outlines the problems with his suggestion: Are there *really* parallel universes? Would a single replicating molecule be enough to start life?. He then tells of some other approaches being considered seriously by physicists and cosmologists to account for the problem of getting the reproducing molecule into our system, but he ends up mostly defending the parallel-universe idea. Note that we are now into the realm of philosophy and far distant from the exact science of quantum mechanics. But McFadden's theory is, in his mind at least, consistent with what is known about quantum mechanics.

Who am I to say that this is all fantasy when, despite my recent studies of quantum mechanics, I would still find it very difficult to converse with any specialist in that field? Maybe Johnjoe McFadden is onto something—or, alternatively, perhaps an Intelligent Creator was involved in the Creation of life on earth, and quantum mechanics had little to do with this Creation. Because of the many yet-to-be solved problems of quantum mechanics, all would agree that Johnjoe has not presented a *truly* convincing scheme to account for those all-important sequences. Yet he *could* have a clue that will some day lead to an acceptable theory for an atheistic origin of life. I'm dubious, but it is way too early to be sure.

Michael Russell:
The most plausible just-suppose story so far

In a recent issue of *American Scientist*, Michael Russell (2006) builds upon much of the work that we have discussed so far to outline a detailed and even plausible story of how life might have originated on the primitive Earth. (He also refers to several colleagues who, during past decades, contributed to his thoughts on life's origin.) In his introductory paragraphs, Russell notes that scientists "don't know for certain how life started....Thus, the question we ask is not 'did it happen this way?' but rather, 'could it have happened this way?' And if we can say at each step 'yes, this is possible,' then we can construct a path that stretches from the raw materials of the universe to ourselves." My first impression was that Russell has certainly spun the most detailed and most plausible what-if tale that I have yet encountered. And that is probably the case.

Here is a much-condensed outline: Because of the dangerous radiation from the early sun and other vicissitudes of Earth's surface conditions, Russell's story takes place in the deep ocean, but not by the "black smokers." They are too hot (400 C) he says. A better location was near warm (90 C) alkaline springs at the bottom of the acidic ocean, which itself contained huge quantities of dissolved carbon dioxide. Russell and a colleague had suggested the existence of such springs, and they were indeed discovered in 2000. The springs provide many dissolved mineral elements, including the iron and nickel sulfides that play roles in Wächtershäuser's and Russell's schemes. Under these conditions, carbon dioxide would combine with hydrogen to form organic compounds, especially acetic acid (vinegar). This has been demonstrated.

The minerals from the springs form precipitates such as calcium carbonate (limestone) as the warm, alkaline, spring water encounters the cooler acidic ocean water, building up huge towers, some as high as sixty meters. (The discovers of these springs and towers called them the "Lost City.") The towers are hollow, and there are small "bubbles" of solid mineral on their surfaces.

Russell suggests that these bubbles acted as cells now act by isolating what was going on inside from the outside environment. Within these *proto-cells*, everything could come together to form the acetic acid and many other compounds, including (Russell says!) RNA and various peptides. As proteins and other substances collected on the inside surfaces of these proto-cells, more typical organic membranes would form. Some of the proteins or RNA would have had catalytic properties, acting as precursors to future enzymes. Once some form of inheritance had developed, probably based on the RNA, then Darwinian selection could go on at the molecular level, gradually over millions of years developing the complex systems we have been discussing in this book. Russell even has some fairly plausible suggestions about how photosynthesis might have developed. (Incidentally, Russell makes no mention of quantum mechanics.)

Russell's scheme is indeed impressive, and much has been learned about the Earth and its chemistry as the proposed events have built up bit by bit in the minds of Russell and his colleagues. Still, I see some problems. Despite the difficulties of forming RNA in a primitive world, as we discussed above, Russell falls back on the presence of RNA to complete his scheme. Perhaps we can *not* say about all of the steps in Russell's scheme: "Yes, it is possible."

I continue to worry about those sequences that are so critical to life. If amino-acid and nucleotide sequences are as essential as they seem to be, based on descriptions such as those in chapter 4, Russell's scheme will face the big numbers at every step, even if RNA and proteins are in great abundance under the postulated conditions. A giant leap is still required.

But we won't know how serious this problem is until we know more about Stuart Kauffman's universal enzyme toolboxes. Maybe there is an astronomical number of sequences that will do any one job, and maybe once one of those has been incorporated in a developing life form, slight changes will lower its effectiveness so that the version with the changes will not survive (as histone IV, the sequences of which were conserved almost intact from the ancestor of peas and calves!). There are certainly reasons to doubt the toolbox idea. For example, the histones have an unusually high number of positively charged amino acids (lysine and arginine), and these positive charges are essential to the function of the histones (which is to organize DNA into chromosomes). Only a tiny portion of possible proteins would have sufficient positive amino acids to act as histones. Many examples could be cited. We'll just have to wait to see about universal toolboxes.

Incidentally, as I was reading Russell's article and learning about the compounds that might be synthesized near those alkaline hot springs, the thought occurred to me that an Intelligent Creator should have many molecular building blocks to work with in creating life on a primitive earth!

Panspermia: Svante Arrhenius and Fred Hoyle

For the sake of completeness, we must mention one more theory of the origin of life on Earth. Maybe life came here from outer space. This concept, called *panspermia*, was first mentioned by the Nobel Prize (1903) winning Swedish chemist, Svante Arrhenius, who proposed in 1908 that life was spread about the universe by bacteria propelled by light pressure. This theory was also seriously proposed by Francis Crick (codiscoverer of DNA structure; chapter 3). Of course, panspermia doesn't solve the origin-of-life problem; it just moves it to somewhere besides the primitive Earth.

Shapiro (1986, chapter 9) has a good discussion of this idea in his book *Origins*, where he mentions Arrhenius and Crick but devotes his most extensive discussion to the proposals of the late Sir Fred Hoyle and

Chandra Wickramasinghe (1981, pp. 139–40, 150). These authors first studied the spectra of inter-stellar clouds, concluding that they contained a plethora of organic molecules (which they do), including cellulose (which is highly suspect). As they published in the scientific literature, their ideas continued to change. Eventually, they decided that bacteria and viruses were forming in space and raining down on Earth, sometimes bringing plagues such as the influenza epidemic of the first world war. Based on calculations of life's complexity, they finally concluded that life was the product of an Intelligent Creator. At one point in their speculations, they wondered if the Creator was based on silicon chips with enormous powers of calculation, dwarfing the best of our modern computers. A strange view of God, but then, as with all of us, they were simply wondering about the nature of their Creator.

Needless to say, their ideas have not received much (if any) support. Shapiro is amazed that such wild notions could come from such a distinguished scientist as Sir Fred Hoyle, who was widely respected and was even Astronomer Royal in England at one time. Hoyle was the first to suggest the origin of heavy elements in stars, these elements being spread through space when the star becomes a nova, which later, along with large amounts of hydrogen, condense into suns and planets like ours. I like the way David Darling (2001, p. 37) puts it: "In a sense, we're all extraterrestrial. The particles in our bodies were once scattered across many light-years, and we're made literally of star dust. Every atom heavier than hydrogen of which we're composed was forged in the deep interior of a star now long dead. This is perhaps the most awe-inspiring truth that science has ever revealed, as wonderful as anything dreamed up in fiction."

Shapiro notes that some of Hoyle's ideas were latent in a popular science-fiction novel that he wrote, *The Black Cloud*, published in 1957. Although Hoyle's "big numbers" are similar to my own, and I even felt a kinship with his reasoning at one time (I once visited him at his home in northern England), his ultimate ideas go too far even for me.

Where Do We Stand?

The soupy sea and RNA world problems, plus the minimum-sequence complexity problems outlined in chapter 4, certainly illuminate the challenge of imagining Creation without intervention from an Intelligent Creator. Faith in the concept of an aetheistic creation remains strong among biologists and origin-of-life researchers. Even Robert Shapiro (1986,

p. 130), whose skepticism of current origin-of-life theories hit me like a breath of fresh air, makes it clear where he stands: "Some future day may yet arrive when all reasonable chemical experiments run to discover a probable origin for life have failed unequivocally. Further, new geological evidence may indicate a sudden appearance of life on the Earth. Finally, we may have explored the universe and found no trace of life, or processes leading to life, elsewhere. In such a case, some scientists might choose to turn to religion for an answer. Others, however, myself included, would attempt to sort out the surviving less probable scientific explanations in the hope of selecting one that was still more likely than the remainder." Shapiro is no creationist.

And yes, I do turn to religion—well, not really; that's where I *start* with my Weltanschauung, rather than going there for answers after science fails. It is, however, surely too early to say that science has failed. Even as my religion sets a foundation for thoughts about Creation, it still leaves me open to consider and to wonder about what science discovers. In common with science, my religion does not even come close to describing exactly how Creation occurred. Yet it does teach that the Creation was, in some way, the work on an Intelligent Creator, and that teaching fits well with all of my other religious convictions. For that matter, it fits well with what science has learned—and failed to learn—about the complexities of life, how it works, and how it originated.

Summary

1. One branch of science attempts to provide a *plausible scenario* of how life might have originated, here on earth or perhaps somewhere else in the universe, by a spontaneous process that did not involve an Intelligent Creation. So far, although progress has been made, all scientists agree that no totally convincing theory has emerged.

2. It is important to note that the idea of *spontaneous generation* of life under present Earth conditions (which was believed during most of human history) has been thoroughly discredited.

3. Most modern theories depend on the presence of *organic molecules* identical with or similar to those presently found in living organisms. There are three popular ideas about how the molecules in the primitive soupy seas (a prebiotic soup) might have originated:

A. Conditions on the early earth might have been such that organic molecules would be formed from simple carbon compounds (methane, CO_2), hydrogen, water, and ammonia, using the energy produced by lightening, geothermal vents, and so forth. In this regard, there is often mention of the *Miller-Urey experiment*, carried out in 1953.

B. It is now known that organic molecules of varying levels of complexity form in *space*. These could reach Earth via meteorites, comets, or by other means. (The question of their absence on the Moon and Mars remains.)

C. Even today, there are *deep-sea hydrothermal vents* that produce extremely hot water along with various minerals and organic molecules. Some scientists suggest that life originated under those conditions.

4. Most scientists agree that it is a *giant leap* to go from relatively simple organic molecules to the complex sequences found in nucleic acids and proteins.

5. RNA is known to have enzymatic properties; it has been suggested that RNA formed early in the earth's history, leading eventually to the complexities of protein synthesis and the role of DNA in preserving information. Thus, *RNA world* was postulated.

A. Rather *elaborate ideas* have been postulated, based on RNA world.

B. But RNA world faces serious, probably *insurmountable problems*.

C. RNA is an extremely *unlikely molecule* to have existed on primitive Earth. One must imagine totally unreasonable conditions that would produce the nucleotides of RNA, and then one must imagine even more unreasonable conditions that would combine these nucleotides to form reproducing RNA.

D. The structure and function of *ribosomes* is now understood, and realizing their complexity (required for protein synthesis) makes RNA world seem even more unlikely.

6. *Some theories* relating to the origin of life include:

A. *Manfred Eigen* worked with viruses, but he has no good suggestions about the origin of required sequences.

B. *Stuart Kauffman's* Complexity Theory suggests that when there are enough proteins floating around in the prebiotic soup, order will grow out of disorder, and life will come into being. Other scientists working in the field are not convinced by Kauffman's suggestions.

C. *Günter Wächtershäuser* suggests that life formed near hydrothermal vents, with reactions being catalyzed by iron and other sulfides. Many investigators are impressed with Wächtershäuser's proposals, but they also fail to suggest the origin of suitable sequences.

D. *A. Graham Cairns-Smith* suggests that the original life on Earth consisted of clays, which gradually were taken over by the organic systems that we presently know. Again, Cairns-Smith has no good suggestions about those sequences or how the change might occur.

E. *Johnjoe McFadden* suggests that the answer to the origin of life is to be found in the strange mysteries of quantum mechanics, specifically the concept of superpositions.

F. *Michael Russell* has presented what is probably the most detailed and the most plausible just suppose story about the origin of life. It is based on the chemistry that must take place near warm, alkaline springs in the deep ocean.

G. Lastly, *Svante Arrhenius* and *Fred Hoyle* (and others) have seriously considered the possibility that life on Earth came from somewhere else in the universe (Panspermia)—but this only puts the problem beyond our reach.

7. Some of us begin with the concept of an *Intelligent Creation*; nevertheless, we enjoy learning what is going on in the science that studies the origin of life. There is much to be learned about nature and how it works—even about the nature of God.

6 A HOUSE DIVIDED: WHO BELIEVES WHAT AND WHY?

It is often said that evolution is neutral; it says nothing about the existence or nonexistence of God. Be that as it may, but not all biologists have responded to the concept in a neutral way. Some have seen in Darwinian, evolutionary theory a scheme that says no Intelligent Creator is necessary to account for life's complexity, so there must be no God. The creationists and others see God's hand in Creation and resist the idea that mutation and selection can ultimately account for the intricate nature of life. Some biologists simply don't talk about their beliefs in God.

In this chapter, we'll first meet a few of those who reject God on the basis of Darwinism. Then we'll meet Michael Behe, who has recently led a contingent of *intelligent-design creationists* who base their concept of Creation on the irreducible complexity in nature. We'll consider whether the atheistic evolutionists have been able to answer the arguments of the intelligent-design creationists. In biology today, Creation or creation makes for a house divided.

The "God-Is-Not-Necessary" Contingent

There are many authors, and even television personalities, who hold that evolution can account for creation; hence, there must not be a God. Of course, their belief that God does not exist is often implied rather than clearly stated. The late Carl Sagan is a good example of an author and television guru who sometimes did make it clear that God was not needed for creation. (I remember reading Sagan's article in *Parade* magazine shortly before his death, written when he knew his days were numbered; there he stated his atheism explicitly.)

Richard Dawkins

Dawkins was born in Nairobi in 1941 and educated at Oxford University in England. One of the most prolific authors in this genre, Richard Dawkins, is also a frequent speaker and television personality. In 1995, he became the first holder of the newly endowed Charles Simonyi Chair of Public Understanding of Science at Oxford University. He has written several books defending Darwinian evolution and is perhaps the most powerful modern proponent of Darwin's natural selection.[1] He writes with authority but in a captivating, almost glib, even breezy style. He pushes some topics to the limits of modern understanding, but his explanations are clever—even ingenious—and always worth pursuing. A touch of humor at frequent intervals makes for easy reading. It was easy to like Richard Dawkins and his writing style. My first reading was *Climbing Mount Improbable*, published in 1996, although *The Blind Watchmaker* (1986; second edition, 1996) and *The Selfish Gene* (1976; second edition, 1989) are better known. His other books include *River out of Eden* (1995), *Unweaving the Rainbow* (1998), and *A Devil's Disciple* (2003), which is a collection of a number of his essays, and *The Ancestor's Tale: A Pilgrimage to the Dawn of Evolution* (2004).

Dawkins makes his position on creation perfectly clear throughout his writing. He does not equivocate about his atheism. Even the subtitle of *Watchmaker* makes it clear: *Why the Evidence of Evolution Reveals a Universe Without Design.* In the first chapter of *Watchmaker,* he quotes William Paley's argument from design (Appendix B), which we discussed in chapter 1. He then states his conviction that there was no Designer of living organisms:

> Paley's argument is made with passionate sincerity and is
> informed by the best biological scholarship of his day, but it
> is wrong, gloriously and utterly wrong. The analogy between
> telescope and eye, between watch and living organism, is
> false. All appearances to the contrary, the only watchmaker

in nature is the blind forces of physics, albeit deployed in a very special way. A true watchmaker has foresight: he designs his cogs and springs, and plans their interconnections, with a future purpose in his mind's eye. Natural selection, the blind, unconscious, automatic process which Darwin discovered, and which we now know is the explanation for the existence and apparently purposeful form of all life, has no purpose in mind. It has no mind and no mind's eye. It does not plan for the future. It has no vision, no foresight, no sight at all. If it can be said to play the role of watchmaker in nature, it is the *blind* watchmaker.

Despite the ardor, Dawkins's paragraph is an unequivocal statement of faith. He has never accounted for the origin of life nor the unlimited origin of variability needed for natural selection to work without God, nor has anyone else. Yes, there might have been prebiotic soupy seas and there are mutations, but who really knows if they will do the job that they are assigned to do by neo-Darwinism? Although their faith remains strong, those whom Dawkins represents never admit to us that it is only faith. It is left up to us to see that for what it is.

In the course of a discussion over dinner with a "distinguished modern philosopher, a well-known atheist," Dawkins says that "although atheism might have been *logically* tenable before Darwin, Darwin made it possible to be an intellectually fulfilled atheist." His statement is quoted in many books on evolution or creationism. I'm struck by the depth of his "passionate sincerity" and conviction, being "informed by the best biological scholarship of his day." In spite of all the unknowns that I'm outlining in this book, Dawkins has no misgivings about how evolution works, or about his rejection of an Intelligent Creator.

As a matter of fact, I've thought of a way to restate Dawkin's statement: "No one has thought of a better way to be an atheist than evolution by natural selection. That is why it is accepted and so strongly defended in spite of all the problems."

Kenneth Miller

Kenneth Miller has written a curious book, *Finding Darwin's God*, in which he uses the first half of his book to shoot down all varieties of creationists from the young-Earthers to the intelligent-design proponents; in the second half, he tells us why he believes in God and God's intervention in Creation—thus qualifying himself as a creationist in the broad sense (the sense in which I admit to being a creationist). The book has an interesting chapter, "The Gods of Disbelief," in which he provides a number of quotations from biologists who are proclaimed atheists (Miller, 1999, chapter 6). Here are some excerpts from a few of Miller's quotations, along with a couple of my comments:

> By coupling undirected, purposeless variation to the blind, uncaring process of natural selection, Darwin made theological or spiritual explanations of the life processes superfluous. (Douglas Futuyma, 1986, p. 8)

> Modern science directly implies that there are no inherent moral or ethical laws, no absolute guiding principles for human society. . . . We must conclude that when we die, we die, and that is the end of us. . . . Finally, free will as it is traditionally conceived—the freedom to make uncoerced and unpredictable choices among alternative courses of action—simply does not exist.. . .There is no way that the evolutionary process as currently conceived can produce a being that is truly free to make moral choices. (William Provine, 1988)

> If humankind evolved by Darwinian natural selection, genetic chance and environmental necessity, not God, made the species.. . .[This] remains the philosophical legacy of the last century of scientific research.. . .Theology is not likely to survive as an independent intellectual discipline. (Edward O. Wilson, 1978, p. 1; Wilson is a Harvard biologist who studied social insects—ants, bees, wasps—and then developed the science he called *sociobiology*)

> Whatever the God implied by evolutionary theory and the data of natural history may be like, He is not the Protestant God of waste not, want not. He is also not a loving God who cares about His productions. He is not even the awful God portrayed in the book of Job. The God of the Galápagos is careless, wasteful, indifferent, almost diabolical. He is certainly not the sort of God to whom anyone would be inclined to pray. (David Hull, 1991, pp. 485–86)

Although Stephen Jay Gould in some of his writings seemed to allow for religious belief by saying that science and religion deal with unrelated ideas that need not intrude on each other's domain, in an interview he said that religion is sweet:

Because it gives comfort to many people. I think that notion that we are all in the bosom of Abraham or are in God's embracing love is—look, it's a tough life and if you can delude yourself into thinking that there's all some warm and fuzzy meaning to it all, it's enormously comforting. But I do think it's just a story we tell ourselves. (Stephen Jay Gould; see Miller, 1999, p. 170; the comments are from a transcript of *CBS Sunday Morning* on November 29, 1998; the interviewer was Rita Braver)

Speaking of the late Stephen Jay Gould, one of the strongest arguments against an Intelligent Creator harks right back to Darwin's frequent comparisons of special creation with natural selection; namely, that God would not create things the way we find them in nature. Just as if he knew how God would create. Consider the arrogance of this statement from Gould:

Orchids manufacture their intricate devices from the common components of ordinary flowers, parts usually fitted for very different functions. If God had designed a beautiful machine to reflect his wisdom and power, surely he would not have used a collection of parts generally fashioned for other purposes. Orchids were not made by an ideal engineer; they are jury-rigged from a limited set of available components. Thus, they must have evolved from ordinary flowers.

. . . But ideal design is a lousy argument for evolution, for it mimics the postulated action of an omnipotent creator. Odd arrangements and funny solutions are the proof of evolution— paths that a sensible God would never tread but that a natural process, constrained by history, follows perforce. No one understood this better than Darwin. (Stephen Jay Gould, 2001, pp. 669–76)

One can't help but wonder what Stephen Jay Gould's relationship with that "omnipotent creator" must have been for him to be so certain about how God would carry out creation. I agree with eighteenth century biologists who thought that studies of creation might well provide insights into God's nature. Could it be that modern biology provides more insights into God's nature than did the deliberations of learned councils, which were trying to reconcile their interpretations of scripture with Greek philosophy (Hopkins, 1998)?

Michael Behe's Irreducible Complexity

Michael J. Behe is a Professor of Biochemistry at Lehigh University. The thesis of his book, *Darwin's Black Box, The Biochemical Challenge to Evolution* (1996), is that Darwin formulated his theory of natural selection without any knowledge of cellular and molecular biology. Darwin knew nothing of genes and virtually nothing about enzymes; that is, about biochemistry and molecular biology. Behe says such knowledge was, for Darwin, locked away in a "black box." Now we have opened the black box; especially during the second half of the twentieth century, we have rummaged around inside, discovering marvelous things about life at the cellular and molecular level. What we have learned, Behe claims, puts a whole new light on Darwinian evolution. Behe defines for us the concept of *irreducible complexity* and then illustrates the concept with some fascinating stories.

Behe's mousetrap

As William Paley in 1802 had his watch, Michael Behe has his mousetrap. He uses his metaphor to define *irreducible complexity* by analyzing the mechanism and function of a mousetrap. He concludes that each part is essential to its function. For example, he notes: "If there were no catch or metal holding bar, then the spring would snap the hammer shut as soon as you let go of it; in order to use a trap like that you would have to chase the mouse around while holding the trap open" (42). Then he goes on to describe eight cellular and molecular functions of life, concluding that each is so complex that, if any part were missing, the function will fail. We'll examine only a couple of his stories.

He wonders just how such a machine could come into being step by step? We must distinguish between *physical precursors* and *conceptual precursors*, he says. Is a bicycle a physical precursor to a motorcycle? No, there is no way that one can convert a bicycle into a motorcycle by small steps. Adding a motor and a gas tank and attaching the sprocket and chain to the motor are *big* steps. Nothing in the bicycle can be modified slightly to produce a motor or a gas tank. And all must be complete if the motorcycle is to function. It is an irreducibly complex machine.

The inventor of the motorcycle, *its intelligent designer*, can *conceive* of how it might be built, but the inventor must see the end from the beginning and then take the steps to reach the goal, even though the steps along the way might first make the bicycle *less* functional rather than *more* functional. The bicycle is a *conceptual precursor* to a motorcycle.

Once the essential parts of a motorcycle have been put together, it is possible to add nonessential parts such as leather fringe hanging from the ends of the handlebars, or painting the gas tank a fire-engine red. Some parts, such as a rear-view mirror or a headlight, may be nonessential under some conditions but essential to a motorcycle *designed* for heavy traffic. It is also possible to improve on the first functional motorcycle by making it even more functional by making the frame heavier, using larger tires, and so on. In any case, the first bicycle converted to a motorcycle by adding the motor and other essential parts might have some of the elements of a physical precursor to a modern Harley Davidson street bike, but in practice it wouldn't work like one. Each motorcycle is the result of an act of special creation. Hence, the analogy with evolution can be pushed only so far.

Nevertheless, in Behe's analogy it should be clear that getting irreducibly complex systems all at once by chance events is in the same category as getting a fully functional, modern enzyme by randomly rearranging amino acids in peptide chains—essentially no chance at all. (Behe does not discuss enzyme structure in detail.) Once the irreducibly complex system has been designed and constructed, however, there may well be ways to improve it by tiny steps. Indeed, we saw in chapter 4 that intelligent creators (molecular biologists) in laboratories all over the world are randomly mutating existing enzymes to better fit them for some desired end. Darwin and Dawkins assume that there will nearly always be something that can become randomly variable, providing raw material for natural selection to work on. Behe and others (including me) strongly doubt that irreducibly complex living systems can come into being that way. Such systems point to an Intelligent Creator.

The Bombardier beetle: irreducibly complex?

The eight stories of cellular and molecular complexity that Michael Behe tells as examples of irreducible complexity include: vertebrate vision, the bombardier beetle, the cilium (perhaps his best example), the bacterial flagellum, the blood clotting mechanism, cellular transport (movement of proteins via the ER and the Golgi apparatus), the immune system, and the synthesis of ADP (an important molecule in several cellular functions).

I would like to summarize all of Behe's stories, but we'll have to settle here for just one: the marvelous bombardier beetle. This bug defends itself by squirting out a boiling-hot solution at an enemy through an aperture in its hind section. To prepare for such an event, specialized structures called secretory lobes make a highly concentrated mixture of hydroquinone and hydrogen peroxide. The mixture goes into a storage chamber, the collecting vesicle, which, in turn, is connected to but sealed off from the appropriately named explosion chamber. Attached to the explosion chamber are small knobs called ectodermal glands that can secrete the enzyme catalase (see Figure 3-1), which breaks down hydrogen peroxide at the rate of thousands of H_2O_2 molecules per catalase molecule each second, releasing oxygen (O_2) and water (H_2O). When the beetle feels threatened, it relaxes the sphincter muscle that otherwise closes the connection between the collecting vesicle and the explosion chamber, at the same time squeezing muscles around the ectodermal glands so that the mixture and the catalase end up in the explosion chamber at the same time. There, the newly released oxygen reacts explosively with the hydroquinone, yielding more water molecules and a highly irritating chemical called quinone. The reaction releases a large amount of heat, so the solution rises to the boiling point as it squirts out at the enemy.

The function is clear: to produce a hot, astringent solution and shoot it at the enemy. The essential parts are also clear. They include all of the structures noted above plus the cells with their enzymes that produce hydroquinone, hydrogen peroxide, and catalase—not to mention the nerve connections from the beetle's eyes to its brain, so that it knows when it is being threatened and the nerves from the brain to the explosion apparatus. Without any *one* of these items, the bombardier beetle won't be able to bomb anything.

This story is so beautiful that it has been told by many creationists and others who fail to see how gradual evolution could account for it. But Richard Dawkins (1986, pp. 87–97) took up the challenge: "As for the evolutionary precursors of the system, both hydrogen peroxide and various kinds of quinones are used for other purposes in body chemistry. The bombardier beetle's ancestors simply pressed into different service chemicals that already happened to be around. That's often how evolution works." And, as we'll discuss in more detail in a moment, that is often how evolutionists counter intelligent-design creationists.

But please note that Dawkins reply is another just-suppose tale. Because both quinones and hydrogen peroxide "happened to be around," Dawkins supposes that suitable cells with suitable enzymes, secretory lobes, a collecting vesicle, a sphincter muscle, ectodermal glands, an explosion chamber, an outlet duct, and the necessary nerves would all come into being by small mutations and natural selection until the whole system was in place. That is a rather wild stretch of the imagination. We know the function and we know the parts, and the function won't occur unless *all* the parts are in place. There we are again. In our present state of knowledge there is no realistic way to imagine how all those parts would evolve by tiny mutations that modify existing parts, each mutation having selective value, until the entire mechanism is in place. Believing otherwise requires much faith in the idea that future knowledge will tell us how it could have worked, and it might, but there is no way to be sure that it will. Isn't Dawkins being a bit overcredulous in accepting the evolutionary explanation on such meager evidence?

Michael Behe's philosophy

In his final three chapters, Behe expands his thoughts about the science and logic of neo-Darwinian evolution, expands on irreducible complexity, and discusses the evidence for intelligent design and an Intelligent Designer. Behe's chapters interject many succinct and pithy statements that I not only high-lighted in yellow but also marked with my red pen. I don't agree with all of Michael Behe's philosophies, but his ideas have had scorn heaped upon them by the anti-creationists. Do they really merit such scorn? Here are a few of them with my comments in square brackets:

> The conclusion of intelligent design flows naturally from the data itself—not from sacred books or sectarian beliefs. (p. 193)
>
> Inferences to design do not require that we have a candidate for the role of designer. We can determine that a system was designed by examining the system itself, and we can hold the conviction of design much more strongly than a conviction about the identity of the designer. (p. 196) [This idea is at least as old as William Paley; see Appendix B.]
>
> As the number or quality of the parts of an interacting system increase, our judgment of design increases also and can reach certitude. (p. 199) [Well, philosophically, our *judgment* of design can increase, but maybe never to the level of certitude.]
>
> The fact that biochemical systems can be designed by intelligent agents for their own purposes is conceded by all

scientists, even Richard Dawkins. (p. 203) [Behe then gives an example from one of Dawkins's books, plus examples of protein and gene design from modern molecular biology.] Therefore we *do* have experience in observing the intelligent design of components of life. (p. 219)

The argument from imperfection [that God would have created a perfect world, but there are imperfections in nature] overlooks the possibility that the designer might have multiple motives, with engineering excellence oftentimes relegated to a secondary role. Most people through history have thought that life was designed despite sickness, death, and other obvious imperfections. (p. 223)

Another problem with the argument from imperfection is that it critically depends on a psychoanalysis of the unidentified designer. (p. 223)

[After listing such recognized processes of speciation as founder effects, genetic drift, and gene flow, Behe concludes:] The fact that some biochemical systems may have been designed by an intelligent agent does not mean that any of the other factors are not operative, common, or important. (p. 230) [That is, the discoveries of evolutionists must apply at a certain level, but can they account for all life as we know it?]

The result of these cumulative efforts to investigate the cell—to investigate life at the molecular level—is a loud, clear, piercing cry of "*design!*" The result is so unambiguous and so significant that it must be ranked as one of the greatest achievements in the history of science. The discovery rivals those of Newton and Einstein, Lavoisier and Schrödinger, Pasteur, and Darwin. The observation of the intelligent design of life is as momentous as the observation that the earth goes around the sun or that disease is caused by bacteria or that radiation is emitted in quanta. The magnitude of the victory, gained at such great cost through sustained effort over the course of decades, would be expected to send champagne corks flying in labs around the world. This triumph of science should evoke cries of "Eureka!" from ten thousand throats, should occasion much hand-slapping and high-fiving, and perhaps even be an excuse to take a day off.

But no bottles have been uncorked, no hands slapped. Instead, a curious, embarrassed silence surrounds the stark complexity of the cell. When the subject comes up in public, feet start to shuffle, and breathing gets a bit labored. In private people are a bit more relaxed; many explicitly admit the obvious but then stare at the ground, shake their heads, and let it go at that. (pp. 232–33)

Behe says that it is the word *God*—the only place in his book that Behe uses the term—that scientists want to avoid (p. 233). Scientists invoke the rule that science cannot study the supernatural. Behe holds that deducing *design* from the facts at hand—that is, arriving at an inescapable conclusion—is not the same as invoking a supernatural explanation for certain facts that seem difficult to explain because the research is not complete; that is, taking an easy way out of some trivial problem by invoking God. I'll agree that deducing design can surely support one's belief in God, but proving that design is the inescapable conclusion may be philosophically beyond us. You decide for yourself.

Atheists have long countered arguments for God based on design in nature by saying that God is a convenient explanation for things that we don't yet understand. Such a God is a "God of the gaps," meaning the gaps in our knowledge. But Behe says that the idea that something is designed is more than intuitive. We can discern its function and examine its parts to see which ones and how many are essential to the function. Then we can calculate the chances that these essential parts could all come into being at once by chance processes. If not, then the only other alternative is that the something was designed, Behe says. The fact that all parts must be present for the system to function eliminates a gradual development, a natural selection of gradual, small changes, each having selection value.

Behe's detractors say that Behe cannot absolutely *prove* that his examples of apparent design are indeed impossible to produce except via the intervention of intelligence, and I must agree with them. Philosophically, it is extremely difficult to prove that something is impossible—that a bombardier beetle, for example, could *only* have been designed and could *not* have been the product of mutations and natural selection.

Still, Behe's final chapters are gems that should be carefully studied by anyone who is interested in the relation between science, philosophy, and religion—or by anyone who is interested in an Intelligent Creation. Now let's be more specific about what the detractors have to say.

Attempts to Refute Behe
and Other Intelligent-Design Creationists

The anti-creationists/evolutionists have picked up the gauntlet. Indeed, Behe seems to have hit a nerve with them, judging by their rhetoric against him. Their retorts, while sticking closely to the scientific facts, are not infrequently sarcastic and almost always presented with great conviction: The tenor of their remarks is that Behe is "not only wrong, he's wrong in a most spectacular way (Miller, 1999, 150)!"

Many biologists besides Dawkins have reacted to Behe's ideas as though they were anathema to true science (and perhaps, in a limited sense, they are).[2] Judging by the tenor of the anti-Behe writing, however, the writers seem to be incensed by this "new" version of the argument from design (at the same time saying that it isn't new)—and they seem to be convinced that their counter arguments refute it *in toto*. No doubt they would deny it, but I sense a bit of *angst* in their writings.[3] Are they perhaps *threatened* by the possibility that God's Creations declare his glory?

The bottom line for me is that some of their arguments are interesting and impressive, but they are far less impressive and conclusive than their proponents would have us believe.

The "old" argument from design

Many of the anti-Behe books and articles begin their tirade against irreducible complexity by noting that it is "just the old argument from design," put forth by John Ray in 1691, by William Paley in 1802, in the Bible, and by others. The implication is that, because the argument has been around for a long time, it is no longer a strong argument. Yet, as far as the *validity* of the argument from design goes, its age is irrelevant. If it is a good argument, who cares how old it is? To quote Kenneth Miller (1999, p. 134), the design argument remains "the oldest, the most compelling, and quite simply the best rhetorical weapon against evolution."

Miller goes on to say, however, that Darwin refuted the argument from design by proposing his theory of natural selection. *That* could be relevant. Does natural selection refute the argument from design? I've been arguing that "just suppose" stories do not constitute a refutation regardless of how *plausible* they might be. True, thanks to these plausibility tales—many of which *are* highly plausible—the argument from design can never have the power that it once had. My point is that we can't really say that Darwin refuted the argument or that he didn't refute it. There are still far too many lacunae in our knowledge of the origin of variability and other matters.

Behe's detractors push one important viewpoint: Many of those who argue from design claim that design *proves* the existence of God, is scientific, and thus should be taught in the schools as science. (Behe claims that it is scientific but does not say that it should be taught in the schools.) Opponents say that it is *not* science and should *not* be taught in the schools. I'll agree: The *conclusions* based on intelligent design should not be taught as *science*, but aren't students entitled to know that there are those who have used the findings of science to build their own view of the universe and that their views may include or exclude an Intelligent Creator?

Six arguments attempting to refute Behe

In a review of Behe's book, Robert Dorit (1997) presented six arguments against Behe's ideas. These are similar to the arguments used by others. Of the six anti-design arguments, all but one seem to me to be mere quibbles—nit-picking, if you will. So Behe made some mistakes and probably over-stated his case; does that prove the design argument invalid? By far the most scientific of the anti-design arguments is the sixth one, which states, in essence, the argument Dawkins used against the notion that the bombardier beetle is the product of design: that the parts really were there all along, and all that natural selection had to do was to piece them together. Well, maybe. Here are the six arguments:

1. Behe implies that there is a boundary between the molecular world and other levels of biological organization. There isn't, but so what? This is a quibble, aimed at Behe but irrelevant regarding the concept of irreducible complexity.

2. No analogy is perfect—and Behe relies heavily on analogies. Most of Behe's analogies in *Darwin's Black Box* are excellent; some are less so. So what? (I did get a little tired of them.)

3. Behe says that no one is working on the problem of how Darwinian natural selection can account for the origin of irreducibly complex biochemical systems. Actually, the anti-Behe contingent cites many papers telling about work that *is* being done, but to some extent it depends on your viewpoint. Behe wants *real* evolutionary mechanisms; his critics are happy with the many just-suppose stories. So okay, maybe Behe was wrong on this point, but that's irrelevant to the concept of irreducible complexity.

4. Behe and the other intelligent-design creationists present no experimental evidence for design—nor do they have peer-reviewed publications in the scientific literature. True, but just how do you present experimental evidence for God? Behe's mistake may be in claiming that his conclusion—that there is an Intelligent Designer—is science. It is really philosophy. Papers claiming to *prove* God's existence don't belong in scientific literature.

5. Behe suggests that, unless we can identify advantages for each imaginary gradual step leading to a contemporary bit of biochemistry, we cannot invoke a Darwinian explanation. Dorit's (1997) review of Behe's book says: "In a narrow sense, Behe is correct when he argues that we do not yet fully understand the evolution of the flagellar motor or of the clotting cascade. Unsolved questions, however, are the hallmark of an exciting science." As we have noted, Darwin was fully aware that all of the steps in the evolution of a complex organ (or biochemical pathway or structure) must have selective value, or perhaps be neutral in their environment. Darwin wrote in chapter 6 of *The Origin*: "If it could be demonstrated that any complex organ existed, which could not possibly have been formed by numerous, successive, slight modifications, my theory would absolutely break down. But I can find no such case."

Biologists who are convinced that evolution by natural selection of random mutations will *eventually* account for everything see the gaps in our knowledge as intriguing "unsolved questions" that will one day be accounted for. That's fine, and that's what keeps science going. It must be good for the exercise of one's creative faculties to dream up just-suppose stories that might even turn out to be true. But let's recognize the element of faith involved in such an approach and allow some possibility that *some* of the difficult steps *might* have involved an Intelligent Creation—or at least admit that science cannot prove otherwise.

6. Behe has not proved that his systems are truly irreducibly complex, nor that their parts can have no other functions. This is the strongest argument being used against irreducible complexity, and many scientists are contributing to it. There are two thrusts to this argument:

First, one can't be sure that some complex structure is really *irreducibly* complex. This is well illustrated by a web site hosted by Prof. John McDonald of the University of Delaware, on which animated drawings illustrate how a mouse trap might be constructed with fewer than the five parts that Behe says are essential (http://udel.edu~mcdonald/mousetrap. html). A rather inefficient but nevertheless workable trap could, according to McDonald, be created with just one part, a wire bent in a certain way! It wouldn't be a very good mouse trap, but it might occasionally catch mice. Then McDonald improves it bit by bit until he has arrived at Behe's trap. It is an ingenious example produced by a most intelligent designer!

Second, the often complex parts needed to create an "irreducibly complex" structure may well have functions other than those that are applied in that structure.

Irreducible complexity: How can we be sure?

In *God the Mechanic*, Kenneth Miller (1999, pp. 129–64, especially pp. 140–43) attempts to refute Behe's contention that the eukaryotic cilium[4] is an irreducibly complex machine. Miller notes Behe's detailed discussion of the eukaryotic cilium, concluding that if any of its parts were to be removed, it would not function. The cilium Behe describes depends on nine doublet microtubules around the circumference of a cross section, with two singlet microtubules in the center. Miller proceeds to give examples of eukaryotic cilia that have different numbers of microtubules arranged in different ways. He says: "What we actually see among cilia and flagella in nature is something entirely consistent with Darwin's call for numerous gradations from the simple to the complex. Once we have found a series of less complex, less intricate, differently organized flagella, the contention that this is an irreducibly complex structure has been successfully refuted."

But who says that the functionality of the cilium depends on the *nine* doublet microtubules around *two* singlet microtubules? Behe never says that the *number* was all that important; indeed, he never mentions the number and even notes that there are apparently parts of the cilium that are nonessential to minimal function, much like the headlights on a motorcycle.

Actually, the functionality of a eukaryotic cilium or flagellum depends on the molecular structures of all the proteins that are involved (their amino-acid sequences—although Behe doesn't mention this). Miller must show us that each of those proteins isn't itself irreducibly complex. Counting microtubules is just another quibble.

For all we know, each of those different cilia and flagella that Miller told us about is itself an irreducibly complex machine. Just showing that there are different kinds of mouse traps doesn't prove that any one kind isn't irreducibly complex, or nonfunctional if any of its parts are missing. The mousetraps on McDonald's website weren't built by removing single parts from Behe's trap; they were built by starting with that specially bent wire (itself irreducibly complex in that it had to be bent a certain way), adding special parts piece by piece and modifying as he went along. That's equivalent to producing new developmental programs by gene mutations, programs that can take existing parts from cells and combine them in ways that produce new functions.

Parts lying around waiting to be used: the blood-clotting system

And that, say biologists, is exactly what evolution does. Richard Dawkins's comment about evolving the defense mechanism of the bombardier beetle is typical. Quinones, hydrogen peroxide, and catalase occur in many cells. All that evolution had to do was mutate sufficient development-controlling genes to produce suitable cells with suitable enzymes, secretory lobes, a collecting vesicle, a sphincter muscle, ectodermal glands, an explosion chamber, an outlet duct, and the necessary nerves, all in the right places. As long as the necessary chemicals were already there, that shouldn't be too much to ask.

This approach has been applied to "explain" the evolution of many complex molecules and structures. As we saw in chapter 3, microtubules have many other functions in cells besides making cilia work. They account for ameboid motion and the contraction of muscle cells, for example. Separation of the chromosomes during mitosis depends on microtubules. All that evolution had to do was to put these structures to work in a new function: the beating of cilia and flagella. That seems plausible enough, doesn't it?

I guess it does, especially because we don't really know how it might have worked. Maybe one or a few simple mutations would be sufficient to gather the microtubules into bundles surrounded by a membrane and protruding from the cell. If that hair-like projection had any movement at all, we can imagine that it would be selected in the struggle for existence, and then natural selection could further improve upon it until it was a fully developed eukaryotic cilium or flagellum. It makes a fairly plausible just-suppose story, and I don't have the knowledge to refute it.

There are many of these stories based on knowledge gained through the analysis of amino-acid sequences. Indeed, such stories are the most common and the most powerful arguments presently being tossed at the concept of intelligent design. Miller (1999, pp. 143–61) presents a number of them.

Kenneth Miller's version of the evolution of blood clotting

One of Behe's prime examples was the blood clotting mechanism. It is a fascinating exercise to read his story in *Darwin's Black Box* and then to read, in *Finding Darwin's God*, what Kenneth Miller has to say about Behe's story. Both authors base their comments on the wonderful work of Russell Doolittle, who is a professor of biochemistry at the Center for Molecular Genetics, University of California, San Diego, and who has spent over a quarter of a century trying to work out a plausible explanation for the evolution of the blood-clotting mechanism. Actually, in reading the two versions of Doolittle's explanation, it is interesting to begin with Miller's (1999, pp. 152–58) comments, although they were written in response to Behe.

As Miller tells it, Doolittle has produced a highly plausible outline of how the clotting mechanism evolved. The existing proteins of the mechanism did not all come into being suddenly; rather, their amino acid sequences clearly show that they came into being by evolutionary modifications of pre-existing proteins (actually, the genes that control the proteins). First, Miller summarizes the complexities of blood clotting, albeit in less detail than Behe did. There is no way to simplify Miller's summary, so let's examine it verbatim:

> At its core, the actual mechanism of clotting is remarkably simple. A fibrous, soluble protein called fibrinogen ("clot-maker") constitutes about three percent of the protein in blood plasma. Fibrinogen has a sticky portion near the center of the molecule, but the sticky region is covered by little amino acid chains with negative charges. Because like charges repel, these chains keep fibrinogen molecules apart.
>
> When a clot forms, a protease (protein-cutting) enzyme called thrombin clips off the charged chains. This exposes the sticky parts of the molecule, and suddenly fibrinogens (which are now called fibrins) start to stick together, beginning the formation of a clot. To start the reaction, thrombin itself must be activated by another protease called Factor X. Believe it or not, Factor X requires two more proteases, Factor VII and Factor IX, to switch it on; and still other factors are required to activate *them*. Why so many steps? The multiple steps of the clotting cascade *amplify* the signal from that first stimulus. . . .
>
> Michael Behe properly emphasizes the intricacy of this

161

process. He is correct to point out that if we take away part
of this system, we're in trouble. Hemophiliacs, for example,
are unable to synthesize the active form of an essential step in
the cascade known as Factor VIII. This makes them unable
to complete the final step of one of the clotting pathways, and
that's why hemophilia is sometimes known as the "bleeder's
disease." Defects or deficiencies in any of the other factors are
equally serious. No doubt about it—clotting is an essential
function and it's not something to be messed with. But does
this also mean that it could not have evolved? Not at all.
(Miller, 1999, pp. 153–55)

Miller fills a few paragraphs with descriptions of clotting mechanisms
in invertebrates like starfish and worms, which are very primitive compared
with those of us vertebrates, but which, Miller suggests, *could*, along with
blood-serum proteases present already in the blood, serve as starting places
for evolution of the complex system that exists in vertebrates now. He then
summarizes Russell Doolittle's findings and exlanation for evolution of
vertebrate blood clotting.

The main key is the proteases. It turns out that nearly all of the
regulatory molecules in blood clotting are related to each other, according
to their amino-acid sequences, forming a class called serine proteases.
There are other serine proteases in blood serum that have nothing to do
with blood clotting, and perhaps the most basic of the serine proteases is
the enzyme trypsin, a serine protease that takes part in digestion and is
produced in the pancreas. Where did all the members of this class come
from? Here Doolittle (and Miller) bring out the most powerful weapon in
the arsenal of molecular evolutionists: gene duplication and subsequent
modification of the new genes for other purposes.

There is evidence that, in the course of cellular reproduction (mitosis
and meiosis), some genes may be duplicated—even entire sequences of
genes located along a chromosome. Some of this evidence is rather circular:
Because there are genes with similar nucleotide sequences, there must
be duplications of genes that sometimes occur during cell divisions, and
because there are duplications of genes that sometimes occur during cell
division, there are genes with similar nucleotide sequences. The evidence
does go beyond that, however, including laboratory observations of gene
duplications in some organisms like the fruit fly. There are also rearrangements of segments of nucleotides in a given gene: Portions of a DNA chain

may be bodily moved from their original location to another location along the chain, or portions of DNA from one chain may end up in another chain. We can call it gene shuffling, and much of the evidence that it occurs is based on the analysis of nucleotide or amino-acid sequences.

In any case, once we have duplicate genes in a given organism, then one of the new genes might mutate without upsetting the life of the organism because the other gene will still be able to carry out its normal and essential function (producing its normal and essential protein). If the new gene is not activated, it can mutate again and again in different ways in the offspring of the organisms in which the original duplication occurred. At some point, the mutations might lead to a gene that, when activated, might code for a protein that can improve some biochemical mechanism such as the blood-clotting system. New serine proteases might appear that would improve the amplification process and thus bestow slightly better survival characteristics on their possessors. True, but this must have happened long ago before the vertebrates appeared because they all have essentially the same clotting mechanism. If this is so, then we should be able to find similar proteins in organisms that are even simpler than the vertebrates, and indeed, we do find a fibrinogen-like sequence in the sea cucumber, a relative of the starfish. Prediction fulfilled.

This just-suppose story, told by Miller but based on the suggestions of Russell Doolittle and his colleagues and students, certainly sounds plausible, even if the proof can never be iron-clad. Indeed, Miller (1999, 158) even uses the word *plausible* in his summary of the blood-clotting story:

> Now, it would not be fair, just because we have presented a realistic evolutionary scheme supported by gene sequences from modern organisms, to suggest that we now know *exactly* how the clotting system has evolved. That would be making far too much of our limited ability to reconstruct the details of the past. Nonetheless, there is little doubt that we do know enough to develop a plausible—and scientifically valid–scenario for how it might have evolved. And that scenario makes specific predictions that can be tested and verified against the evidence.

Michael Behe's version of the evolution of blood clotting

Hold on; not so fast. Let's see what Behe (1996, pp. 90–97) had to say in *Darwin's Black Box* and whether Miller really answered the points brought up by Behe. Actually, as I reread both Miller and Behe, it was as if Miller had written first and Behe had written to answer him. First, Behe quotes extensively from a summary article by Russell Doolittle (1993), who talks about the appearance of first one factor (by gene duplication and rearrangement) and then the protease that activates it, going down the list of about 17 proteins. Then Behe elaborates on four critical questions (that Miller never addresses) brought up by Doolittle's scheme. We'll have to settle for part of the first question (which is reminiscent of the numbers presented in my chapter 4; items in quotation marks are from Doolittle's article):

How's That Again?

Now let's take a little time to give Professor Doolittle's scenario a critical look. . . . Doolittle appears to have in mind a step-by-step Darwinian scenario involving the undirected, random duplication and recombination of gene pieces. But consider the enormous amount of luck needed to get the right gene pieces in the right places. Eukaryotic organisms have quite a few gene pieces, and apparently the process that switches them is random. So making a new blood-coagulation protein by shuffling is like picking a dozen sentences randomly from an encyclopedia in the hope of making a coherent paragraph. Professor Doolittle does not go to the trouble of calculating how many incorrect, inactive, useless "variously shuffled domains" would have to be discarded before obtaining a protein with, say, TPA-like activity.

To illustrate the problem, let's do our own quick calculation. Consider that animals with blood-clotting cascades have roughly 10,000 genes, each of which is divided into an average of three pieces. This gives a total of about 30,000 gene pieces. TPA has four different types of domains. By "variously shuffling," the odds of getting those four domains together is 30,000 to the fourth power, which is approximately one-tenth to the eighteenth power[a]. [That is, one chance in $30,000^4 = 10^{18}$.] Now, if the Irish Sweepstakes had odds of winning of one-tenth to the eighteenth power, and if a million people played the lottery each year, it would take an average of about a thousand billion years before *anyone* (not just a particular person) won the lottery. A thousand billion years is roughly a hundred times the current estimate of the age of the universe.

Doolittle's casual language ("spring forth," etc.) conceals enormous difficulties. The same problem of ultra-slim odds would trouble the appearance of prothrombin ("the result of a. . .protease gene duplication and. . .shuffling"), fibrinogen ("a bastard protein derived from . . ."), plasminogen, pro-accelerin, and each of the several proposed rearrangements of prothrombin. Doolittle apparently needs to shuffle and deal himself a number of perfect bridge hands to win the game. Unfortunately, the universe doesn't have time to wait.

Behe offers two interesting endnotes. One of these (superscript [a]) is in relation to the above quotation; the other (superscript [b]) is in relation to a point made in the further discussion:

[a]This calculation is exceedingly generous. It only assumes that the four types of domains would have to be in the correct linear order. In order to work, however, the combination would have to be located in an active area of the genome, the correct signals for splicing together the parts would have to be in place, the amino acid sequences of the four domains would have to be compatible with each other, and other considerations would affect the outcome. These further considerations only make the event much more improbable.

[b]It is good to keep in mind that a "step" could well be thousands of generations. A mutation must start in a single animal and then spread through the population. In order to do that, the descendants of the mutant animal must displace the descendants of all other animals.

Behe's second question concerns how a new gene produced by gene duplication and shuffling changes to one that differs from the original and is effective. Presumably, that is a matter of gradual mutations—mutations that are not eliminated by natural selection.

Behe's third question asks how one might account for the quantitative aspects of all these changes in new genes and the like. It is critical to have just the right amount of clotting. Too much might clog up the system, and too little won't prevent bleeding.

The most serious objection, Behe says, goes right back to irreducible complexity. Natural selection "only works if there is something to select—something that is useful *right now*, not in the future." In Doolittle's scheme, no blood clotting occurs until at least the third step. What happens to those first three genes and their enzymes while they are waiting for the ones that will make coagulation possible? (Miller would probably say that they are doing something else, although we may not know what it is.) If the new protein has no function, it might gradually be eliminated by natural selection.

Behe notes that these problems would be solved "by the guidance of an intelligent agent."

(There is one other complexity story that is actually my favorite but unrelated to those mentioned by Behe. It concerns the processes of photosynthesis, cellular respiration, and the ATPase rotary motor. I have included a brief version as Appendix C.)

Has Miller demolished irreducible complexity?

When I recently reread Kenneth Miller's book, not having read Behe for a year or so, I was indeed impressed. Miller's (1999, pp. 160–61) positive style of writing is difficult to resist; he harbors no doubts that Behe has gone completely astray: "Michael Behe's purported biochemical challenge to evolution rests on the assertion that Darwinian mechanisms are simply not adequate to explain the existence of complex biochemical machines. Not only is he wrong, he's wrong in a most spectacular way. The biochemical machines whose origins he finds so mysterious actually provide us with powerful and compelling examples of evolution in action. When we go to the trouble to open that black box, we find out once again that Darwin had it right."

Well, that depends on how you look at the cases that Behe presents. If it is enough to dismiss each case of irreducible complexity by proposing a just-suppose story that seems like a plausible way to arrive at the structure or system, then it must be admitted that Behe has not proved his case. And there must be an almost infinite number of those what-if tales that can be created in the minds of ingenious evolutionists, those stories being based on the evidence of homologous organs or amino-acid sequences or even fossils. This being the case, it may well be impossible to prove a case of irreducible complexity and to deduce from such a case that there must be an Intelligent Creator. Science cannot prove the existence of God.

Nevertheless, others of us will examine those feasibility stories and see that they are never conclusive. We'll decide that some complex systems possibly "could not have been formed by numerous, successive, slight modifications." Always there are gaps in the feasibility stories, sometimes rather important gaps as Behe pointed out in Russell Doolittle's just-suppose story. Please note that Kenneth Miller, in his attempt to demolish Michael Behe's argument for the irreducible complexity of the blood clotting system, only presented the standard version of gene duplications and gene shuffling, never actually taking on what Behe had to say about the chances of getting those genes shuffled in the right way. For Miller, the possibility that a complex system can come from gene duplications, gene shuffling, mutations, and selection is enough; it all sounds *plausible*. Michael Behe sees all this as quite *implausible*, recognizing that an Intelligent Designer *could* put it all together. Science cannot disprove the existence of God.

Richard Dawkins and others love to say that the only evidence for design is the incredulity of those who believe in it—that they cannot believe the what-if stories. But this statement strongly implies its counter idea: The only critical evidence for the *truth* of the just-suppose stories (in addition to the starting details; amino-acid sequences or fossils) is the credulity (the willingness to believe) of those who think the stories solve the mystery.

God, the Divine Engineer

Much of the work backing up Miller's approach is indeed impressive. Still, most of it is based on similar amino-acid sequences, which leads to the assumption that they must have had a common ancestor. That is well and good, but clearly an Intelligent Creator could have created things that way—and not for some unfathomable reason of his own but simply because it made sense. If an amino-acid sequence has been constructed that will provide a desired or required function, and some related function is also necessary, why not modify the sequence just enough to produce the needed function? Any engineer would surely do it that way. Although at this point we don't have the *knowledge* to do it, we can improve enzymes with random, small mutations; surely God might also have used that approach. How's that for a just-suppose story?

Stephen Jay Gould asked why God would use "spare parts" to build his orchids—or his structures in general? Why not? When I first encountered the question, my reaction to learning that similar parts were assembled in various ways to accomplish different functions in living organisms was that it provided great insight into the nature of God. He must be an efficient engineer. All of which puts me right back there with Carolus Linnaeus in the eighteenth century as he tried to discern the mind of God from his creations. So be it.

One problem might be the kind of God that is taught in many churches: a Great Spirit with magical powers that can call things into being. My concept of God as it has developed over the years (and I can support it within my church's theology) is that he is an *engineer*, not the scientist that I thought he was when I was a young lad aspiring to be a scientist. A scientist attempts to *learn* the laws of nature. An engineer *knows* enough of those laws to create. Hence, God is an engineer with all knowledge of how the universe works and with the creative mind as well as the means and desire to put that knowledge into practice. Since we have actually reached the stage of *evolving enzymes*, it is not difficult to imagine God the Divine Engineer.

Hence, the bottom line for me is that each of us can use the findings of science and our other encounters with religious (spiritual) matters to build a *personal* weltanschauung, but we can't expect science to take us directly to God. I like the way Robert Dorit (1997, p. 475) says this as he ends his review of *Darwin's Black Box*:

> Behe's argument for intelligent design ultimately fails because it is a belief and not a potential explanation. The hand of God may well be all around us, but it is not, nor can it be, the task of science to dust for fingerprints.

Summary

1. Some biologists and other scientists have decided that the "facts" of evolution lead to the conclusion that there is *no Intelligent Creator* (no God).

2. Examples of *atheist scientists* briefly reviewed in this chapter include Carl Sagan, Richard Dawkins, Douglas Futuyma, William Provine, Edward O. Wilson, David Hull, Stephen Jay Gould, and Richard Dawkins.

3. *Richard Dawkins* is one of the most eloquent writers who hold that there is no God—that there is no "watchmaker" or Intelligent Creator analogous to William Paley's intelligent watchmaker. Dawkins claims that the universe has no Designer, no planner; it is analogous to a "blind watchmaker."

4. The biochemist, *Michael Behe*, on the other hand, describes the concept of irreducible complexity, arguing that even the lowly mousetrap testifies of its designer because it would not function unless all of the parts were available and assembled together in the proper way.

5. Behe's thesis is that when Darwin (and Wallace) proposed the

theory of natural selection, they did so in ignorance of the intricacies of biochemical systems, as we understand them today. For those early pioneers, *biochemistry was hidden* in a "black box"—Darwin's Black Box.

6. Behe is one of the *intelligent-design creationists*, whose argument is essentially the same as that of William Paley in 1802 and those who preceded him: *The Argument from Design*.

7. Behe provides eight biological *examples* to illustrate his concept of irreducible complexity; one of these stories is summarized in some detail here: the bombardier beetle.

8. Behe's philosophy is suggested with a number of *quotations* from Darwin's Black Box.

9. Many evolutionists have attempted to counter the concept of irreducible complexity. Often their arguments are trivial. For example, those who counter the argument from design often do so by pointing out how old it is—but that is clearly irrelevant. Robert Dorit summarizes the arguments against Behe, and most of these seem trivial.

10. Yet, their point that it may well be *impossible to know* and to prove that some complex structure could not come into being without a designer could certainly be valid. It is simply impractical (if not impossible) for any individual to imagine all of the ways to account for any natural, complex machine.

11. These thoughts, if valid, confirm the conclusions of this book: *science can neither prove nor disprove the existence of God.*

12. Among those who will counter irreducible complexity is *Kenneth Miller*, who argues against all varieties of creationists and then tells of his own belief in God as Creator.

13. Miller and others who attempt to explain specific examples of apparent irreducible complexity do so by pointing out that the parts for some structure or function that has been said to be irreducibly complex were available for evolution to work on, being present in proposed ancestors of the organism with the complex structure or function. *Evolution only had to put the parts together* in the apparently irreducibly complex way.

14. *Dawkins* takes this approach in relation to the *bombardier beetle* but falls far short of providing a plausible story about the evolutionary steps needed to give the beetle its mechanism.

15. The evidence for this approach is often based on *observed* amino acid and/or nucleotide *sequences* that have some function other than the one in question that would provide the needed molecules for natural

selection to act upon to produce the function in question.

16. Miller uses Behe's example of the vertebrate *blood-clotting mechanism* as an example of this approach, basing his discussion on the work of Russell Doolittle. Yet, one might decide that Miller completely fails to answer Behe's arguments that the mechanism is irreducibly complex—it is as if Behe had written to answer Miller instead of the other way around.

17. If those who reject some or all of the concepts of evolutionary doctrine are being *incredulous* (unable to believe the "obvious" evidence), are those who do accept the evidence being *credulous* (too ready to accept doubtful evidence)? (See the following chapter.)

18. Some argue that an Intelligent Creator would not use parts already in existence when creating some new organism or biochemical mechanism. Why not? Some of us conclude that God *did indeed do what any intelligent engineer would do* in creating some new mechanism: take what was available and modify it.

CHAPTER

7

CHOOSE YOUR WELTANSHAUUNG: AN INTELLIGENT CREATION?

It's time to consolidate and review the main themes I've been following in the preceding chapters. First, there is an implied question behind almost everything: Can Darwin's natural selection, with all that has been added to the concept since his time, particularly mutation as the source of variability, truly provide a *plausible* explanation for the origin of earth's organisms as we know them today *without the intervention of an Intelligent Creator?* Scientifically, my reason for suspecting that a positive answer to this question may never be achieved is that we face huge problems in accounting for the origin of those minimally complex (required) sequences, either protein or nucleic acid. Then, of course, come the problems of cellular organization, development, and such.

Second, most everyone who understands modern biology realizes that the origin of amino-acid and nucleotide sequences is a truly serious problem, yet mainstream biologists seem to have ways to, temporarily at least, ignore the problem by believing that it will some day be solved. They create just-suppose stories and put much more faith in them than seems to be justified. The stories are almost always based on *mutations* and *small steps*, but there are good reasons for doubting that this combination can do the job.

Third, some scientists reconcile their understanding of biology with their belief in God. Some of those are, of course, the creationists, but they have certainly received a bad press from the mainstream! Kenneth Miller, one of the creationists' most vocal opponents, still defends a faith in God. We'll take a closer look at how he does it.

Finally, we'll face the challenges of building a weltanschauung in today's scientific world. That worldview can, of course, be built on more than modern biology in particular and science in general. Its foundations can include one's personal reasons for believing in God.

Whence the Minimally Complex Sequences?

Kenneth Miller (1999, p. 104) says, "Since mutations can duplicate, rearrange, or change literally any gene, it follows that they can also produce any variation." I've been mulling that statement over in my mind, and I'll have to admit that in some theoretical sense it must be true. But the question isn't whether any variation *can* be produced from any gene; the question is, is there a reasonable *probability* that such duplications, rearrangements, or changes can account for all the genes in the world? Are such changes really *plausible*? Even if we assume that "changes" can include additions and deletions? As Michael Behe calculated in relation to supposed evolution of the blood-clotting mechanism (chapter 6), the probabilities may be minuscule indeed.

Then there is, of course, the question of how you get the genes in the first place: the problem of the origin of life. It should be clear that we really have no more than speculative ideas, each troubled by serious problems, of how life might have begun in the first place, let alone how we could develop complex assemblies of enzymes, membranes, organelles, and on and on. Your biology teacher might have told you that evolution is a *fact*, the natural selection part as well as the unity of life part. If we are improving some highly complex enzyme as we discussed in chapter 4, it *is* a fact. But does that truly tell how an atheistic creation might have worked? Not on your life. Don't give up your faith in God because some evolutionists think they have proved that there is no God. They haven't.

Christian de Duve (2002, pp. 77–79) thinks that the origin of variability isn't much of a problem. Among other things, he calculates that *all* the possible proteins about twenty amino acids long—and proteins with only twenty amino acids are known to have some minimal catalytic activity—would fit in a "moderate-size lake measuring, for example, 20 by 50 kilometers in surface and one hundred meters in depth." Well, that sounds pretty good, but remember the problems of getting *any* RNA (chapter 5), plus the problems of getting amino acids to form large peptides (proteins) controlled someway by RNA. These problems also apply to Kauffman's "universal enzyme tool boxes" (chapter 4). Then, how do you get appropriate proteins together to make metabolic pathways and the like? In a way, de Duve's calculation *sharpens* the problems rather than tending to solve them. De Duve's proposals are another what-if story.

With the pace of scientific discovery continuing to accelerate, perhaps this century will see a solution to the problems of the origin of variability for natural selection to act upon. Or perhaps new knowledge will not solve those problems. Our only precedent is the last half century, during which the challenges to evolution by natural selection became much more serious than they appeared to be during the first half of the twentieth century. Still, most biologists would say that there aren't any problems, that we *know* the origin of variability as mutations and all that they imply, as illustrated by Kenneth Miller's statement, which takes us to the next topic.

The Power of Just-Suppose Stories

Remember that anticreationists like to point out that the power of the Intelligent-Design idea is also its weakness: It can be used to "explain" everything. The same can be said for the just-suppose stories put forth by those who would "explain" everything *without* Intelligent Design. Stuart Kauffman (1995, p. 42) recognizes this in his discussion of an RNA world: "The best answer that the advocates of an RNA world can offer is an evolutionary just-so story, in honor of Rudyard Kipling and his fanciful tales about how different animals came to be.. . .Evolution is filled with these just-so stories, plausible scenarios for which no evidence can be found, stories we love to tell but on which we should place no intellectual reliance."

Kauffman is not the only one to quote Kipling, but I think that "just suppose" or "what if" are more descriptive than "just so." A huge part of evolutionary theory consists of these "explanations" that are always preceded by an implied: "Just suppose that it happened like this," or, "What if it happened like this?" or, "What I'm going to tell you sounds plausible." In many cases, there is no way to subject the ideas to scientific testing. Things happened in the distant past, and we don't have a time machine— or for that matter the time—to go back and see, or even to wait and see. Of course there are exceptions, cases where we really can study evolutionary processes in the laboratory, as in the improvement of enzymes discussed in chapter 4.

Just-suppose stories have their place. They sometimes point out avenues that can be followed by experiment or observation in the field, and they are almost always at least thought provoking. In a sense, the hypotheses upon which science depends might be called just-suppose stories. We say: "Suppose such and such is the explanation." Then we devise experiments to test the idea. The problem with studies of evolution or the origin of life is that the hypotheses may be difficult or impossible to test because they involve long time intervals or require historical conditions that no longer exist—and maybe never did exist. Hence, we must be very careful when we evaluate these tales, especially when they depart significantly from what is really known.

UFOs and walking on water

The worst of these examples remind me of what I encountered many years ago when I tried to take a scientific approach to the phenomenon of unidentified flying objects (Salisbury, 1967, 1974a, 1974b). There were believers and nonbelievers. I did my best to be objective and neither believe nor disbelieve—not an easy task. The exercise highlighted many points of scientific philosophy. There were believers who had some good evidence (mostly witness accounts but a few more tangible things) but who extrapolated this evidence to various solid beliefs that probably were not warranted.

The nonbelievers were mostly *explainers* who took the same kind of just-suppose approach that we encounter in the field of evolution. What if such and such *really* happened, said the explainers, instead of what the witnesses *thought* happened? The explainers assumed that they could tell when witnesses were deceived.

The basic data pertaining to a given case are not always agreed upon by all the believers, let alone the explainers; there is often room for argument. However, I found a nice example in a book by two explainers, Harvard astronomer Donald H. Menzel and the psychoanalyst Ernest H. Taves (1977, pp. 21–21, 34). They not only "explained" the UFOs, but they also took on some of the miracles of the Bible as well. A good example is the legend (their term) of Jesus walking on water. They devote a page and one photograph to the phenomenon of the inferior mirage, in which a person standing on a spit of land at some distance from the observer is both magnified in apparent size and seems to be standing on the water. The conclusion: The "legend" originated as an inferior mirage!

Well, that's nice, but it has little relevance to the *only data* available, the accounts in Matthew 14:24–31, Mark 6:44–51, and John 6:16–21. Here is the King James Version from Matthew:

> But the ship was now in the midst of the sea, tossed with waves: for the wind was contrary. And in the fourth watch of the night Jesus went unto them, walking on the sea. And when the disciples saw him walking on the sea, they were troubled, saying, It is a spirit; and they cried out for fear. But straightway Jesus spake unto them, saying, Be of good cheer; it is I; be not afraid. And Peter answered him and said, Lord, if it be thou, bid me come unto thee on the water. And he said, Come. And when Peter was come down out of the ship, he walked on the water, to go to Jesus. But when he saw the wind boisterous, he was afraid; and beginning to sink, he cried, saying, Lord, save me. And immediately Jesus stretched forth his hand, and caught him, and said unto him, O thou of little faith, wherefore didst thou doubt?

Now I'm not concerned here with whether the event actually occurred as described. My point is that Menzel and Taves, to "explain" this "legend," implied just-suppose explanations for all the primary data except the idea of walking on water. Inferior mirages occur under a warm sun and involve objects far enough away so that the atmosphere can have its lensing effect. They don't occur "in the fourth watch of the night," involving someone walking on the water right up to the boat. Hence, Menzel and Taves implicitly said, "Just suppose that it was really day and not night, that there wasn't a storm, that Jesus was a few hundred meters away, and that Peter's experience was added as the legend grew. See, the legend is explained!"

RNA world

There is much of this in the field of evolution and neo-Darwinism. The RNA world provides a good example. The basic facts are that RNA can act as an enzyme in some limited situations, and in the best case, it plays a critical role in forming peptide bonds—making proteins. That's the good news (equivalent to the inferior mirage). The bad news is that RNA is an extremely unlikely prebiotic molecule, as we saw in chapter 5. Nevertheless, Michael P. Robertson and Stanley L. Miller (1996; see discussion in Shapiro, 1999, pp. 111–16) reported that cytosine and uracil would form under certain laboratory conditions. Then they said in essence: "Just suppose that an isolated lagoon would evaporate down until the urea had been concentrated about a million times, and just suppose that certain special compounds were present! And just suppose that there were no other compounds, especially the very common amino acid glycine, present to interfere with the reaction. Wow! We're well on our way to making RNA! What if the other two RNA bases could some way be synthesized? Then all four bases could combine with the sugar ribose and even be phosphorylated and put together without interfering substances so that RNA could form. Then the RNA might have enzymatic properties, making proteins, and in a few million years, life would appear!"

There is much bad news apparent in my fanciful story put into the mouths of Miller and Robertson, a story that must be accepted, at least in essence, by all those who believe in the RNA world, and that is probably a majority of those working in the field. The problems of concentration are relegated to the just-suppose evaporating lagoon. The problem of interfering substances like glycine is simply ignored, as is the problem of getting the other bases and the very unlikely sugar ribose. (If it did form from formaldehyde, it would do so along with many other sugars, all of which might also react with the purine and pyrimidine bases.) Forget the difficulties of an energy source to add the phosphate—or just suppose that this might happen around those black smokers. Forget the problems of getting nucleotide *sequences* that are enzymatically active, and while we're at it, forget the problem of going from a ribozyme (enzymatically active RNA) to the amazingly complex ribosomes, which now depend on tRNA and mRNA to do their thing.

Clearly, RNA world is one huge just-suppose tale that seems highly implausible to many of us, although it must have some plausibility for those who continue to follow its trail off into the great beyond. I continue to see references to the RNA world in *Science*, which arrives in my mail weekly, and the 24 February 2003 issue of *U. S. News & World Report* (p. 41) celebrates the fifty-year anniversary of the double helix and refers to the RNA world.

The "Church of Natural Selection"

It's one thing to try to solve a mystery by proposing ideas to consider and, when possible, test those just-suppose tales. But what we see in today's society of biologists is the tendency to accept the concepts of neo-Darwinism and an atheistic origin of life as a starting place for all other ruminations about how life works. Indeed, acceptance of these concepts is a kind of article of faith. For many, neo-Darwinism serves as a religion, even if it is *in addition to* more traditional religions to which some of them might also adhere.

What is religion?

I mentioned this idea, which was anything but unique with me, in a letter to the editor (Salisbury, 1974c) in relation to an article by Monroe W. Strickberger (1973). Strickberger replied that science is based on testable data while religion is based on records of human interactions with the supernatural and as such cannot be tested with the tools of science. Religion puts faith in a *God*, or some comparable concept, that depends on the religion. Of course, Strickberger is nearly correct. (One can test religious principles personally, but not scientifically, by putting them to practice in one's life.) Nevertheless, one definition of religion suggests what I mean. Here, of several that are listed, are two pertinent definitions of religion from Webster's Collegiate Dictionary: "1. The service and worship of God or the supernatural. . . . 4. A cause, principle, or system of belief held to with ardor and faith."

The first definition covers traditional religions, but that fourth definition covers many of the neo-Darwinians. We have seen that the *facts* of modern cellular and molecular biology outline many systems of high complexity, and that such systems are consistent with an Intelligent Creation. Yet today's high priest of "The Church of Natural Selection," Richard Dawkins, vehemently rejects the argument that *complexity* means *design*. We've noted his subtitle for *The Blind Watchmaker: Why the evidence of evolution reveals a universe without design.* Yet a reading of Dawkins's books makes it clear that his evidence is for the most part a series of just-suppose stories. Dawkins writes as if such "evidence" is *proof,* but when we see that it isn't, we understand that Dawkins is really telling us, and most arduously, about his *faith.* His religion requires much faith, as does mine, which is the first kind of religion defined in Webster. Dawkins and many others are the theologians of their faith; my faith also has many good theologians.

Bearing testimony: faith and weltanschauung

The amazing thing is that modern biologists of all persuasions who are acquainted to some extent with the role of enzymes and other complex systems believe (publicly, at least) that random chemical events, plus Darwin's natural selection—always with no Designer—can account for life. Furthermore, there seems to be a need among the faithful to *bear testimony* to their beliefs (as there is in any religion). In countless articles and books that may have nothing to do directly with evolution, their authors pay homage to the evolutionary article of faith. They seem to want to let their colleagues know that they are staunch members of the congregation of believers; they want to be included in the fold.

Appendix C is a summary of the processes of photosynthesis, cellular respiration, and the ATPase rotary motor, perhaps the most amazing example of biological complexity currently known. Much of the discussion about ATPase is from David W. Lawlor (2001), and it has nothing to do with evolution. Nevertheless, after describing the ATPase motor, Lawlor bears his testimony on evolution by saying, "Clearly, [parts of the ATPase system] were developed early in evolution and, despite the great changes that organisms have undergone since, the enzyme has not changed radically." (See the complete quotation in Appendix C.)

I see no need to invoke evolution when it isn't needed to put over a point but rather is only invoked to show one's faith in the Church of Natural Selection. Just the facts would do fine. Isn't it as inappropriate to present in a public school the evolution part of such statements as *fact* as it would be to present creation as fact? Somewhere, authors should make it clear that, based on the meager evidence available, this is what most biologists believe—it isn't actually known. (The attempts to legislate teaching of creationism in public schools is nicely documented by Bleckmann, 2006.)

Although many biologists simply accept neo-Darwinism because that is what they were taught (they accept it on authority—blind faith), there are certainly many true believers such as Dawkins who would readily tell you why they believe, but their reasons would mostly boil down to those just-suppose stories. Do they really *know* that there will be enough mutations for the required small steps; that is, that there will always be a source of variability? I think not. Such a thing can't be proved at this stage of our science and possibly never will be proved. It must be accepted on faith.

I think there is an element of circular reasoning in the development of that faith, as we've already seen: Because life in all its diversity is here—there *must* have been enough mutations! But how do you know that these weren't the acts of an Intelligent Creator? Because God doesn't exist. How do you know that God doesn't exist? Because He is not needed to account for life in all its diversity. But how do you know that when you don't know if it is possible to produce by pure chance all the mutations that are required? It must be possible because life exists and God does not. How do you know that? I just know! (Or maybe: Because I know of no direct evidence for God's existence.)

So if you are uncomfortable when I refer to belief in total evolution without intervention of an Intelligent Creator as a religion, at least you should agree that it is a weltanschauung, founded on how one prefers to interpret the findings of science and not an inescapable conclusion of science. Based on what we now know about what life is and how little we actually know about how life came into being and progressed to its present complexity, this seems clear. One can take the facts of modern cellular and molecular biology and with some logic arrive at a no-God weltanschauung, or one can take those same facts and with good logic arrive at an Intelligent-Creation weltanschauung. Neither view can be called scientific in the sense that things "scientific" are limited to *conclusions* based only on available data.

God and Quantum Mechanics: The Faith of Kenneth Miller

Because of his powerful defense of neo-Darwinism in particular and evolution in general, and because of his sometimes devastating attacks on creationists of all stripes, we have often made reference to Kenneth Miller's (1999) book: *Finding Darwin's God: A Scientist's Search for Common Ground Between God and Evolution.* Miller is considered by anticreationists as the standard bearer against Intelligent Design. If a debate is held between creationists and anticreationists, the organizers will most likely ask Miller to take the anticreationist position. He is an excellent writer and debater, and those who would put down Michael Behe typically quote Miller.

All of which makes it most interesting that the second half of his book is a defense of belief in God, and for that matter, a God who took an active part in creation. Under the broad definition that makes me admit that I am a creationist, Miller is also a creationist. Amazing!

The Uncertainty Principle: the death of mechanism and determinism

The key to Miller's reconciliation of God and evolution is quantum mechanics, particularly Heisenberg's uncertainty principle. Unlike John-joe McFadden (2000), Miller doesn't push quantum mechanics to the levels of superpositions and such other far-out notions as coherence and entanglement, but he does a credible job of describing the consequences of the uncertainty principle and the fact that most biologists don't appreciate those consequences (Miller, 1999, chapter 7).

Miller begins his discussion by emphasizing the materialist views of the late nineteenth century. If the universe ran strictly on Newtonian laws combined with the other laws of physics and chemistry known by then, *in principle* (although certainly not in practice), knowledge of the positions and momentums of all particles at any moment in the present would allow calculation of where they would be and what they would be doing at any given moment in the future. This is strict determinism, and it fortified the beliefs of the deists (including Franklin and Jefferson among our found-ing fathers) that God set the universe in motion at some time in the past, and that it has simply been running like clockwork ever since. Such a view implies a predestination in everything that happened or happens in history and in our own personal lives. (Even fellow members of my own church have argued this viewpoint; namely, that our "free will" consists of our lack of knowledge of what will happen, although God knows every detail of the future—and that he knows those details because the universe is mechanis-tic and his mind can comprehend it.)

Werner Karl Heisenberg's *indeterminacy* or *uncertainty principle* was published in 1927. Most of us nonphysicists tended to think that this was just an expression of how measuring something might change the prop-erty of what is being measured. (I used to tell my classes that inserting a mercury thermometer in a beaker of water might change the temperature of the water because the thermometer could be warmer or cooler than the water and would thus warm or cool the water until both were at the same temperature.) Actually, this is not the principle at all. The principle proves to be a fundamental law of nature that means that we can never think of the universe as a deterministic machine.

The actual principle is significant only at the atomic level. Heisenberg formulated an equation that gives the uncertainty in momentum if posi-tion is measured—or visa versa. The equation says that measurement of an object of one gram mass to a precision of 0.000001 meter (1 micrometer) will leave an imprecision of only $1/10^{25}$ m/s in its momentum—hardly any-thing to worry about. But if the position of an electron in an atom about

0.0000000001 m (0.1 nanometer) diameter is measured, the uncertainty in its momentum is about one million meters per second (10^6 m/s)—a very large uncertainty! Please be clear that this has nothing to do with techniques used in making the measurements. *In principle*, even if the measurement techniques have no limitations at all, the greater the precision of one measurement, the greater the uncertainty of the other. In developments well beyond this brief summary, it was found that this law of nature impacts everything in the quantum world. For example, energy and time are also *complementary variables*; if one is known with absolute precision, the other remains unknown.

Miller gives examples of unpredictability, and he notes that these quantum uncertainties can be magnified to the macro-world (pp. 202–3). Say we surround a bit of radium with four detectors of the emitted radiation, and then we connect these detectors to a mechanical mouse such that response of one detector moves the mouse in one direction, and responses of the others move the mouse in the other three directions. The result will be movement of the mouse in totally unpredictable ways. *In principle*, there is no way to predict the mouse's movements.[1]

In a beautiful discussion extending over several pages, Miller tells how the discovery of quantum mechanics freed the world of absolute materialism. Sure, we can predict many events in the physical world because of the large number of particles involved and the statistics of large numbers, but unpredictable quantum events at the atomic level can have their effects on the macro-world, and one way is in the changes in DNA that we recognize as mutations. Miller (1999, p. 203) says, "Quantum reality is strange, troublesome, and downright illogical, but its unexpected discovery solves one of the key philosophical problems faced by any religious person: How could a world governed by precise physical law escape a strictly deterministic future?"

Miller (205–9) refers to Erwin Schrödinger's book, *What is Life*, published in 1943, in which the great physicist asked why our bodies must be so large compared with the atom?

> The answer he gave was that we are big relative to the atom
> to insulate us and our senses from atomic-level [quantum]
> events. . . . As a result, events with quantum unpredictability,
> including cosmic ray movements, radioactive disintegration,
> and even molecular copying errors, exert direct influences on
> the sequences of bases in DNA. . . . Mutations . . . are just as

unpredictable as a single photon passing through a diffraction slit. . . . This is something biologists, almost universally, have not yet come to grips with. And its consequences are enormous. . . . The *true* materialism of life is bound up in a series of inherently unpredictable events that science, even in principle, can never master completely. Life surely is explicable in terms of the laws of physics and chemistry, just as Schrödinger hoped, but the catch is that those laws themselves deny us an ultimate knowledge of what causes what, and what will happen next.

Miller's God

Based on these ideas, Miller fills many pages with an excellent discussion of how his God, the God given the freedom of quantum mechanics, has operated via the laws of physics and chemistry through the beginning of Creation until the very present, perfectly able, as taught by the three great Western religions (Islam, Judaism, and Christianity), to intervene when ever it suited him, answering prayers, and even performing things that to us appear miraculous. He is a genuine, personal God, and we are his intentional creations. This we know because he has revealed himself to us. I noted in the margin of the following quotation that these words must be a key to how Miller (pp. 238–39; see p. 222 about God's revelation of himself) reconciles evolution and God:

> Given evolution's ability to adapt, to innovate, to test, and to experiment, sooner or later it would have given the Creator exactly what He was looking for—a creature who, like us, could know Him and love Him, could perceive the heavens and dream of the stars, a creature who would eventually discover the extraordinary process of evolution that filled His earth with so much life.

Your Choices

I like Kenneth Miller's view of his God, even though there are certainly points that I would like to discuss with him. But say that you are constructing your own origins weltanschauung—your philosophy of where life came from and, for that matter, where *you* came from. Your worldview can be based on a purely "natural" (no-God) philosophy, or you can accept the idea that an Intelligent Creator was responsible for life. Or you can keep an open mind and decide not to decide at all—just yet! There are scientists in both camps.[2] I've boiled the arguments down to three in each of the two categories. Here they are:

I. A Creation without Intervention from an Intelligent Creator: The atheistic/agnostic view based on *chance* and *selection*.

1. Science has come an immense distance in understanding evolution and the origin of life since the middle of the nineteenth century. Granted, we still don't know all of the answers, but a highly logical story can be told, based on Charles Darwin's *natural selection* and chance changes in the genetic material—*mutations*, recombinations, and so on. The idea is supported by the fossil record (with a few problems, it's true) and other evidences outlined briefly in chapter 2. There are direct observations of the operation of natural selection in many situations, most of them not requiring new mutations but some (at the level of the viruses and bacteria) actually demonstrating sequence changes that lead to more rapid reproduction, antibiotic resistance, and even improved enzymes. True, we do not yet completely understand how life could have originated, although several suggestions being pursued in laboratories all over the world have merit. History suggests that, given more time, it is likely that the remaining gaps in our knowledge will be filled.

2. As to the existence of a benevolent and loving God who oversees the world, why would he allow the existence of evil—even in the natural world? And why would he consign otherwise good men and women to eternal damnation because of their unbelief?

3. Where could God have come from? An Intelligent Creator responsible for life as we know it would be even more complex than that life! Could such a God exist?

II. An Intelligent Creation: The religious, theistic view, based on such lines of thought as witness testimony and personal experience.

1. Yes, we have learned a great deal, but one critical part of neo-Darwinism must, at this time, be accepted largely on faith: the origin of suitable sequences for natural selection to act upon. It is by far the weakest link in current theories about the origin of life, and it applies to the evolution of advanced species as well as to evolution leading to the first living cell. The nature of the problem seems to be understood by everyone who is acquainted with modern biology including all of the evolutionists and those working on the origin of life, but after stating the problem and providing the huge numbers that show how improbable it is to expect meaningful

sequences to appear by chance, they then move on as though the answer will some day be forthcoming—based on mutation and selection of small steps. Their faith is strong!

Historical considerations don't necessarily provide comfort and support for that faith. True, we have learned a great deal in a century and a half of modern research, but much of what we have learned has only illustrated the levels of complexity, especially the problems of achieving suitable sequences by random events. To those who see no need for an Intelligent Creator, the vast body of knowledge that has accumulated provides hope. For those who believe that an Intelligent Creator accounts for life, the amazing complexity that has become apparent is consistent with an Intelligent Creation. Although there may be other explanations for complexity, they are not now apparent, while it is clear that Creation *could* have required input and guidance from an Intelligent Creator. The workings of nature really do declare the glory of God, just as the scriptures and many great religious thinkers have always said.

2. Evil in the world poses no problem for those who believe in a God who might well have his reasons for permitting the existence of evil. The most obvious reason is the importance of *agency* or *freedom of choice* in the development of human beings—even of life in the natural world. Humans are part of God's plan, and agency is a critical part of that plan. This is what all the great religions tell us, and their faith is that the knowledge came from God himself. Further, I speculate, if mutations *do* account for changing species, there might be a sort of "freedom to mutate," which does not exclude a Creator's ability to intervene when it seemed or seems appropriate.

As to consigning unbelieving but otherwise good people to eternal damnation, that is simply not a part of my theology.

3. As science can neither prove nor disprove the existence of an Intelligent Creator, so science can certainly have nothing to say about the *origin* of such a Creator. Only God could tell us, and to the best of my knowledge, this information has not been forthcoming. Some solace is provided by the precedence for intelligence in the universe: our own existence. A Creator God would indeed have to be intelligent—and thus complex—beyond anything we can know, yet collectively we humans have discerned within less than 150 years much of the fantastic complexity of life. We obviously possess great collective intelligence. Given eternity, why not God? Much solace is provided by God's revelation of himself, which in the last analysis I must accept on the basis of my experience and my faith.

Does It Matter?

We saw in the previous chapter that some thinkers have rejected God on the basis of their understanding of evolutionary and even molecular biology. Modern biology, even if the public knows little about it except for the "hearsay" that appears in the media, can certainly have an impact on our collective thinking about and belief in God. It matters!

The creationists make a large issue of the idea that the "Godless doctrine" of evolution is at heart responsible for much of the moral decay they see in our society: loose sexual behavior, abortion, cheating, lying, and so forth.[3] Lack of belief in a God who gives us righteous commandments permits one's breaking of those commandments without fear of punishment. The anticreationists counter this assertion by pointing out that there has always been evil in the world, and much of it has been perpetrated in the name of God (Eldredge, 2000, chapter 7; and Pennock, 1999, chapter 7). We need only think of the inquisition, the Crusades, slavery, and now the horrible attacks in the name of God on the World Trade Center and the Pentagon. Furthermore, there have always been those who, having at least some belief in God, were still willing to ignore his commandments and do as they pleased.

It is easy for me to relate to both of these viewpoints. The world has both good and evil, believers and nonbelievers. Yet at some level, the question of creation touches the lives of us all. To some extent, we live our lives in a manner that is influenced by whether or not we believe in God. It is ideal if we work through the logic of living moral lives in a perfect society whether we believe in God or not, deciding that it makes sense to treat each other as we would like to be treated. But the evils in today's society suggest that without God in their lives many have not come to that conclusion. Belief in God and an eternal justice, tempered by God's mercy, *can* have a strong positive influence on how we live and act—even if that doesn't always happen. On the one hand, we may fear God's punishment for our sins. On the other hand, we may be touched by our understanding of God's love for us and have no desire to harm others for the sake of our own pleasure or even to harm our future selves for the sake of immediate pleasure. If in the minds of some, the "doctrine" of evolution has led to rejection of belief in God, even if that doctrine says nothing about God and is only superficially understood by many who use it as an excuse to reject God, the possible positive influence of such a belief in God will have been lost.

In our present society with all its ills and evils, it's easy to get the idea that there is no God, indeed that there are no rules or absolutes. Although this worldview may derive primarily from the idea that a benevolent God would not permit the ills and evils, it is short-sighted to suggest that this impression is not influenced by the notion that God was not needed in creation. If the philosophy of an Intelligent Creation helps one formulate better moral values and actions in today's world, so be it! But each individual must choose, and knowledge of modern biology just might help. Does it matter? I think it *can* matter, and for many, it *does* matter.

What Is Truth?

Based on scientific knowledge alone (and the problem of God's origin), I see the choice between the two possibilities of God or no God as a very difficult one. The case for science is very strong, and even from where I stand, including my belief in an Intelligent Creator, I'm convinced that scientists should keep looking. Such a search for life's beginnings and continued progress may never reach its goal, but much is bound to be learned along the way. Personally, I find other aspects of science more intriguing (how plants work), but those whose drive is to seek understanding of how life could originate and evolve without divine intervention, in the postulated primeval soup or over the course of evolution, should follow their star. Science knows no boundaries of what is "legal" to study. We try only to understand the universe, to find truth.

The God of the gaps

If one chooses the worldview of Intelligent Creation based *only* on what science has failed to learn about the nature of life, one is in a real sense choosing the "God of the gaps." That is, one places one's faith in a God who fills the gaps in our present knowledge. This is derisively pointed out by anticreationists. Or, if one chooses the no-God worldview, one can place one's faith in the future findings of science to fill the gaps. Make no mistake, the gaps are there, and they are more important than most modern biology texts might have you believe. It takes faith to believe that they will be filled, either with or without an Intelligent Creation.

Incredulity

As noted earlier, another form of this "gap" argument used by anticreationists is to insist that the creationists' attitude is based on "the argument from personal incredulity." For example, Kenneth Miller (1999, p. 111) says, "The only compelling case [creationists] can make against evolutionary theory is that the mountain of historical and experimental evidence supporting evolution hasn't yet convinced *them*." Of course the creationists' retort could be that evolutionists are too credulous, willing to believe too readily, especially without adequate evidence. Remember that much of that "mountain of. . .evidence" consists of those "what-if" stories. Evolutionists seem to assume that if a scenario is *plausible* it must represent what actually happened—or at least close to it.

Credulity

I find this very interesting. Science is reputed to be based on skepticism: "Show me the evidence!" But when the creationist says the evidence is almost totally based on "plausibility" rather than demonstration (except in some laboratory studies with viruses and microorganisms, from which much "evidence" is induced or extrapolated), and that we still have a long way to go before we understand how those minimal amino-acid sequences can appear and how they can be properly integrated into the respective developmental programs. The evolutionist says, "Oh, you are just *too* incredulous." The term seems to have a negative ring, impugning the weak-minded personality of someone who "just doesn't get it." In my defense, I replace the term "incredulity" with its near synonyms: *skepticism* or *doubt*. Yes, it is interesting that scientists can be proud of being skeptical, yet they can be totally *credulous* when it comes to evolution. Because of this switch in attitude in today's world, it is almost impossible to be accepted by mainstream science if one is openly skeptical about evolution.

Personal belief

In any case, I didn't invent God to fill the gaps or because of my incredulity. I knew about God long before I knew about the gaps. Science cannot tell us about God, but God could reveal himself. With just as much logic and careful thought as has gone into writing this book—or that goes into a book by, say, Richard Dawkins—I believe that God has revealed himself. My faith is not blind faith any more than faith in neo-Darwinism needs to be a blind faith; much evidence is involved in either case. Furthermore, it is not only my understanding of scientific method that convinces me that science can neither prove nor disprove the existence of God; my theology supports the same conclusion. I believe that we are indeed here on earth, among other reasons (especially how we react to innate moral principles), to be tested based on faith. Part of that faith is accepting the existence of God. If God's existence is *proved* by scientific means, the nature of the test is destroyed.

I promised not to get into theology in this book, so I'll stop now to keep my promise. Still, I have decided to add Appendix D to summarize some of what my fellow church members have had to say about these matters.

Let me leave you with three thoughts: First, it is up to you to decide— or to decide not to decide yet. Second, it is implied in many presentations that the problems with evolutionary theory are relatively simple and that some day we will have *all* the answers as to how life originated and evolved to its present level of complexity without God. I hope that this book helps you to see that the problems are anything but simple. And third, my faith in an Intelligent Creation, developed some years before and many years during my study of biology, greatly intensifies my appreciation of what we have been learning about biology in general and cellular and molecular biology in particular. Life, with its complexity and order, is truly beautiful, just as we might expect from an Intelligent Creator, a God who wanted us to have the freedom of choice to love him or reject him, all in a world of living things that exhibit their own freedom to mutate, change, and otherwise interact according to the natural laws of this stage of our existence. Eyes up in the Lord God's garden!

Summary

1. A personal weltanschauung should take into account the difficulties in accounting for the complexities of living things, especially the minimum amino acid and nucleotide sequences. Can these sequences be achieved by the natural selection of random changes in the genetic material? There are valid reasons for doubt.

2. Some scientists (Kenneth Miller and Christian de Duve) see no problem in getting the necessary sequences, suggesting (with circular logic) that the mechanisms of genetic change are well known, and since the necessary sequences exits, there must have been a way to produce them by random changes.

3. By now, the role of "just suppose" stories in explaining creation by natural selection should be apparent. This is sometimes mentioned by evolutionists (Stuart Kauffman). And such stories can also be thought of as

being the hypotheses necessary to advancing science.

4. What-if stories are often based on many assumptions that can be neither proved nor disproved. An example is the "explanation" (by Donald Menzel and Ernest Taves) for the "legend" of Jesus walking on water, based on the phenomenon of the inferior mirage. The "explanation" works only by ignoring the available data relating to the reported event.

5. Michael Robertson and Stanley Miller base a just-suppose story about the origin of RNA for an RNA world on many assumptions about conditions that seem highly unlikely.

6. If a "cause, principle, or system of belief held to with ardor and faith" can be considered as a religion, many evolutionists qualify as supporting the "religion of natural selection." Richard Dawkins's statement about the blind watchmaker provides a good example.

7. It is common, apparently almost essential, for modern biologists to mention evolution regardless of whether the subject being discussed has any direct relationship to evolutionary theory. David Lawlor's statement on the time of the evolution of ATPase is a good example.

8. Kenneth Miller emphasizes the importance of the uncertainty principle in our understanding that the universe is not deterministic or purely materialistic. Miller builds on these ideas to reconcile evolution and God.

9. The atheistic weltanschauung can be based on one's acceptance of an atheistic evolution to account for living organisms, the existence of injustice and evil in the world, and the impossibility of accounting for the origin of God.

10. The theistic weltanschauung (an Intelligent Creation) can be partially based on one's knowing the limitations in our ability to account for living organisms based only on an atheistic evolution and natural selection (especially in accounting for those sequences), acceptance of the concept that evil and injustice are inescapable consequences of chance and free choice (free will or agency) in the world, and the realization that, although there is no way for us to account for God's origin, this does not mean that he does not exist.

11. Although humans can be evil whether they believe in God or not, one can make a case that rejection of belief in God can increase the amount of evil (if evil can be quantified)—as some creationists point out. Accepting God based on Creation can matter.

12. Belief in God should in no way halt the pursuit of scientific knowledge, including studies of evolution and the possible atheistic origin of life.

13. Faith should be more than accepting a "God of the gaps." The gaps in our knowledge are certainly there, but there are better reasons to believe in God.

14. Creationists (in the broadest sense of the word, which includes me) may reject evolution because they cannot accept the "what-if" stories that support it: They are too incredulous. This suggests that evolutionists are too credulous about those stories. Remember that incredulous can mean being skeptical, and credulous can mean not being skeptical.

15. In the last analysis, whether one's weltanschauung is atheistic or theistic is a personal matter, and it can apparently be almost independent of one's personal theology. Whatever it might be, hopefully it will include an appreciation for the beauties of our natural world!

A CREATION AND CREATIONISTS

Although anti-creationists sometimes berate creationists for not saying just how an Intelligent Creation might have taken place, believing in an Intelligent Creation does not obligate anyone to tell how such a Creation might have taken place. How should we know? Yet it seems appropriate to review some of the possibilities that have been suggested, both natural and with intervention from a Creator—ignoring the unknown details, of course. Some of these suggestions have little or no merit; others may at least provide food for thought. Clearly, there can be no scientifically proved conclusion, although science might *eliminate* some of the possibilities. As far as I know, there can also be no theologically proved conclusion. (The religious suggestions presented in this appendix are based on the Judeo-Christian Bible and ignore other world religions, which I have not studied.)

For all of my scientific lifetime, I have been practicing the art of objectivity—fence-sitting, one might say. I've become quite good at it. Thus, I cannot even say that I *favor* one of the eight possibilities outlined below. Some go against our current science or (in the case of the last one) my theology. They are arranged roughly beginning with the greatest degree of Intelligent Intervention (and/or the most magical) and ending with no intervention at all. Sometimes, however, that is not easy to do. For example, where should we put the intelligent-design creationists? Actually, the first seven of these eight categories qualify in at least some sense as creationist, although the fifth category rejects the traditional God of Judeo-Christianity and other great religions but still insists on "special creation." You'll note that the first four, and probably number six, begin with a religious conviction and build from there.

1. Omphalos

We encountered Phillip Gosse in chapter 2. He published his book, *Omphalos*, in 1857, two years before Darwin's *Origin* was published. Omphalos is the Greek word for *navel*, and Gosse's inspiration came with his realization that God *might* have created Adam and Eve with navels although they never had a natural birth. If that were the case, then God could have created the trees in the Garden of Eden already fully grown but with annual rings that normally would be formed one at a time during each year of their life. Gosse wondered, Why stop there? God might have created the earth with layers of sediments that contained fossils of animals that never lived, or God might have created all of the universe as well as the earth with the *appearance* of age, all in an instant, and from nothing. Light might have been created in space as though it came from a distant galaxy beginning ten billion years ago.

Interestingly, the anticreationists who relate the Omphalos story, and virtually all of them do, say that it is logically infallible. The logic must follow this simplified syllogism:

> **Major premise:** Omnipotence is the power to do absolutely anything that can be imagined.
>
> **Minor premise:** God is omnipotent and could imagine an *Omphalos* creation.
>
> **Conclusion:** Therefore, God could have accomplished such a creation.

The conclusion is logically valid, but is it true? I don't know because I don't know if the major or the minor premises are true. The major premise could be true by definition, or one could hold that omnipotence is the power to do anything that is possible within the laws of physics and chemistry. Personally, I prefer the anything-that's-possible definition of omnipotence, but some (many, most?) theologians would prefer the first. They might say that God *created* the laws of physics and chemistry and could do what he wanted with those laws. I withdraw from the argument at that point, but it seems that an Omphalos creation stretches physical law so far that it becomes magic and not within the power of the Intelligent Creator who is part of *my* theology. That's why it is at the top of the list: the most magical and unreasonable of the scenarios (but not far above the next one). Furthermore, such a creation would be a colossal act of deception fostered upon human kind. No doubt, that is one reason why it has never really been taken seriously (as far as I know), even by the most ardent creationists today and in Gosse's time.

2. Creation Science: Young Earth, Flood Geology

Next in line are the young-earth creationists, especially those espousing "flood geology," who call their doctrines *creation science* or *scientific creationism*. These were the ones who were most vocal during the twentieth century and who tried and are still trying to get their ideas taught in the schools. A most valuable book by Ronald Numbers (1992), which outlines the history of creationists in general and this group in particular, notes that they are a phenomenon of the twentieth century, surprising as that might seem. Few indeed are those who championed such notions during the nineteenth century. Their beliefs are nicely outlined and defined in a 1981 Arkansas Law (Numbers, 1992, p. x), which states that:

> Creation-science includes the scientific evidences and related inferences that indicate:
> 1. Sudden creation of the universe, energy, and life from nothing;
> 2. The insufficience of mutation and natural selection in bringing about development of all living kinds from a single organism;
> 3. Changes only within fixed limits of originally created kinds of plants and animals;
> 4. Separate ancestry for man and apes;
> 5. Explanation of earth's geology by catastrophism, including the occurrence of a worldwide flood; and
> 6. A relatively recent inception of the earth and living kinds.

As Numbers (1992) relates it, the history of the development of scientific creationism is a fascinating story. Although there were some who preceded George McCready Price during the early decades of the twentieth century, it was he who was highly effective in insisting that the appearance of life on earth was a recent event (perhaps as recent as 10,000 years ago), and that the world's geology was rearranged by the Noachian flood, described in Genesis 6–8. Price was a self-proclaimed geologist who wrote many books and articles and strongly influenced creationist thinking during most of his 93 years. He had no formal training in science but early on made a living by selling books (especially the Seventh-Day Adventist books of Ellen G. White, who taught a literal seven-day creation with the seventh day devoted to honoring God). Later, he obtained a one-year teaching degree and taught school. His goal in life was to be a writer, however, and when he became converted to young-earth creationism, he spent his life writing about it.

An example of creation geology is Chief Mountain in Canada (see chapter 2), which is considered by geologists to be a prime example of an *overthrust*; it was Price's showcase example of an exception to the fossil record in the geological column. For a time, Price and his colleagues pushed an observation in Texas of supposed dinosaur and human footprints in the same riverbed; it is now agreed that both prints are those of dinosaurs.

Price's influence was at first mostly within his small Seventh-day Adventist group, and his arguments are the classic example of beginning with a specific interpretation of the Genesis account of Creation and then attempting to make science fit that interpretation (for example, that there was no death of any organisms before the fall of Adam and Eve, which implies that all the organisms that became fossils lived after Adam and Eve). Better-trained geologists took up the baton, however, and continued Price's approach, notably Henry M. Morris and John C. Whitcomb Jr. with their book, *The Genesis Flood*, first published in 1961 but with several revised editions. Other fundamentalist religionists outside of Seventh-Day Adventism joined the crusade.

This brand of creationism, although it was by far the best known during the twentieth century, is so vulnerable to scientific examination that its widespread influence seems almost ludicrous. The young-earth idea goes against all scientific methods used to date the earth, and the notion that earth's geology can be accounted for by a Noachian, worldwide flood requires numerous assumptions that are truly impossible to support scientifically. Nevertheless, some proponents of these doctrines continue to garner strong support among a high percentage of Americans today. Is this a comment on the level of science teaching in our schools? How can one avoid such a conclusion?

In addition to the young-earth and flood doctrines, creation science notes the details of the complexity of life that we have summarized in this book. They claim that these items *prove* the existence of the Intelligent Creator who formed the earth in seven, 24-hour days, resting on the seventh.

Incidentally, the definition given above lets me off the hook of being called a creationist. The dictionary definition of *creationism* also lets me off the hook: "The doctrine ascribing the origin of all matter and living forms as they now exist to distinct acts of creation by God." That goes way beyond my belief. I believe that God played some critical role in creation, but I don't think that he was responsible for "all matter and living forms as they now exist," unless that role was some kind of guidance of evolutionary creation at every step, and I strongly doubt that. (Furthermore, my personal theology rejects the widely held belief in creation *ex nihilo*: creation of matter, energy, and time out of nothing. My theology holds that God created or *organized* from matter that already existed.)

Still, most of us feel that the term *creationist* goes beyond the dictionary definition. Wouldn't most biologists today agree that the term includes those who believe God played some "critical role in creation" whatever it might have been? In that sense, I certainly qualify, and most of the Intelligent-design creationists would also say they qualified on that basis, while admitting that many "living forms as they now exist" came into being via Darwinian evolution. Kenneth Miller (1999) is a good example, as we saw in chapter 7. After presenting his excellent anti-creationists arguments, he goes on to tell why he believes in God and speculates on how God might have been responsible for creation, thus qualifying himself as a creationist in the broad sense (but never admitting it).

3. The Day-Age Interpretation of the Genesis Account

The rise of "scientific creationism" during the twentieth century is surprising because up to the late nineteenth century, even the most conservative Christian apologists readily conceded that the Bible allowed for an ancient earth and life and death before the Garden of Eden. One approach was to consider the Genesis "days" of Creation to actually represent geological ages. In such an interpretation, matter was created on day one, life was created on day three, and days four and five allowed time for the fossils to form. Humans were created on day six. Some time well after Eden, Noah's flood occurred. For example, the much misunderstood William Jennings Bryan read the Genesis "days" as geological "ages" and even allowed for the possibility of organic evolution—so long as it did not produce Adam and Eve.

There are problems with this approach, in particular that one must rearrange the days of creation a bit to make them match up with the geological record, but it does allow for a fair amount of agreement between science and religion. Some theologians have even suggested that when God told Moses about creation, he simply organized the story around various days, each "day" representing something that had to be accomplished. God didn't mean for them to be thought of as being sequential. In any case, the day-is-an-age idea is a view that is held by many religious people today.

4. The Gap or Ruin-and-Restoration Interpretation of the Genesis Account

Another approach followed by many creationists of the nineteenth and early twentieth centuries was to insert, between the first and second verses of Genesis, the vast amounts of time needed to account for the findings of geology. The first verse tells of the creation of matter and energy ("In the beginning God created the heaven and the earth."), now thought by many Evangelicals to be a description of the "big bang" (Strobel, 2004). This was followed by a long period (billions of years, we might say now) during which the earth supported life, fossils were formed, and God might have even carried out several creations of life. This period ended with a cataclysmic destruction of all life, leaving an earth that, as noted in the second verse, was "formless and empty" (New International Version [NIV: very close to original Hebrew], or in King James, "was without form, and void," or in the *New American Bible* [Catholic]: "a formless wasteland," or in Luther's Bible: "wüst und leer" = "desolate and empty"). Then the second and following verses tell of a much later creation of life, the Garden of Eden, and Adam and Eve, perhaps adding the idea noted above that the "days" of creation were a literary device used by God to tell Moses about creation. As far as I know, this approach is not taught by modern creationists, but I'm not aware of all that is taught today by the various creationists. It was an important interpretation during Darwin's time.

Modern creationists *could* point out that this scenario might be supported by our current conviction that the dinosaurs were eliminated by a cataclysmic impact of a large meteor, which sent up clouds of dust and debris that led to the extinction of many species. Paleontologists assume that some species survived and went on to repopulate the earth, but the gap creationists could note that *all* life might have been eliminated, with God then carrying out another creation, replacing some of the same species as before the catastrophe. Such events could have happened several times, accounting for the extinctions seen in the fossils of the geologic column. Could such an extinction event followed by re-creation have happened relatively recently, say within the last ten to twenty thousand years? One would expect that there would be much geologic evidence if that were the case. If such evidence exists, I'm unaware of it.

5. Chariots of the Gods: The Raëlian Movement

There are those out there who believe that the "gods" who created life on earth were a group of extraterrestrials who visited earth at intervals in their space ships, genetically engineering the development of all the prokaryotic and eukaryotic species and eventually humans. This would be a sort of intelligent creation in lower case. Such an idea has been suggested by various authors, including Erick von Däniken (1968), who was one of the first to cite ancient carvings, illustrations, monoliths, and other physical artifacts that he believed support the idea that the earth was visited by ancient astronauts, extraterrestrials in unidentified flying objects. Von Däniken mentioned Ezekiel's vision of the "wheel in a wheel" and argued that this was a space vehicle and could not be the transportation system of an almighty God, although it was so interpreted by Ezekiel (Ezekiel 1–3). At the same time that von Däniken was pushing his views (with much success; his books were best sellers), the Reverend Barry H. Downing (1968) examined the Bible as a source of UFO accounts, concluding that many Biblical miracles could be viewed as UFO visitations but that this in no way diminished the concept of an Almighty God.

The Raëlian movement is a somewhat more recent version of this "UFO" approach. In May 2003, the movement claimed 60,000 members who adhere to the doctrines of "Raël," the former Claude Vorilhon, a French journalist and race-car enthusiast.[1] Raël claims to have been twice contacted by an alien in a flying saucer who revealed to him the true story of the creation of life on earth. Raël's accounts of these visitations were published in 1974 (with an updated version in 1986). The Raëlians were recently in the news for claiming to have cloned a human infant.

According to Raël, eons ago on a distant planet these aliens—the *Elohim*[2] —advanced in their science until they could create primitive cells in the laboratory. They were afraid of contaminating their own planet with these cells, however, so they found another suitable planet—our earth, of course. As their science advanced (presumably while countless generations came and went), they were able to create all kinds of plants and animals, and with the help of their artists, some of these were spectacular indeed. There was not only a great variety of flowers, but some birds were so adorned with colorful feathers that they could not fly. Their greatest challenge was to create beings after their own images, but there were some failed attempts along the way (the fossil pre-humans). They ended with what we recognize as the races of humans, but all were in the fundamental image of their creators.

The Raëlians consider evolution to be a myth. The increasingly complex fossils in the geological column are the evidences of how the Elohim scientists improved in their special creations. Raël relates all of this to the Biblical account of creation, as you surely have already guessed. Raëlians hold that the Bible contains a partial but somewhat corrupted version of the true story of creation. Although the Biblical authors had been told the story of their creation, they were too primitive to understand it correctly. This is a story by a special, "scientific" brand of creationists, who reject both the more traditional religious accounts of creation *and* the evolutionists!

Their mechanisms of creation—careful genetic engineering plus the knowledge of how to control development from a single cell (a surrogate fertilized egg without the previous sperm and egg)—come close to what might be suggested by intelligent-design creationists. Much of what I have written in this book could be thought of this way. It seems to differ from the next topic only in theology.

6. A Directed, 4.3-Billion-Year Evolution of Life

Do the intelligent-design creationists fit here?

Many scientifically inclined creationists, both early and modern, have held to the theist view that creation was indeed along the lines described by paleontologists and modern evolutionists, but that an Intelligent Creator intervened in the process at many steps along the way. This would be much like the Raëlian story, but proponents of an Intelligent Creation would insist that their Creator (one God) differed in fundamental ways (which I won't try to describe) from the Raëlian Elohim. Most of Darwin's friends held to such a view, one that grew out of their religious up-bringing and not out of their science. Many of today's scientists might also fit in this or the next category. The great geneticist Theodosius Dobzhansky (1973) could be a good example, although he may fit even better in the next category (see chapter 3, footnote 2).

The intelligent-design creationists are a more recent (not mentioned by Ronald Numbers, who published in 1992) group who, like William Paley, argue that the intricacy of life, particularly at the molecular and cellular levels that were unknown to Paley, *proves* that there must be an Intelligent Designer. Whether they adhere to the young-earth, gap, destruction-restoration views, or something else was not apparent to me in their writings. Michael Behe (1996) is perhaps the best known and one of the most scientific spokesman for these creationists. We met him in chapter 6. Behe is an active Catholic.

While Behe and many others of the "new creationists" are trained in the sciences and mathematics (William A. Dembski, 1998; Behe et al., 2000) the most vocal seems to be Phillip E. Johnson, a professor of law at the University of California, Berkeley. He has written numerous articles and three books contending that neo-Darwinian evolution is false science, that science should incorporate his views of creationism, and that teaching evolution has led to many of our current social ills. Although I can't agree with all that he says, some of his arguments appeal to me, and he must have "hit a nerve" in creationism's critics because he is singled out by those critics more than anyone else. Robert Pennock (1999) in his *Tower of Babel* fills many pages in many chapters with arguments against Johnson's philosophies and contentions, which are mostly against Darwinism and the negative effects that *naturalism* has had on our society.[3] Johnson is a Protestant Christian.

Perhaps Johnson's most influential book is *Reason in the Balance* (1995), but in his book, except for mentioning "Michael Behe's forthcoming book," he has little to say about intelligent design, although he notes that the argument from design goes back at least to New Testament times almost two thousand years ago. In support of intelligent design, he (as other creationists) quotes the apostle Paul in Romans 1:20, which I have quoted in chapter 1. Creationists also take the idea back to the time of David, about three thousand years ago. For example, the psalmist David seemed to be well aware of the design exhibited in his own body. "I will praise thee; for I am fearfully and wonderfully made.. . .I was made in secret, and curiously wrought.. . .In thy book all my members were written. . .when as yet there was none of them" (Psalm 139:14–16).

As we have noted again and again, the scientific method can neither prove nor disprove the existence of God, but the intelligent-design creationists *strongly suggest* that the discovery of design in nature (especially Behe's *irreducible complexity*) *does* prove God's existence, although these creationists occasionally note that science can *never prove* God's existence. Furthermore, the anti-creationists accuse the intelligent-design creationists of having a "hidden agenda," which is to convert their readers to their version of Christianity and to push evolution out of the public schools. Barbara Forrest (2001) documents this "hidden agenda." Behe's (1996) book does not give the impression of such an agenda, but Johnson (1995) states his agenda rather clearly, which means that it is not "hidden" after all.

In any case, although my views come very close to their views, I'm uncomfortable being placed in the intelligent-design group partially because it really is a *group* of individuals who have met together, corresponded, and formed organizations, while I have never met those people, joined their organizations, or even corresponded with them. (Which is not to say that I never will.)

7. Darwin's Tangled Bank: Creation of Life and Then Evolution

Charles Darwin mostly rejected the idea of the Creation as is made clear in his many letters and other writings (see Francis Darwin, editor, 1892, pp. 59–69), but he kept the last "tangled bank" paragraph of *The Origin* through all of its six editions: "It is interesting to contemplate a tangled bank, clothed with many plants . . . birds . . . insects . . . worms. . . . There is grandeur in this view of life, with its several powers, having been breathed by the Creator into a few forms or into one. . .from so simple a beginning endless forms most beautiful and most wonderful have been, and are being evolved." This may have been in deference to his believing wife, or it might have been his honest conviction. In any case, in this paragraph he suggested that the Creator established life on earth in some very simple form and that evolution took over from there, producing all the planet's species including us. This would at least solve the problem of the origin of life. And that is about all that science can have to say about this approach. It is probably fair to say, however, that many people today who believe in God, especially scientists, would claim this deist view as most closely related to their own.

8. The Blind Watchmaker: There Is No Intelligent Creator

This viewpoint could have about as many subheadings as the views listed above, but there is no need to discuss them in this appendix because we have already referred to them throughout the text. The headings would first break down according to the various theories of the origin of life, all of which attempt to account for a spontaneous generation of life under earth's primeval conditions, which we described in chapter 5.

Moving beyond the origin-of-life theories, we would encounter various ideas about how evolution took place, but virtually all of them would be based on natural selection of random mutations, or transferring genomes among species. There would be Darwin's original ideas of very gradual changes, these ideas being strongly defended by Richard Dawkins (*The Blind Watchmaker*, 1986). We could list the "punctuated equilibria" theory (that evolution proceeded slowly during long periods of "stasis," with more rapid changes after times of extinction and/or climatic change) of Niles Eldredge and Stephen Jay Gould (1972), which is still being discussed and debated. Science, which cannot logically discuss the role of an Intelligent Creator, continues to be anxiously engaged in the search for naturalistic truth—as it must be.

Where Do I Stand?

I would like to avoid answering this question, and indeed I am unable to give a meaningful answer except to say that I am still sitting on the fence. *Omphalos* or creation by magic is easy to reject, as are both young-earth "scientific creationism" and the atheistic approach that many scientists take. Science itself must be agnostic. I can reject the atheistic approach because of my personal convictions about God, but at the same time I can encourage agnostic scientific research and discussion among the researchers simply because that is the only logical way for science to function. Because the Raëlian doctrine is essentially also anti-God, I reject it, yet I'm tempted by the closely similar *directed* evolution approach, which often encompasses the concept of intelligent design—that is, an Intelligent Creation. Sometimes I find myself also tempted by the gap or the ruin-and-restoration ideas, but then at other times Darwin's tangled bank intrigues me. For now, except for the rejections, I'll await more science and continue to sit on the fence.

B RETURN TO WILLIAM PALEY

Since Paley has taken such bad press, it seems appropriate that we see what he really said about the watch, back in 1802, or at least as much of it as space will allow (see Danielson, 2000, pp. 191–93). The concept of minimum or irreducible complexity is clearly evident in his analogy:

> In crossing a heath, suppose I pitched my foot against a *stone*, and were asked how the stone came to be there. I might possibly answer that, for anything I knew to the contrary, it had lain there for ever; nor would it perhaps be very easy to show the absurdity of this answer. But suppose I found a *watch* upon the ground, and it should be inquired how the watch happened to be in that place. I should hardly think of the answer which I had before given—that, for anything I knew, the watch might have always been there. Yet why should not this answer serve for the watch as well as for the stone? Why is it not as admissible in the second case as in the first? For this reason, and for no other, [namely] that, when we come to inspect the watch, we perceive (what we could not discover in the stone) that its several parts are framed

and put together for a purpose—that they are so formed and adjusted as to produce motion, and that motion so regulated as to point out the hour of the day; that, if the different parts had been differently shaped from what they are, of a different size from what they are, or placed after any other manner, or in any other order, than that in which they are placed, either no motion at all would have been carried on in the machine, or none which would have answered the use that is now served by it.. . .This mechanism being observed. . ., the inference we think is inevitable, that the watch must have had a maker: that there must have existed, at some time, and at some place or other, an artificer who formed it for the purpose which we find it actually to answer, who comprehended its construction, and designed its use.

Nor would it, I apprehend, weaken the conclusion, that we had never seen a watch made; that we had never known an artist capable of making one; that we were altogether incapable of executing such a piece of workmanship ourselves. . ..

Neither, second, would it invalidate our conclusion, that the watch sometimes went wrong, or that it seldom went exactly right. The purpose of the machinery, the design, and the designer, might be evident, and in the case supposed would be evident, in whatever way we accounted for the irregularity of the movement, or whether we could account for it or not. . ..

Nor, third, would it bring any uncertainty into the argument, if there were a few parts of the watch, concerning which we could not discover, or had not yet discovered, in what manner they conduced to the general effect; or even some parts concerning which we could not ascertain whether they conduced to that effect in any manner whatever. . . . .

Nor, fourth, would any man in his senses think the existence of the watch, with its various machinery, accounted for, by being told that it was one out of possible combinations of material forms; that whatever he had found in the place where he found the watch, must have contained some internal configuration or other; and that this configuration might be the structure now exhibited, [namely] of the works of a watch, as well as a different structure.

Nor, fifth, would it yield his inquiry more satisfaction to be answered, that there existed in things a principle of order, which had disposed the parts of the watch into their present form and situation. He never knew a watch made by the principle of order; nor can he even form to himself an idea of what is meant by a principle of order, distinct from the intelligence of the watch-maker.

Note that no one—including Charles Darwin, Richard Dawkins, and Kenneth Miller—has refuted Paley's argument as presented here. Indeed, it is interesting to see that in his five points he anticipates many theories of Creation that have been proposed even in recent years. The concept of irreducible complexity is clearly evident in his first paragraph. In his second, he notes (as does Behe) that we don't need to understand or know the watchmaker to know there was one. Even if the watch isn't perfect, the evidence of design is there. Even if we couldn't understand all the parts of the watch, we would still know that it had a maker. We wouldn't ever think that the watch came into being by itself from the materials on the heath. And finally, we would be hard to convince that some "principle of order" other than intelligent design helped it come into being.

Paley's detractors side-step the issue, as Behe (1996, pp. 210–16) nicely points out. Neither Dawkins nor any of the other detractors tells us how the watch was produced without a designer. Instead, they point out the imperfection of analogies leading to the small mistakes that Paley made, and such things. For example, in sections left out above, Paley specifically mentions that the wheels were brass to avoid rust and that the crystal protected the hands. Behe notes that these are not *essential* parts for the function of telling time. Paley could have honed his analogy to make it sharper, perhaps, but it continues to call our attention to the possible implications of biological as well as man-made complexity.

Actually, there is one way to refute Paley's argument, but it is not by claiming that complexity can be produced by natural selection (and to some *unknown* extent it can). The way to refute Paley is to point out that, analogies being imperfect, a watch with its designer may not be perfectly analogous to the natural world with its postulated Intelligent Creator; perhaps there is some way—and it could be natural selection when all the problems have been solved—to account for increasing complexity in the natural world without an Intelligent Creator. Science and logic can neither prove nor disprove the existence of God!

C

PHOTOSYNTHESIS, CELLULAR RESPIRATION, AND THE ATP SYNTHASE MOTOR

Virtually every metabolic reaction or the transport of some molecule involves an exchange of energy. For the most part, those reactions that require an energy input get their energy from adenosine triphosphate (ATP). Usually this means that one phosphate group is removed from the ATP, leaving ADP (adenosine diphosphate), with the energy of ATP being transferred to where it is required and with the phosphate being released. There must then be a mechanism to add the phosphate back to the ADP to restore ATP, and this mechanism will require an input of energy (because energy can neither be created nor destroyed, only transferred). We can think of three aspects of this process: *photosynthesis* (which captures the energy of light), *cellular respiration* (which "burns" various molecules, usually to produce CO_2 and H_2O, releasing the energy held in those molecules), and *ATP synthase* (which actually produces the ATP in response to conditions set up by photosynthesis or by cellular respiration). Biochemists studied these processes during much of the twentieth century, and they proved to be fiendishly complex with many of the earmarks of Michael Behe's irreducible complexity.

Chapters and books have been filled with descriptions of this complexity. Here, we'll have to be restricted to very brief overviews plus some illustrations of photosynthesis, respiration, and ATP synthase—the most marvelous molecular machine that I know about (with cilia and flagella running a close second). The following discussion is mostly condensed from a book by David Lawlor (2001).

Photosynthesis

Yes, it's those green chlorophyll molecules that capture the energy of light, but they aren't just floating around inside the chloroplasts. Some 300 to 400 chlorophyll molecules (made up of two kinds in higher plants) are grouped together (forming *photosystems*) in membranes in the chloroplast, with two molecules in each forming a *reaction center* (RC). As photons are absorbed by the various molecules, their energy is passed around until it reaches the RC. Absorption of the photons changes the RC so that is can accumulate electrons, which come from water through a complex of proteins that includes manganese atoms. As the electrons are removed from water, hydrogen ions (H^+) and oxygen (O_2) are released. The H^+ ions act later in the process; the O_2 is released to the environment. The electrons go from one RC through a series of protein/enzymes, ending at the RC of a second kind of photosystem and then being passed through more proteins. Various things happen at the proteins as the electrons move along the chains. At some enzyme steps, the energy from the electrons is used to pump H^+ ions to the inside of a double-membrane system. This pumping builds up a higher concentration of H^+ inside than outside the double-membrane system, and it is this concentration difference that drives the ATP synthase.

Some of the H^+ ions end up in another high-energy compound (abbreviated NADPH), and this compound, plus ATP, is used in a cycle of enzymatically controlled steps to "fix" CO_2 from the atmosphere and from it to form two kinds of three-carbon molecules, which can, in turn, combine and react to form sugars, starch, and ultimately all the molecules of life. Please note that all the pigments (chlorophyll and other light-absorbing molecules) and proteins must be arranged in a specific way within the chloroplasts, forming thousands of photosystems within each chloroplast, of which there are a few hundred within each green plant cell. Remember also that each protein is synthesized under the control of a specific gene, some genes being within the chloroplasts and others within the nucleus. Everything must be exactly coordinated or the system won't form and function.

Figures C-1 and C-2 (on the following page) illustrate the above discussion—and add a few details—but they are oversimplifications of the incredible complexity of photosynthesis.

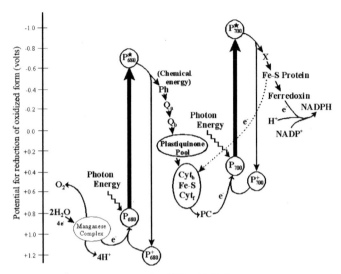

Figure C-1

The so-called Z-scheme. This diagram outlines the steps following absorption of light (photon energy) by two "reaction centers" (P_{680} & P_{700}) to the point where the energy from the light is converted into a compound called NADPH. Electrons (e-) move in such a way that hydrogen ions (H^+, not shown) are concentrated on one side of an internal chloroplast membrane. The details of the process won't be explained here, but basically, light energy raised the energy level of a reaction center, which then loses an electron and falls back to its original energy level, ready for another photon. The electrons go through many steps before NADPH is formed and H^+ ions have been pumped across a membrane. The point of this figure is only to illustrate the extreme complexity of just one part of photosynthesis.

Cellular Respiration

Cellular respiration takes place within the mitochondria (or within prokaryotic cells that don't have mitochondria). There, all kinds of molecules, especially sugars (glucose) are broken down in a highly complex series of steps called glycolysis, the citric-acid cycle, and the electron transport system. Over 50 enzymes are involved in these three systems.

THE CALVIN CYCLE

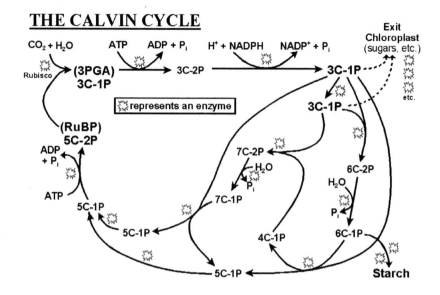

Figure C-2

The so-called Calvin Cycle. Using the energy in the form that it was produced in the first part of photosynthesis, carbon dioxide (CO_2) is taken through a series of highly complex reactions, each controlled by a special enzyme, until starch and other compounds are formed. Melvin Calvin at the University of California, Berkeley, received the Nobel Prize for working out this series of reactions, in which a compound abbreviated RuBP is combined with CO_2; the reactions eventually restore the RuBP. Each time six CO_2 molecules pass through the cycle, one six-carbon sugar molecule is produced (combined with phosphate); these molecules eventually form starch and all of the other molecules of life found in green plants.

(It is possible for glycolysis alone to produce some ATP in the absence of oxygen; this is often called fermentation.) As electrons are passed along the electron transport system, H^+ ions are again pumped to one side of a membrane system, producing a much higher concentration of H^+ on one side of the membrane than the other. Eventually, the electrons are combined (by cytochromes) with H^+ and O_2 to form H_2O, the carbon atoms from the sugars and such being released as CO_2. Except for the spectacular functions of plant pigments in capturing light energy, cellular respiration is as complex as photosynthesis. Again, we are dealing with highly organized groups of enzymes, each controlled by its gene (some genes in mitochondria, and some in the nucleus). A bottom line so far is that both photosynthesis and respiration cause a build-up of H^+ ions on one side of a membrane. And it is within those membranes that the amazing ATP synthase motor resides. Figure C-3 summarizes some of the complexity of cellular respiration.

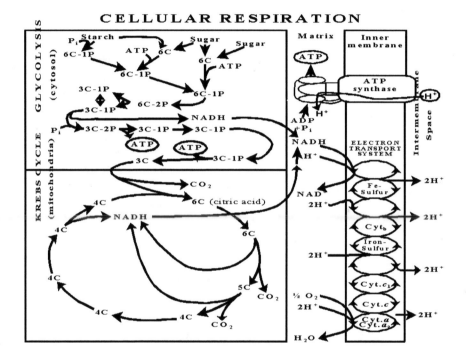

Figure C-3

The reactions of cellular respiration. This diagram illustrates the steps involved in three phases of cellular respiration: Glycolysis, the Krebs Cycle, and the Electron Transport System. Each step is controlled by a separate enzyme, all of which are synthesized on ribosomes in response to the RNA information coming from genes (at least one for each enzyme) located in the mitochondria or the cell's nucleus. Obviously, a full explanation of these three figures would require many pages, but the figures should make it clear that life at the cellular level consists of some complex molecular machinery, and this is duplicated many times in each chloroplast or mitochondrion.

ATP Synthase (ATPase)

In 1963, M. Avron detected a protein (protein complex, as it turns out) that when removed from the surface of certain membranes prevented ATP synthesis, which would resume when the protein complex was restored. This complex is called *coupling factor one* (CF_1). (The system *couples* H^+ movement through the membrane to ATP synthesis.) Then it was found that this complex was part of another complex that existed within the membrane itself, now called *coupling factor zero* (CF_0). By the 1990s, the various proteins of CF_1 and CF_0 were well understood, and it was even possible to visualize the complete *ATP synthase* structure and mode of operation (Boyer, 1997; McCarty et al., 2000; Stock, 1999). Although not everyone agrees on the details, here is a condensed description (see Figure C-4):

The part of the protein complex that is on the surface of the membrane (CF_1) is composed of five kinds of protein labeled with the Greek letters α (alpha), β (beta), γ (gamma), δ (delta), and ε (epsilon) in a ratio of 3:3:1:1:1. Their arrangement is shown in the figure. Much is known about the amino-acid sequences of these proteins and how they relate to function. For example, the amino acids of the α and β subunits at the point where the elongated γ unit contacts them are highly hydrophobic, so there are no hydrogen bonds between them and the tip of the γ protein. This point where all the α and β subunits meet acts as a bearing such that the γ unit can rotate as shown in the figure. The amazing thing about the complex is that it is a rotary motor that spins about 1000 times per second, achieving rapid ATP synthesis. (Indeed, both the synthesis and the use of ATP in cells is rapid, with a complete turnover about every half second.)

The CF_0 part of the synthase complex consists of three proteins, a, b, and c, in the ratio of 1:1:9–12. The c proteins form a ring within the membrane and make up the rotor of this molecular machine. Thanks to the steep gradient in H^+ ions (and electrical charge), there is a strong tendency for the H^+ to move through the CF_0, and the CF_0 is highly capable of allowing this to happen. Indeed, 200,000 H^+ ions can move through each complex each second, which is about a thousand times faster than ATP can be synthesized; hence, the synthesis of ATP actually limits the rate at which H^+ can move through CF_0. The H^+ ions move through a channel in the a-protein of the CF_0, and this movement is what causes the rotor, consisting of c-proteins, to spin. How that happens is not yet completely clear, although suggestions have been made. It appears that 9 to 12 H^+ must

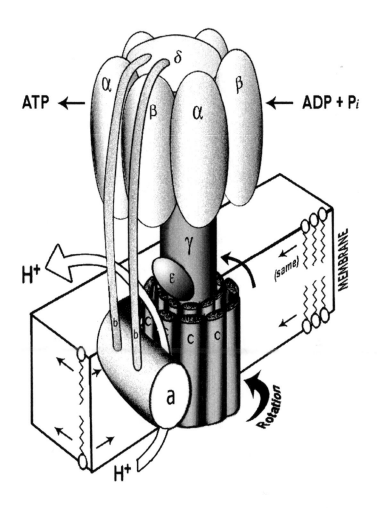

Figure C-4

The ATP-synthase molecular motor. Each single letter (except H^+ and P_i) repre-sents a protein. There are three molecules each of α and β, and one each of δ, γ, and ϵ. The rotor is shaded in the figure and consists of 10 c molecules plus one γ and one ϵ; this structure spins as H^+ ions move through molecule a. (The exact mechanism of how this works is unknown.) The two b molecules stabilize the structure where ATP synthesis takes place (α, β, and δ). As the rotor spins, it opens and closes a site in each α so that inorganic phosphate (P_i) can couple to ADP (adenosine di-phosphate), producing ATP (adenosine tri-phos-phate). Remember that this amazing piece of molecular machinery is duplicated thou-sands of time in every living cell and that each protein owes its functionality to the sequence of its amino acids. (Computer drawing by Tami Allen Salisbury) move through CF_0 for a single rotation. In chloroplasts, a single rotation produces three ATP molecules, so three to four H^+ ions are required for each ATP molecule that is synthesized.

The b-proteins form the attachment between the CF_0 and the δ protein of the CF_1, and rotation of the c-protein rotor causes the γ and ε proteins to spin along with the rotor. As the γ and ε-protein rotates, it acts as a cam to open and close active sites in the α-protein. There are three positions for each active site, and there is an active site on each of the three α-proteins of CF_1. In the first position of a given active site, the site is open, and in that configuration it can accept a molecule of ADP plus an inorganic phosphate. Then, as the cam spins by, the site is closed, allowing the ADP and the P_i to bond, forming ATP. As the cam passes, the site again opens, releasing the ATP. All of this is possible because of the detailed configuration of the active site caused by the amino-acid sequences that make it up. Because of that configuration, of the thousands of possible kinds of molecules in the vicinity of the active site, only ADP and P_i will fit into their proper places where the energy of the spin can cause them to form the bond needed to make ATP. In photosynthesis, that energy was initially the energy of the photons absorbed by the chlorophyll and other pigment molecules, or it is the energy produced by oxidation in cellular respiration.

The Challenge of ATP Synthase

David Lawlor (2001, p. 129) notes in his discussion of the ATP synthase that it is "the first and smallest rotary mechanism known in biology." His description of the mechanism made me draw in my breath in wonder. If ever there was an irreducibly complex piece of living machinery, the ATP synthase rotary motor in particular and photosynthesis in general should qualify. This never seems to occur to Lawlor, or if it did, he did not feel compelled to mention it. Instead, in virtually every chapter of his fine book, there is a sentence or two paying his respects to neo-Darwinian evolution. In Lawlor's ATP chapter, he says:

> It has been described by Boyer (1997) as a "splendid molecular machine," a fitting description of what is a nano-sized rotary motor, driven by protons [H^+ ions] and coupled to the active catalytic sites of ATP synthesis. Coupling factors are of very similar subunit structure in all organisms, with extensive homology in the amino acids of the polypeptides of the subunits. Clearly, the nature of coupling factor and

the mode of catalysis were developed early in evolution and, despite the great changes that organisms have undergone since, the enzyme has not changed radically.

So, the complexity of the ATP machine and its presence in all living things merely indicates that it came into being so early in the game of evolution that all living things have descended from the cell where it first appeared (but in what cell that didn't already need ATP?), as the result, of course, of tiny mutations, each with selection value until eventually the whole system had evolved. Well, maybe so, but can you blame anyone for doubting? Whatever he might say in his excellent review of photosynthesis, Lawlor must not mention the possibility of an Intelligent Creation (and yes, that *would* be out of place). Yet the first article of faith of modern biology is that everything can be accounted for by neo-Darwinian mechanisms; that is simply taken for granted. Although his book is not about evolution, Lawlor feels compelled to pay homage to the doctrine anyway.

APPENDIX D

EVOLUTION, NATURAL SELECTION, AND THE CHURCH OF JESUS CHRIST OF LATTER-DAY SAINTS

The original envisioned audience for this book included people of all faiths or no faith, with only a few being members of my own church. Thus, I referred to my theology only in a few places where I just couldn't resist. It now appears that members of my church may make up a significant portion of the audience.

There is, however, a considerable division among the members of my church about the topics of this book. There are those who sympathize with the young-earth creationists who might think my book is far too liberal because I reject that viewpoint. There are also those who think evolution, even of humans, was God's mechanism of creation, and they might think my book is far too conservative because I wonder if natural selection based on purely random mutations will really work on a grand scale. That's the danger of being a fence-sitter: It's impossible to please anybody. (Actually, there are also many others in my church with philosophies like mine, in between these extremes.) In any case, some LDS readers might not be aware of the divisions within the Church, so I feel that I need to summarize three points:

First, different leaders within the church (the general authorities, as we call them) have, during the past century or so, expressed vastly different viewpoints about the means of creation. In addition to various commentaries that touch on these matters, I am aware of six excellent summaries: Ash (2002); Jeffery (1974); Jeffery and Norman (2002); Evenson and Jeffrey (2005); Numbers (1992, pp. 308–14); and Talmage (2001). Except for Jeffery and Norman, which is an interview with Duane E. Jeffery, these summaries include many documented quotations from the General Authorities. (See also Stephens et al., 2001.) This material is far too extensive to repeat, but here are a few summary ideas:

Beginning not long after Darwin (1859) published *The Origin*, members of the church have held differing opinions on evolution and the origin of humans. Finally, in 1909, the First Presidency issued an official statement regarding this matter (*Improvement Era*, November, 1909, pp. 75–81) in which it was stated that Adam was "the first man of all men" (Moses 1:34), but the statement did not take an official position on evolution in general, even leaving open the possibility that Adam was the product of an evolutionary process (neither accepting nor rejecting the idea).

The controversy continued, especially at the Brigham Young University. Some of the apostles and other general authorities took an interest in the matter, but two diametrically opposed schools of thought developed. Joseph Fielding Smith, who became an Apostle in 1910 at age thirty-three, was strongly opposed to the "theory of evolution," and even became enamored with the writings of George McCready Price who espoused and defended a young-earth flood geology (see Appendix A). Smith corresponded with Price and based much of his thinking on Price's arguments. Price held, based on Genesis, that there was no death of any organism before the Fall. This was an old sectarian doctrine, but Smith found support for it in the Book of Mormon (2 Nephi 2:22), although that scripture is open to other interpretations. Clearly, the concept of no death before the Fall means that *all* the organisms that became fossils were alive *after* Adam and Eve, and most were killed in the Flood. The doctrine also means that there were no carnivorous animals and that plants that are eaten did not die. These concepts are impossible for a biologist to accept.

In 1927, Elder Brigham H. Roberts (see two versions of his works, both published with extensive commentaries in 1994), one of the Seven Presidents of the Seventy (since 1888), began preparing notes that he hoped would become a study guide for the Seventies Quorums. There were chapters in which Roberts considered favorably the possibility that there were human beings before Adam ("pre-Adamites") and that the evolution of species was a likely possibility. He suggested that these pre-Adamites were destroyed in a great cataclysm after which Adam and Eve were placed on the earth (see appendix A: "4. The Gap or Ruin-and-Restoration Interpretation of the Genesis Account"). Roberts's notes were submitted to a publication committee consisting of five Apostles, who rejected his work primarily because of his stand on pre-Adamites. This led to much controversy among the Brethren, especially with Joseph Fielding Smith on the young-earth side and three scientifically trained Apostles on the side of an ancient earth and evolution, sometimes with misgivings, James E. Talmage (a respected geologist and broadly trained scientist), John A. Widtsoe (who had a Ph.D. in biochemistry from the University of Göttingen in Germany), and Joseph F. Merrill (also a scientist). There was also much correspondence on the topics of creationism and evolution between Elder Talmage and his son, Sterling Talmage (2001), also a geologist.

By 1954, most of the General Authorities with viewpoints favorable to evolution had passed away, leaving little opposition to Joseph Fielding Smith's views. He then published *Man: His Origin and Destiny*, in which he expanded on the creationist approach of Price, emphasizing such ideas as a young earth and no death before the Fall. He went so far as to say (p. 276) that one cannot be a "true member of the Church" and "accept organic evolution." This book was met with both opposition and praise, and it can be thought of as the beginning of a fundamentalist and anti-science stance among many members of the Church. Joseph Fielding Smith's opinions were supported by his son-in-law, Elder Bruce R. McConkie, and the explosives chemist, Melvin A. Cook (professor of metallurgy at the University of Utah). He was opposed by many other scientists, including Henry Eyring, Dean of the Graduate School at the University of Utah, and William Lee Stokes, head of the Department of Geology at the University of Utah.[1]

Although many members of the Church, probably a higher percentage than at the beginning of the twentieth century, currently espouse the views of Joseph Fielding Smith, many others, and especially those with some training in the sciences, take the opposite viewpoint, while remaining strong and active members of the Church. (My position is clear. I greatly admire Joseph Fielding Smith, Bruce R. McConkie, Melvin A. Cook, and others who took the anti-evolution stance—but I disagree with their views on evolution.)

Perhaps the best illustration of support for evolutionary theory within the Church is the approach taken at BYU, a university owned by the Church (see Ash, 2002, p. 33). Zoology 475 is a course in evolutionary biology that has been taught for at least the past fifteen years, and the First Presidency has given its approval for the course. Indeed, evolutionary biology is one of the largest and most successful graduate programs at BYU. It seems like the Utah news media report some new BYU study on fossils, especially the dinosaurs, about every week or so, noting the estimated ages of their finds in the tens of millions of years. Many of the biologists at BYU are involved in research that depends upon their full acceptance of evolutionary theory, including natural selection. Thus, it is safe to say that many of the LDS faithful are not upset by the concept that creation followed natural principles.

Second, the above-mentioned sources clearly show that the Church (specifically, the First Presidency) has never taken an official stand on evolution or the origin of humans, except to say that Adam was a real person and the progenitor of the human race. In 1957, William Lee Stokes wrote a letter to President David O. McKay inquiring about the Church's position on Smith's book and theories. President McKay's response is often quoted: "On the subject of organic evolution the Church has officially taken no position. The book *Man; His Origin and Destiny* was not published by the Church and is not approved by the Church. The book contains expressions of the author's views for which he alone is responsible."[2] The documents referenced above contain many other statements of this kind, which emphasize that the Church has avoided any official statement on organic evolution.

Third, let me once again state my views as a scientist and active, practicing member of The Church of Jesus Christ of Latter-day Saints, this time with a few additions:

The doctrine that Adam (with Eve) was the progenitor and great leader of the human race as it now exists is so central to our theology that I accept it completely, but I wonder how it will some day be reconciled with the findings of science, though I'm sure that it will. That reconciliation has been promised in Doctrine and Covenants 101:32–34: "Yea, verily I say unto you, in that day when the Lord shall come, he shall reveal all things— Things which have passed, and hidden things which no man knew, things of the earth, by which it was made, and the purpose and the end thereof— Things most precious, things that are above, and things that are beneath, things that are in the earth, and upon the earth, and in heaven." I have called this time of revelation "The Millennial Symposium." It would be wonderful to attend.

I accept the doctrine that we are spirit children of God, created in his image, but again, I have no idea about how this was accomplished. The placing of a spirit into a human body that was the product of evolution is a possibility, but I suspect that it was not that straight forward.

I totally reject young-earth, flood geology; the evidence for an ancient earth on the order of 4.65 billion years old is overwhelming.

I accept the doctrine that an Intelligent Creator was responsible for the creation of the earth in its present state, although I don't know how it was done. It seems clear to me that the Creator must have intervened in creation, but I have no idea of the extent of that intervention, whether it was minor or major.

Natural selection as Darwin and Wallace proposed it is a process that operates in nature; much of its operation is conservative, but I don't know how much leads to evolution in the broad sense—probably a lot over the long time intervals involved in earth's history.

Random mutations clearly function in nature, but there is no way for us to know whether some mutations are or were influenced by an Intelligent Creator.

If evolution was the mechanism of creation, it must have been guided to reach the Creator's goals (an idea totally rejected by most biologists, especially the atheistic ones).

I support the general authorities of my church as my ecclesiastical leaders without reservation, but realize that it is my right to disagree with their personal opinions, as they have stated.

NOTES

Preface

1. I'll capitalize Creation when it refers to Creation by God; when discussing atheistic creation, I'll use lower case.
2. Here's my translation of the German definition from *Meyers Grosses Handlexikon in Farbe.* (1983; 13th Edition. Meyers Lexikonverlag, Mannheim, Wien, Zürich): Weltanschauung: Collective conception of the universe, from nature and the essence of man and his history, growing out of previous nonrational intuition or out of a scientific world picture. [Gesamtauffassung vom Weltganzen, von der Natur, dem Wesen des Menschen und seiner Geschichte, entstanden aus Vorwissen irrationaler Intuition oder aus wissenschaftlichem Weltbild.]

Chapter 1

1. The law of gravity is not that apples fall from trees—that had been noticed before Isaac Newton. The law is Newton's mathematical formulation that predicted, to a high degree of accuracy, such things as how the Moon orbits the Earth. Basically, it states that the gravitational attraction between two

bodies is proportional to the product of their masses and inversely proportional to the square of the distances between them.

2. Incidentally, the God of the Old Testament is by no means always a tyrant; see Micah 6:8; Ezekiel 18; Isaiah 1:18; and many other scriptures.

3. The examples of testimony and revelation that follow are based on the *Christian* God, in whom I believe. Yet it is my conviction that God might, for his own purposes, allow different cultures among his children to understand him in different ways. Ultimately, however, I believe that there can be only one true description of the real God (and it is likely that no one on Earth knows that true description). A verse from my religion from The Book of Mormon, expresses the thought so well that I'm constrained to quote it. "For behold, the Lord doth grant unto all nations, of their own nation and tongue, to teach his word, yea, in wisdom, all that he seeth fit that they should have; therefore we see that the Lord doth counsel in wisdom, according to that which is just and true" (Alma 29:8).

4. Two books from the evangelical literature serve as good examples of scholars who accept the accounts. The logic of Frank Morison (1930) in *Who Moved the Stone?* is impressive. I also found the logic penetrating and the scholarship excellent in a book by Lee Strobel (1998), *The Case for Christ: A Journalist's Personal Investigation of the Evidence for Jesus.* Strobel relates interviews with thirteen Bible scholars, providing *data* that counter such movements as the so-called Jesus Seminar, which rejects essentially everything supernatural found in the New Testament writings.

5. Most scientists and theologians of that time, like Paley and Ray, accepted Creation virtually as a given.

6. Astronomer Royal Martin Rees (2000) in *Just Six Numbers* (see also an article by Rees in the July 2000 *Astronomy* magazine, pages 54–59) describes six physical constants that, if they varied only slightly, would radically change the way the universe functions. Was the suitability of these numbers coincidence, the product of design (God), or is there an infinite number of universes, and just ours happens to be the one in which these numbers allow our kind of life? Rees tends to favor the explanation of an infinite number of universes (which we'll briefly mention in chapter 5). This is another notion that science can't really prove (although science can narrow the possibilities).

Most evangelical theologians believe that current scientific concepts of the "big bang" support the doctrine of creation ex nihilo—creation of time, matter, and energy out of nothing. This is their interpretation of Genesis 1:1: "In the beginning, God created the heaven and the earth." That is, in the beginning God initiated the big bang. The arguments presented by these theologians are summarized in some detail by Lee Strobel (2004). Kenneth Miller (1999, p. 194) also seems to assume that God created the universe at the big bang. (My own theology rejects creation ex nihilo.)

7. We probably know more about the life of Charles Darwin than we do about

almost any other historical character. Darwin kept extensive diaries, and virtually all of his correspondence, notebooks, and other materials were meticulously archived. Most have by now been published, some as recently as the 1990s. Biographies that I consulted include:

> Adrian Desmond & James Moore (1991). This is probably the most definitive biography of Charles Darwin, portraying him very much within his times.
> Irving Stone (1980). Although written in the style of a novel, this book is historically accurate and easy to read.
> Patrick Tort (2000). This small book is filled with illustrations, many in color.
> Janet Browne (2002). This book concentrates on the second half of Darwin's life.

8. The idea of natural selection was called the "Struggle for Existence" by Ernst Haeckel (1834–1919), and it was Herbert Spencer (1820–1903) who coined the phrase "the Survival of the Fittest." Darwin disliked Spencer but borrowed his phrase because it was so descriptive (see Tort, 2000, pp. 130 and pp. 133–35).
9. Wallace's paper was published just as he submitted it to Darwin (see Wallace, 1858). It has recently been reprinted in Jane R. Camerini (2002, pp. 142–51). I have not seen Darwin's papers, but they were probably modified before publication.
10. Because of this, I at first tried to avoid use of *theory* in relation to evolution, but it is still the term found in many books on evolution, and I finally gave up trying to avoid it. I'll agree that the "theory" of evolution is as well established as many other modern "theories" such as the big bang, plate tectonics, and so on.

Chapter 2

1. Evolution from animals with tails to humans may be called *phylogeny*. When I was a student, this idea was summarized by the phrase: *ontogeny recapitulates phylogeny*, and I loved to spout that phrase among my nonbiologist friends.
2. Petroski (1992) mentions a book called *The Evolution of Technology* (Basalla, 1988) and tells about the evolution of the paper clip in an article called "The Evolution of Artifacts."
3. Some time ago, based on figures for dolomites, limestones, coal, and bitumen in my old geochemistry text (Mason, 1951), I calculated 163 kilograms of "flesh"/cm^2 (1,630 metric tons/m^2). Considering just coal and bitumen alone, the figure came out to 16.9 kg/cm^2. More modern estimates would not reduce these figures. ("Flesh" includes mostly algae and other plants, but animals as well.)

Writing in the 1920s and 1930s, Vladimir Vernadsky (2005) gave figures for the quantities of fossilized organic matter; the quantities were even larger than those in Mason's text.

Incidentally, note the tremendous importance of *life* in removing all that carbon from Earth's atmosphere, originally spewed into the atmosphere as CO_2 from volcanoes. If that carbon still existed as atmospheric CO_2, our planet would be a boiling caldron nearly as hot as Venus.

4. Miller (1999, pp. 69–72) nicely summarizes the evidence from radioactive decay, including the interesting fact that no elements with half lives of less than 80 million years (all created in the laboratory) are found naturally on earth, except for those that are being created continually, such as carbon 14, which is created in our upper atmosphere when a nitrogen atom absorbs a free neutron.

5. I recently encountered the story again in a book by Martin Gardner (2000, pp. 7–14). *Omphalos* appears in various anti-creationist books, and all that I've read state that it is logically infallible.

6. The National Geographic Society provided a grant to David Lordkipanidze, the Georgian scientist whose team found the skull. The find is described in the August 2002 issue of the National Geographic magazine (Gore, 2002).

7. This is an important part of creationist *flood geology*, outlined in many creationist books but especially in Morris and Whitcomb (1964), noted above.

8. J. John Sepkoski Jr (1993) tells about the Burgess Shale, an outcropping of rock only about 60 meters long and 2.5 meters thick, which was discovered in British Columbia, Canada, in 1909, by Charles Doolittle Walcott, secretary of the Smithsonian Institution. He eventually collected 65,000 Cambrian fossils from this small formation, and it has been studied by many others since. Some 120 or more animal species found in the Shale provide much insight into that early Cambrian period. Many specimens are strange and otherwise unknown to science.

9. The creationist Jonathan Wells (2000, pp. 29–58), for example, in his book *Icons of Evolution*, gives details of the Cambrian explosion story, suggesting that biology students are being misled.

Chapter 3

1. In manuscript versions of this book, I tried to reach that goal by writing more than two hundred pages in five long chapters. Although those chapters were still just an outline of our knowledge, the book would have been so large that few would have bothered to read it. Hence, I'll have to settle for a brief overview in this chapter. If you have never studied the material in this chapter, the going could be rough. But stick with it and remember that there is no simple way to explain the complexity of living cells. *Simple* and *complex* don't mix. I'll try to help with a few illustrations and by

italicizing some important terms—just like in a textbook!

2. Actually, Dobzhansky, a deeply religious person, argues in the article that evolution and belief in God are compatible; he summarized his views as follows. "The organic diversity becomes, however, reasonable and understandable if the Creator has created the living world not by caprice but by evolution propelled by natural selection. It is wrong to hold creation and evolution as mutually exclusive alternatives. I am a creationist *and* an evolutionist. Evolution is God's, or Nature's, method of Creation." Many religious biologists reconcile their faith this way.

3. See the Protein Data Bank at http://www.rcsb.org/pdb/.

Chapter 4

1. It seems to me that the nature of nucleic acid or protein information is easier to understand than is the information of a written sentence, because that information depends on a brain that understands the language, and at that point, our comprehension of how the process works breaks down. Still, although imperfect, language information as an analogy for protein information can be useful, as we'll see.

2. We could fill pages speculating on the nature of *complexity*. Suffice it to say, based on our intuition of how things are, that a machine is *complex* if it is capable of some fairly intricate function and if it must be fairly intricate to accomplish its task. An automobile is obviously complex; I'd say a can opener is also complex, though much less complex than an automobile, and capable of far fewer functions. An enzyme is complex to the extent that it can catalyze reactions. But obviously, there is much more to *complexity* than that.

3. I'll admit that, to make things less laborious, I also converted from a thirty-letter alphabet to a 10-letter number system by using logarithms (a little more than simple multiplication but not much):

$$10^X = 30^{45}, X \log 10 = 45 \log 30, X = 45 \times 1.477 = 66.47; 10^{66.47} = 2.954 \times 10^{66}$$

4. Earth's surface: 5.10501×10^8 km^2, times 10^{12} dm^3/km^3 times $2 = 1.021 \times 10^{21}$ computers, times 3.1557×10^{16} sentences/year $\cdot$ computer $= 3.1557 \times 10^{37}$ sen/earth $\cdot$ y; divide that figure into 2.954×10^{66} sentences to get 9.36×10^{28} years.

5. Actually, this would be true if we started with a sentence of *any* length. If the sentence were only one letter long, however, the result would not have any real meaning. A short sentence, say six letters long, would produce all possible words or fragments of words and thus fragments of sentences, but still not much meaning. A twenty-letter sentence would produce a much smaller data base and much smaller sentence fragments than our 45-letter sentence.

6. Such ruminations became possible after we learned the importance of *sequence*. I first got involved in the big numbers game with a book

published for members of my church (Salisbury, 1965, pp. 148–50). And a seminar on the big-numbers problem was held and published, but only a few participants really grasped the seriousness of the problem (Moorhead and Kaplan, 1967).

I further published some big numbers in *Nature*, perhaps the granddaddy of scientific journals (Salisbury, 1969). That paper was "answered" in *Nature* by the famous evolutionist John Maynard Smith (1969), but it was then defended by a mathematician from MIT (Spetner, 1970). I had two more publications on the topic (Salisbury, 1971 and 1976).

7. This group also has a website with a list of their many publications and the several different enzymes with which they have worked: http://chem. che.caltech.edu/groups/fha.

8. Robert Shapiro, personal communication.

9. Some of the cytochrome *c* discussion here is modified from Salisbury (1976, pp. 254–65).

Chapter 5

1. Darling (2001, p. 39). Darling's chapter 3, Star Seed, is an excellent review of this topic. See also Bailey et al. (1998), an article in which it is suggested that polarized light in space might control right or left "handedness" in molecules that were being formed; see also Alper (2002).

2. Although much of the discussion of the next few pages emphasizes Shapiro's (1986,1999) approach to the problems of the RNA world in particular and soupy-seas scenarios in general, McFadden (2000, see especially pp. 95–98) also has an excellent discussion of the problems involved.

3. See especially two technical reports in *Science*, 4 May 2001: Ysupov et al. (2001) and Ogle et al. (2001). These studies confirm the role of both ribosomal protein and rRNA in protein synthesis on ribosomes.

Chapter 6

1. According to the cover of *The Blind Watchmaker* (Dawkins, 1985), a review in *The Economist* says, "As readable and vigorous a defense of Darwinism as has been published since 1859," and, "Acclaimed as perhaps the most influential work on evolution written in this century." There is even a website by John Catalano devoted to "The World of Richard Dawkins," with the disclaimer that "This web site is unofficial, and Richard Dawkins is NOT associated with it." (However, it illustrates that some of his fans come close to worshiping him.) The site contains a voluminous amount of material relating to Dawkins's writings and activities. (See: www.world-of-dawkins.com)

2. Some examples of books, articles, and a web site that try to answer

Behe: Eldredge (2000), Gardner (2000), Pennock (1999, 2001), Dorit (1997), and Miller (1999). The web site edited by John Catalana contains numerous references (most of them incomplete) to anti-Behe articles, as well as to articles that (might) show examples of how irreducible complexity has been explained; that is, how various complex systems might have evolved (articles with rather plausible just-suppose stories). (See http://www.world-of-dawkins.com/box/published.htm.)

3. A good example of the angst that sometimes appears in the anti-creationist literature is found in Pennock (2001). This book claims to present both sides of the intelligent-design story, but in my browsing of the book (one could spend weeks reading it carefully), it seems to consist of a few articles by intelligent-design creationists, included as strawmen for other authors to knock down. For example, there is an article by Michael Behe (chapter 10) originally published in 1998, which is essentially an abstract of *Darwin's Black Box*. I can't find any response of Behe to his critics, but there are numerous articles claiming to answer the intelligent-design hypothesis. The title of chapter 1, by Barbara Forrest, says it all. "The Wedge at work: How intelligent design creationism is wedging its way into the cultural and academic mainstream." The Wedge group includes Behe, Phillip Johnson, and other intelligent-design creationists. The Forrest chapter includes 130 footnotes, many of them containing more than one reference; these would be a rich source of information if one had the months necessary for a detailed study of the movement and its opponents. Many of these references are to web sites, where much of the discussion has apparently taken place.

4. A *cilium* (plural: *cilia*) is a structure on the surface of a eukaryotic cell that looks like a relatively short hair and beats like a whip, moving the cell or moving some substance (mucus) on its surface; if the "hair" is longer, it may be called a *flagellum* (plural: *flagella*). Bacterial cells may have similar "hairs," and they are called *flagella*, but their microscopic structure and mechanism of action are different from those of eukaryotic cells.

Chapter 7

1. This is because quantum mechanics states that there is no way to predict which atom of radium will give off radiation at any given moment, or to predict which direction the radiation will go. According to Miller, those phenomena are governed by the uncertainty principle.

2. Larson and Withal (1999) point out: "Science and religion are engaging in more active dialogue and debate, but a survey suggests that scientists' beliefs have changed little since the 1930s, and top scientists are more atheistic than ever before."

3. An oft-quoted spokesman is Phillip E. Johnson, who has written several

books, including *Darwin on Trial* (Johnson, 1991 & 1993), and *Reason in the Balance: The Case Against Naturalism in Science, Law, and Education* (1995).

Appendix A

1. Raël (1986) is an official account of the movement. There are many details on the Raëlian website, http://www.rael.org/english/pages/home. html. A website designed to counter the Raëlian movement is http://skepdic.com/raelian.html. This website says, among other things, that "Raël's success seems to derive from providing a structured environment for decadent behavior: He offers a no-guilt playground for hedonism and sexual experimentation." My brief summary here is from a longer account found in Pennock (1999, pp. 233–40).

2. *Elohim* is the Hebrew plural of *El*, the word for God.

3. The index to Pennock's (1999) book includes 193 references to Johnson and his ideas.

Appendix D

1. It seems worth noting that, to the best of my knowledge, and others have confirmed this in private conversations, Joseph Fielding Smith did not press his views on evolution in particular and science in general after he became president of the Church.

2. This letter, which is quoted here from Ash (2002, p. 29), also appears in a brief paper by Stokes (pp. xli–xliii) that is included in Sterling B. Talmadge's *Can Science be Faith-Promoting*, edited by Stan Larson (2001).

I was personally deeply troubled by Smith's book when it came out, and a few years later when I was thinking of writing on the subject, I traveled to Salt Lake City from Fort Collins, Colorado (where I was a professor at Colorado State University), to talk with Apostle Spencer W. Kimball (with whom I had had some dealings). After saying that he knew little about the science involved in evolutionary theory and had no personal convictions on the matter, he told me essentially the same thing that President McKay wrote in his letter to Stokes, that the book expressed Elder Smith's ideas, which were not to be considered Church doctrine.

GLOSSARY

Angstroms: A unit of measurement equal to one hundred-millionth of a centimeter, used especially to specify wavelengths. Also called "Angstrom Unit."

Anthropocentrism: Regarding human beings as the central element of the universe; interpreting reality exclusively in terms of human values and experience.

Anthropoid: Belonging to the group of great apes of the family Pongidae; resembling a human; characteristic of an ape; apelike.

Catalysis: The action of a catalyst, especially an increase in the rate of a chemical reaction.

Catastrophism: The doctrine that major changes in the earth's crust result from catastrophies rather than evolutionary processes.

Deductive logic: A process of reasoning in which the conclusion is guaranteed to follow from the premises, given that they are based upon facts.

Deleterious: Having a harmful effect; injurious.

Diatoms: Any of various microscopic one-celled or colonial algae of the class *Bacillariophyceae*, having cell walls of silica consisting of two interlocking symmetrical valves.

Homologous: Similar in structure and evolutionary origin, though not necessarily in function, as the flippers of a seal and the hands of a human; having the same morphology and linear sequence of gene loci as another chromosome.

Inductive logic: A process of reasoning in which the conclusion of an argument is likely to be true, but not certain, given the premises.

Metamorphoses: A change in the form and often habits of an animal during normal development after the embryonic stage.

Morphology: The branch of biology that deals with the form and structure of organisms without consideration of function; the form and structure of an organism or one of its parts.

Ontogeny: The origin and development of an individual organism from embryo to adult.

Pangenesis: A theory of heredity proposed by Charles Darwin in which gemmules containing hereditary information from every part of the body coalesce in the gonads and are incorporated into the reproductive cells.

Panspermia: The theory that microorganisms or biochemical compounds from outer space are responsible for originating life on Earth and possibly in other parts of the universe where suitable conditions exist.

Superposition: The geological principle that in a group of stratified sedimentary rocks, the lowest were the earliest to be deposited.

Syllogism: A form of reasoning consisting of a major premise, a minor premise, and a conclusion; reasoning from general to specific; deduction.

Tautology: An empty or vacuous statement composed of simpler statements in a fashion that makes it logically true whether the simpler statements are factually true or false.

Teleology: The study of design or purpose in natural phenomena; the use of ultimate purpose or design as a means of explaining phenomena.

Uniformitarianism: The theory that all geologic phenomena can be explained as the result of existing forces having operated uniformly from the origin of the Earth to the present time.

Weltanschauung: German; literally, "worldview"; the overall perspective from which one sees and interprets the world.

SOURCES

Achenbach, Joel. 2006 (March). The Origin of Life . . . Through Chemistry. National Geographic, p. 31.

Alper, Joe. 2002 (November). It came from outer space. *Astronomy*. pp. 36–41. This article includes a summary of recent studies of meteorites and formation of organics in space; also, the estimate of how much meteor dust falls on Earth each day.

Arnold, Frances H. 1999. Unnatural selection: Molecular sex for fun and profit. *Engineering & Science* [The Caltech alumni journal], No 1 / 2, pp. 40–50.

Ash, Michael R. 2002. The Mormon Myth of Evil Evolution. *Dialogue: A Journal of Mormon Thought* 35 (4):19–38.

Bailey, Jeremy, Antonio Chrysostomou, J. H. Hough, T. M. Gledhill, Alan McCall, Stuart Clark, François Ménard, and Motohide Tamura. 1998. Circular polarization in star-formation regions: Implications for biomolecular homochirality. *Science* 281:672–74. (See also the perspective by Robert Irion on pp. 626–27 of that issue.) This article suggests how polarized light in space might control right or left "handedness" during formation of molecules.

Basalla, George. 1988. *The Evolution of Technology*. Cambridge Univ. Press, New York.

Behe, Michael J. 1996. *Darwin's Black Box, Biochemical Challenges to Evolution*. Touchstone Simon and Schuster (first Touchstone edition 1998), New York, New York.

Behe, Michael J., William A. Dembski, and Stephen C. Meyer. 2000. *Science and Evidence for Design in the Universe*. Wethersfield Institute Proceedings, 1999. Ignatius Press, San Francisco.

Bleckmann, Charles A. 2006. Evolution and Creationism in Science: 1880–2000. *BioScience* 156(2):151–58.

Bolles, Edmund Blair. 2004. *Einstein Defiant. Genius versus Genius in the Quantum Revolution* Joseph Henry Press, Washington, D.C.

Bonner, James F. 1994. Chapters from my life. *Annual Review of Plant Physiology and Plant Molecular Biology* 54:1–23.

Boyer, Paul D. 1997. The ATP synthase—a splendid molecular machine. *Annual Review of Biochemistry* 66:717–49. (Lawlor, 2001, describes the ATP synthase structure on pp. 128–34.)

Brown, Janet. 2002. *Charles Darwin: The Power of Place*. Alfred A. Knopf, New York. This book, a second volume of a Darwin biography, covers the period after publication of *The Origin*.

Cairns-Smith, A. Graham. 1985. *Seven Clues to the Origin of Life: A Scientific Detective Story*. Cambridge University Press, Cambridge.

Camerini, Jane R. (ed). 2002. *The Alfred Russel Wallace Reader: A Selection of Writings from the Field*. The Johns Hopkins University Press, Baltimore & London.

Crease, Robert P. and Charles C. Mann. 1986. *The Second Creation: Makers of the Revolution in 20th-Century Physics*. MacMillan Publishing Company, New York.

Dahlberg, Albert E. 2001. The ribosome in action. *Science* 292; 868–69.

Danielson, Dennis Richard (ed). 2000. *The Book of the Cosmos, Imagining the Universe from Heraclitus to Hawking*. Helix Books, Perseus Publishing, Cambridge, Massachusetts.

Darling, David. 2001. *Life Everywhere: The Maverick Science of Astrobiology*. Basic Books, New York.

Darling, David. 2005. *Teleportation: The Impossible Leap*. John Wiley & Sons, Hoboken, New Jersey.

Darwin, Charles R. 1859. *The Origin of Species by Means of Natural Selection or the Preservation of Favoured Races in the Struggle for Life*. Although the book was first published in 1859, it eventually appeared in six editions, each extensively edited by Darwin with answers to his critics and addition of other new material. It has since been published in various versions. Mine is an old paper-back copy (sixth edition, 1872) published by Collier Books of Collier-MacMillan Ltd, London, in 1962 (1969 printing), with a Foreword by George Gaylord Simpson.

Darwin, Charles R. 1860. *The Voyage of The Beagle*. Several versions of Darwin's account of the voyage are available. My copy (1962) was edited by Leonard Engel and was published by Doubleday and The American Museum of Natural History (Anchor Books) in Garden City, New York. The 1860 edition was the last to be revised by Darwin; the first edition appeared in 1839.

Darwin, Erasmus. 1794–796. *Zoonomia or the Laws of Organic Life*. In this volume, Charles Darwin's grandfather, Erasmus, published his ideas of evolution—and wrote his theories in verse! His proposed mechanism of evolution was essentially the inheritance of acquired traits later published by Lamarck, who is usually given credit for the concept. It is interesting that Charles often cited Lamarck's work but never mentioned his grandfather.

Darwin, Francis (ed). 1892. *The Autobiography of Charles Darwin and Selected Letters*. The version of this book that I have (which is an exact copy of the 1892 publication) was first published by Dover Publications, Inc., New York, in 1958.

Dawkins, Richard. 1976 (second edition, 1989). *The Selfish Gene*. Oxford University Press, Oxford.

Dawkins, Richard. 1986 (new introduction added in 1996). *The Blind Watchmaker*. W. W. Norton & Co., New York.

Dawkins, Richard. 1995. *River Out of Eden*. Basic Books, New York.

Dawkins, Richard. 1996. *Climbing Mount Improbable*. W. W. Norton & Co., New York and London.

Dawkins, Richard. 1998. *Unweaving the Rainbow*. Allen Lane/Penguin Press, London.

Dawkins, Richard. 2003. *A Devil's Chaplain. Reflections on Hope, Lies, Science, and Love*. Houghton Mifflin Co., Boston & New York.

Dawkins, Richard. 2004. *The Ancestor's Tale: A Pilgrimage to the Dawn of Evolution*. Houghton Mifflin Do., Boston & New York.

de Duve, Christian. 1995. The beginnings of life on Earth. *American Scientist* 83:428–37.

de Duve, Christian. 2002. *Life Evolving: Molecules, Mind, and Meaning*. Oxford University Press, New York.

Delsemme, Armand H. 2001. An argument for the cometary origin of the biosphere. *American Scientist* 89:432–42.

Dembski, William A. 1998. *The Design Inference*. Cambridge University Press, Cambridge.

Desmond, Adrian & James Moore. 1991. *Darwin: The Life of a Tormented Evolutionist*. W. W. Norton, New York. Many references in this book are to *Correspondence of Charles Darwin*, edited by F. Burkhardt and S. Smith, and published 1985–1991 in seven volumes by Cambridge University press, Cambridge.

Dobzhansky, Theodosius. 1973. Nothing in biology makes sense except in the light of evolution. *The American Biology teacher* 35:125–29.

Doolittle, Russell F. 1993. The evolution of vertebrate blood coagulation: A case of yin and yang. *Thrombosis and Haemostasis* 70:24–28.

Dorit, Robert. 1997. Molecular evolution and scientific inquiry, misperceived. *American Scientist* 85:474–75. This is a review of *Darwin's Black Box* and a succinct summary of the arguments most commonly used against Behe in particular and intelligent design in general.

Downing, Barry H. 1968. *The Bible and Flying Saucers*. J. B. Lippincott Co., Philadelphia and New York.

Eigen, Manfred with Ruthild Winkler-Oswatitsch. 1992. *Steps towards Life. A Perspective on Evolution*. (Translation by Paul Woolley) Oxford University Press, New York.

Eldredge, Niles. 2000. *The Triumph of Evolution. And the Failure of Creationism*. W. H. Freeman and Company, New York.

Evenson, William E. & Duane E. Jeffery. 2005. *Mormonism and Evolution: The Authoritative LDS Statements*. Greg Kofford Books, Salt Lake City.

Falk, Dean. 1998. Hominid brain evolution: Looks can be deceiving. *Science*. 280:1714. The point of this one-page article was to note that, in light of recent fossil discoveries, the accepted picture of hominid evolution (specifically, brain size) might have to be changed.

Forrest, Barbara. 2001. The Wedge at work: How Intelligent Design Creationism is wedging its way into the cultural and academic mainstream. *In:* Robert T. Pennock (ed). *Intelligent Design Creationism and its Critics: Philosophical, Theological, and Scientific Perspectives*. A Bradford Book, The MIT Press, Cambridge (MA) and London. pp. 5–53.

Futuyma, D. J. 1986. *Evolution*. Sinauer Associates, Sunderland, MA.

Gardner, Martin. 2000. *Did Adam and Eve Have Navels?* W. W. Norton & Company, New York.

Gershenson, A., J. A. Schauerte, L. Giver, and F. H. Arnold. 2000. Tryptophan phosphorescence study of enzyme flexibility and unfolding in laboratory-evolved thermostable esterases. *Biochemistry* 39:4658–665.

Gingerrich, Philip D.; Munir ul Haq, Iyad S. Zalmount, Intizar Hussain Khan, and M. Sadiq Malkani. 2001. Origin of whales from early artiodactyls: Hands and feet of Eocene Protocetidae from Pakistan. *Science* 293:2239–242.

Gore, Rick. 2002 (August). National Geographic Research and Exploration New Find. *National Geographic*. The first forty-four pages in this issue are not numbered. This eight-page article is placed just before page 2, where the first article in the table of contents is listed.

Gosse, Phillip Henry. 1857. *Omphalos: An Attempt to Untie the Geological Knot*. Van Voorst, London.

Gould, Stephen Jay (general ed.). 1993 (reissued in 2001). *The Book of Life*. W. W. Norton & Co., New York & London.

Gould, Stephen Jay. 2001. The Panda's thumb. *In* Robert J. Pennock (ed). *Intelligent Design Creationism and its Critics: Philosophical, Theological, and Scientific Perspectives*. A Bradford Book, The MIT Press, Cambridge (MA) and London. pp. 669–76.

Grant, Peter R. 1991 (October). Natural selection and Darwin's finches. *Scientific American*. 265:82–87.

Guterl, Fred. 2002. All in the Family. *Newsweek*, July 22, 2002, p. 46–49.

Harder, Ben. 2002. Water for the rock? Did Earth's oceans come from the heavens? *Science News* 161(Mar):184–86. Spectral observations of isotope ratios in comets Halley, Hyakutake, and Hale-Bopp have led several planetary scientists to question details of Delsemme's scenarios. An extra-terrestrial source of organics still seems plausible, however.

Harris, Henry. 1999. *The Birth of the Cell*. Yale University Press, New Haven and London. This is a fascinating book, telling how the cell doctrine was developed over a period of several decades. It is a history that is surprisingly different from the way it appears in standard biology textbooks.

Hazen, Robert M. 2001 (April). Life's rocky start. *Scientific American* 284:76–85.

Hey, Tony and Patrick Walters. 2003. *The New Quantum Universe*. Cambridge University Press, Cambridge.

Hopkins, Richard R. 1998. *How Greek Philosophy Corrupted The Christian Concept of God*. Horizon Publishers, Bountiful, Utah.

Hoppert, Michael and Frank Mayer. 1999. Prokaryotes. *American Scientist* 87:518–23. This excellent summary outlines the high degree of subcellular organization in prokaryotes.

Horgan, John. 1991 (Feb.). In the beginning. . . . *Scientific American* 264:116–25. This is an excellent summary of work in the field of the origin of life, hardly out of date after more than a decade.

Horowitz, Norman H. 1945. On the evolution of biochemical syntheses. *Proceedings of the National Academy of Science* 31:153–57.

Hoyle, Fred and Chandra Wickramasinghe. 1981. *Evolution from Space.* J. M. Dent & Sons, London.

Huber, Claudia and Günter Wächtershäuser. 1998. Peptides by activation of amino acids with CO on (Ni, Fe)S surfaces: Implications for the origin of life. *Science* 281:670–72. (See also perspective by Gretchen Vogel, p. 628–29.)

Hull, D. 1991. The God of the Galapagos. *Nature* 352:485–86.

Jeffrey, Duane E. 1974. Seers, Savants and Evolution: The Uncomfortable Interface. *Dialogue: A Journal of Mormon Thought* 8(3/4):41–75.

Jeffrey, Duane E. and Kieth E. Norman. 2002. Thoughts on Mormonism, Evolution, and Brigham Young University. *Diaglogue: A Journal of Mormon Thought* 35(4):1–18.

Johnson, Phillip E. 1991 (1993, 2nd Ed). *Darwin on Trial.* Regney Gateway, New York.

Johnson, Phillip E. 1995. *Reason in the Balance. The Case Against Naturalism in Science, Law & Education.* InterVarsity Press, Downers Grove, Illinois.

Jukes, Thomas H. 1966. *Molecules and Evolution.* Columbia University Press. New York and London.

Kauffman, Stuart A. 1993. *The Origins of Order: Self-Organization and Selection in Evolution.* Oxford University Press, New York.

Kauffman, Stuart. 1995. *At Home in the Universe. The Search for the Laws of Self-Organization and Complexity.* Oxford University Press, New York & Oxford.

Kauffman, Stuart. 2000. *Investigations.* Oxford University Press, New York & Oxford.

Kettlewell, H. B. D. 1959 (March). Darwin's missing evidence. *Scientific American* 200:48–53.

Klawans, Harold L. 1983. Huntington's Chorea. *1983 Medical and Health Annual,* Encyclopædia Britannica, Chicago. pp. 162–74.

Knoll, Andrew H. 2003. *Life on a Young Planet.* Princeton University Press, Princeton & Oxford. Although the specific ages for the earth are being questioned, there is agreement that life got a relatively early start on Earth.

Lamarck, Jean-Baptiste de Monet, Chevalier de. 1802. *Recherches sur l'organisation des corps vivants* (Researches on the Organization of Living Bodies). 1809. *Philosophie zoologique.* (Zoological Philosophy). It was especially in his 1809 publication that Lamarck proposed the inheritance of acquired traits, citing the famous example of the forelegs and neck of the giraffe.

Larson, Edward J. and Larry Withal. 1999 (Sept.). Scientists and religion in America. *Scientific American* 281:88–93.

Lawlor, David W. 2001. *Photosynthesis, Third Edition.* Springer-Verlag, New York.

Lazarus, D. 1986. *Paleobiology* 12:175–89. This reference is cited by Miller, 1999, p. 45. I have not seen the original paper.

Levinton, Jeffrey S. 1992 (Nov.). The big bang of animal evolution. *Scientific American* 267:84–91.

Liboff, Richard L. 2002. *Introductory Quantum Mechanics, Fourth Edition.* Addison Wesley, San Francisco. I cannot claim to have studied in depth this purely mathematical tome.

Lyell, Charles. 1830–1833. *Principles of Geology.* 3 volumes. Murray, London. Darwin took the first volume with him on the *Beagle* and received other volumes while on the voyage.

Maddox, Brenda. 2002. *Rosalind Franklin: The Dark Lady of DNA.* Harper-Collins, New York.

Margulis, Lynn & Dorion Sagan. 2002. *Acquiring Genomes: A Theory of the Origins of Species.* Basic Books, New York.

Majerus, Michael E. N. 1998. *Melanism: Evolution in Action.* Oxford University Press, Oxford.

Malacinski, George M. and David Freifelder. 1998. *Essentials of Molecular Biology, Third Edition.* (Fourth Edition, Malacinski sole author, 2003) Jones and Bartlett, Boston.

Malthus, Thomas. 1826. *An Essay on the Principle of Population.* 6th ed., 2 vol., Murray. In 1798, Malthus published anonymously the first edition of *An Essay on the Principle of Population as it Affects the Future Improvement of Society, with Remarks on the Speculations of Mr. Godwin, M condorcet, and Other Writers.* The work received wide notice.

Mason, Brian. 1951. *Principles of Geochemistry.* John Wiley & Sons, New York.

McCarty, R. E., Y. Evron, and E. A. Johnson. 2000. The chloroplast ATP synthase: A rotary enzyme? *Annual Review of Plant Physiology Plant Molecular Biology* 51:83–109.

McFadden, Johnjoe. 2000. *Quantum Evolution.* W. W. Norton & Co., New York & London.

Meierhofer, Hans. 1947. *Die Augen auf in unseres Herrgotts Garten!* Fretz & Wasmuth Verlag Ag., Zürich. The book describes the beauties of life during the four seasons with virtually no mention of God except in the title.

Menzel, Donald H. and Ernest H. Taves. 1977. *The UFO Enigma: The Definitive Explanation of the UFO Phenomenon.* Doubleday & Co., Garden City, New York.

Miller, Kenneth R. 1999. *Finding Darwin's God: A Scientist's Search for Common Ground Between God and Evolution.* Cliff Street Books, An Imprint of HarperCollins Publishers. New York.

Morgan, Kendall. 2003. A rocky start: Fresh take on life's oldest story. *Science News* 163:264–66.

Moorhead, P. S. and M.M. Kaplan (eds). 1967. *Mathematical Challenges to the Neo-Darwinian Interpretation of Evolution.* Wismar Institute Press, Philadelphia.

Morison, Frank. 1930. *Who Moved the Stone?* Faber and Faber, London. (My edition was first published in 1958 by Zondervan Publishing House, Grand Rapids.)

Morris, Henry M., and John C. Whitcomb Jr. 1964. *The Genesis Flood. The Biblical Record and Its Scientific Implications.* The Presbyterian and Reformed Pub. Co., Philadelphia.

Numbers, Ronald L. 1992. *The Creationists: The Evolution of Scientific Creationism.* University of California Press, Berkeley.

Ogle, James M., Ditlev E. Brodersen, William M. Clemons Jr., Michael J. Tarry, Andrew P. Carter, and V. Ramakrishnan. 2001. Recognition of cognate transfer RNA by the 30S ribosomal subunit. *Science* 292:897–902.

Oparin, A. I. 1968. *Genesis and Evolutionary Development of Life.* Academic Press, New York. Chapter 3, Formation of the "Primitive Soup," reviews several experiments performed before 1966, when the book was originally published in Russian. This book has an excellent summary of the history of origin-of-life studies including the story of spontaneous generation.

Paley, William. 1802. *Natural Theology; or, Evidences of the Existence and Attributes of the Deity, collected from the Appearances of Nature.* A few passages from Paley are included in: Dennis Richard Danielson (2000, pp. 291–93) and in Appendix B of this volume.

Pennock, Robert T. 1999. *Tower of Babel. The Evidence against the New Creationism.* The MIT Press, Cambridge, Massachusetts.

Petroski, Henry. 1992. The evolution of artifacts. *American Scientist* 80:416–20.

Provine, W. 1988. Evolution and the foundation of ethics. *MBL Science* 3:25–29.

Quastler, Henry. 1964. *The Emergence of Biological Organization.* Yale University Press, New Haven and London.

Raby, Peter. 2001. *Alfred Russel Wallace. A Life.* Princeton Univ. Press, Princeton & Oxford.

Raël, Claude Vorilhon. 1986 (1974). The Book Which Tells the Truth. In *The Message Given to Me By Extra-terrestrials.* AOM Corporation, Tokyo.

Ray, John. 1691. *The Wisdom of God Manifested in the Works of the Creation.*

Rees, Martin. 2000. *Just Six Numbers.* Basic Books, New York.

Ridley, Mark. 2001. *The Cooperative Gene: How Mendel's Demon Explains the Evolution of complex beings.* The Free Press (Simon & Schuster, Inc.), New York. Mark Ridley strongly emphasizes the role of meiosis as being absolutely essential for development of multicellular organisms. "Mendel's Demon" is meiosis, according to Ridley.

Ridley, Matt. 1999. *Genome: The Autobiography of a Species in 23 Chapters.* HarperCollins, New York.

Roberts, Brigham H. 1994a. *The Truth, the Way, the Life.* Edited by Stan Larson with Forwards by Thom D. Roberts and Leonard J. Arrington and Introductions by Sterling M. McMurrin and Erich Robert Paul. Smith Research Associates, San Francisco. In Chapter XXX, Roberts presents his scriptural interpretations that led to his theory of a cataclysmic cleansing before Adam was placed on the earth.

Roberts, Brigham H. 1994b. *The Truth, the Way, the Life.* Edited by John W. Welch with some 14 articles, by several authors, on various topics related to Roberts's manuscript. BYU Studies, Provo, Utah. In Chapter 30, Roberts presents his scriptural interpretations that led to his theory of a cataclysmic cleansing before Adam was placed on the earth.

Robertson, Michael P. and Stanley L. Miller. 1996. An efficient prebiotic synthesis of cytosine and uracil. *Nature* 375:772–74.

Russell, Michael. 2006 (January–February). First Life. *American Scientist* 94 (1):32–39.

Salisbury, Frank B. 1965. *Truth: By Reason and By Revelation.* Deseret Book, Salt Lake City.

Salisbury, Frank B. 1967. The Scientist and the UFO. *BioScience* 17:15–24.

Salisbury, Frank B. 1969. Natural selection and complexity of the gene. *Nature* 224:342–43.

Salisbury, Frank B. 1971. Doubts about the modern synthetic theory of evolution. *The American Biology Teacher* 33:335–338, 354.

Salisbury, Frank B. 1974a. Recent developments in the scientific study of UFOs. *BioScience* 25(8):505–12.

Salisbury, Frank B. 1974b. *The Utah UFO Display: A Biologist's Report.* Devin-Adair, Old Greenwich, CT.

Salisbury, Frank B. 1974c. Letter to the editor; reply by M. W. Strickberger. *BioScience* 24:6–8.

Salisbury, Frank B. 1976. *The Creation.* Deseret Book, Salt Lake City.

Salisbury, Frank B. 1997. James Frederick Bonner 1910–1996. *Biographical Memoirs.* National Academy Press, Washington, D.C. 73:100–123.

Sayre, Anne. 1975. *Rosalind Franklin and DNA.* W. W. Norton, New York & London.

Sepkoski, J. John, Jr. 1993 (reissued in 2001). Foundations: Life in the Oceans. In Stephen Jay Gould (ed.). *The Book of Life.* W. W. Norton & Co., New York, pp. 37–63. This is a beautiful book (256 large-format pages), lavishly illustrated, mostly with color paintings but also with some black & white, summarizing in detail what is known from fossils about the parade of life on Earth since its beginnings (but emphasizing mostly *animal* life; only occasional references to plants). The chapter cited here gives an excellent overview of what is known of Earth's history before the Cambrian, and then during the Cambrian explosion. That period represents 88 percent of Earth's history.

Shapiro, Robert. 1986. *Origins: A Skeptic's Guide to the Creation of Life on Earth.* Summit Books, New York.

Shapiro, Robert. 1999. *Planetary Dreams: The Quest to Discover Life beyond Earth.* John Wiley & Sons, New York.

Shapiro, Robert. 2000. A replicator is not involved in the origin of life. *IUBMB Life* 49:173–76.

Sheehan, William & Stephen James O'Meara. 2001. *Mars: The Lure of the Red Planet.* Prometheus Books, New York.

Simpson, Sarah. 2003 (April). Questioning the oldest signs of life. *Scientific American* 288:70–77.

Smith, John Maynard. 1969. Natural selection and the concept of a protein space. *Nature* 225:563–64.

Smith, John Maynard and Eörs Szathmáry. 1999. *The Origins of Life: From the Birth of Life to the Origin of Language.* Oxford University Press, Oxford. This book is another excellent summary of current theories.

Smith, Joseph Fielding. 1954. *Man: His Origin and Destiny.* Deseret Book, Salt Lake City.

Stephens, Trent D., D. Jeffrey Meldrum, with Forrest B. Peterson. 2001. *Evolution and Mormonism: A Quest for Understanding*. Signature Books, Salt Lake City.

Spetner, L. M. 1970. Natural selection versus gene uniqueness. *Nature* 226:948–49.

Stone, Irving. 1980. *The Origin, a Biographical Novel of Charles Darwin*. Doubleday & Company, New York.

Stickberger, Monroe W. 1973. Evolution and religion. *BioScience* 23:417.

Stock, Daniela, Andrew G. W. Leslie, and John E. Walker. 1999. Molecular architecture of the rotary motor in ATP synthase. *Science* 286:1700–705. (Perspective by Robert H. Fillingame, Molecular rotary motors, pp. 1687–688.)

Strobel, Lee. 1998. *The Case for Christ: A Journalist's Personal Investigation of the Evidence for Jesus*. Zondervan, Grand Rapids.

Strobel, Lee. 2004. *The Case for a Creator: A Journalist investigates Scientific Evidence that Points Toward God*. Zondervan, Grand Rapids, Michigan 49530.

Stokes, William Lee. 2001. David O. McKay's Position on Evolution. *In* Sterling B. Talmadge (Stan Larson, ed). 2001. *Can Science be Faith Promoting*, Blue Ribbon Books, Salt Lake City. pp. xli–xliii.

Talmadge, Sterling B. (Stan Larson, ed). 2001. *Can Science be Faith Promoting*, Blue Ribbon Books, Salt Lake City. This book provides much in-depth insight into the counter position on evolution among some of the General Authorities, various scientists, and others. In addition to the text by Talmadge, there are essays by David H. Bailey, William E. Evenson, William Lee Stokes, and Stan Larson. Especially valuable are letters written by Heber J. Grant, Joseph Fielding Smith, James E. Talmadge (the author's father), and John A. Widtsoe.

Tegmark, Max. 2003 (May). Parallel Universes. *Scientific American* 288:41–51.

Tegmark, Max and John Archibald Wheeler. 2001 (February). 100 Years of quantum mechanics. *Scientific American*. 284:68–75.

Tort, Patrick (translated from the French by Paul G. Bahn). 2000. *Darwin and the Science of Evolution*. Harry N. Abrams, Inc., New York. This small book is filled with illustrations, many in color.

Travis, John (reporter). 2002. Channel surfing: Atomic-resolution snapshots illuminate cellular pores that control ion flow. *Science News* 161:152–54.

Tunnicliffe, Verena. 1992. Hydrothermal-vent communities of the deep sea. *American Scientist* 80:336–49. This article describes some of the organisms in the vent communities.

Vernadsky, Vladimir I. 2006. *Essays on Geochemistry* and *The Biosphere*. (Translated by Olga Barash, scientific editor F. B. Salisbury) Synergetic Press, Santa Fe, New Mexico. These two volumes were written in Russia during the 1920s and 1930s. Vernadsky had deep insights into how our biosphere functions; he was especially aware of the role of "green matter."

Von Däniken, Erich. 1968. *Chariots of the Gods: Unsolved Mysteries of the Past.* G. P. Putnam's Sons, New York.

Wächtershäuser, Günter. 2000. Life as we don't know it. *Science* 289:1307–308. This is a brief summary of Wächtershäuser's ideas with references to earlier literature. Details of Wächtershäuser's theory were published in various journals including several issues of the *Proc. of the National Academy of Sciences, USA* (e.g., 87:200–04; 89:8117–120; 91:6721–728), which I have not seen. I found an excellent review of the theory (albeit in German) by Julius Rabl at http://www.julius-rabl.de/leben/wachter.html

Wallace, Alfred Russel. 1858. *Proc. Linnean Soc. of London* 3, no. 19:53–62.

Watson, James D. 1968. *The Double Helix*. Atheneum, New York. (I have a 2001 version published by Touchstone, New York.) The book is fascinating reading but has long been controversial because of its treatment of Rosalind Franklin. See: Maddox, 2002; and Sayre, 1975.

Wells, Jonathan. 2000. *Icons of Evolution: Science or Myth? Why Much of What We Teach About Evolution Is Wrong.* Regnery Publishing, Inc., Washington, D.C. Wells, an intelligent-design creationist claims that the newest findings are often left out of most modern biology text books. His review of the literature relating to his "icons" presents both sides in much detail—although his biases are intentionally obvious.

Whittaker, Robert H. and P. P. Feeny. 1971. Allelochemics: Chemical interactions between species. *Science* 171:757–70.

Wilson, E. O. 1978. *On Human Nature*. Harvard University Press, Cambridge, MA.

Wise, Donald U. 1998. Creationism's geologic time scale. *American Scientist* 86:160–73. This is an excellent refutation of the young-earth creationists' strange flood geology.

Wolpert, Lewis; Rosa Beddington, Thomas Jessell, Peter Lawrence, Elliot Meyerowitz, & Jim Smith. 2002. *Principles of Development, 2nd Edition.* Oxford University Press, Oxford & New York.

Yusupov, Marat M., Gulnara Zh. Yusupova, Albion Baucom, Kate Lieberman, Thomas N. Earnest, J. H. D. Cate, and Harry F. Noller. 2001. Crystal structure of the ribosome at 5.5 Å resolution. *Science* 292:883–96.

INDEX

A

Absolute zero, 52
Achenbach, Joel: on molecular
  evolution, 129
Actin filaments, 60–61, 62, 80
Adaptations: advantageous, 43;
  chemical, 104; with little survival
  value, 44–45, 47
ADP, (adenosine diphosphate), 151,
  207, 213–14
Age of reproduction, 43–44, 47
AIDS (see HIV)
Alper, Joe, 117
Alternation of generation in plants,
  78–79, 82
Altman, Sidney: on the RNA world,
  120
Alvin, 117–18
American Scientist magazine, 137
Amino acid chains: active sites,

52–53, 54, 67, 69, 79, 83, 88–89,
  91–92, 93–94, 97–98, 100–01,
  102, 107–08, 119, 131, 214;
  codons, 69–70; folding, 51–52,
  58, 70; groups, 51; peptide bonds,
  50–53, 70, 79, 124, 151; possible
  combinations, 84; role of genes,
  58; sequences, 51–52, 54, 81,
  83, 92, 106–7, 139, 159–61;
  translation, 69, 81
Analogous structures, 27–28, 46
*Ancestor's Tale: A Pilgrimage to the
  Dawn of Evolution, The*, 146
Archaea, 50, 55, 118
Aristotle, 3
Arnold, Francis H.: on improving
  enzymes, 89, 91
Arrhenius, Svante: on panspermia,
  139, 143
At Home in the Universe, 127–28

ABOUT THE AUTHOR

Frank Boyer Salisbury grew up in Springville and Salt Lake City, Utah. After a year in the Army Air Force, he served as a missionary in Switzerland. As a teenager, he led hikes and taught nature and crafts at two scout camps, where he began a lifelong fascination with biology in general and botany in particular—as well as with all the physical sciences.

After earning bachelor's and master's degrees in botany and biochemistry at the University of Utah, he earned his doctorate in plant physiology and geochemistry in 1955 at the California Institute of Technology. After teaching ecology, general biology, and other subjects at Pomona College for one year, he spent eleven years at Colorado State University before moving in 1966 to Utah State University to become the department head of the newly organized Plant Science Department in the College of Agriculture. He resigned as department head after four years to spend more time writing, continuing at Utah State for a total of thirty-one years.

He has written or cowritten fourteen books, including a basic text in plant physiology that went through four editions and was translated into several languages. His two books on science and religion are *Truth: by Reason and by Revelation* and *The Creation*. His research projects have involved the physiology of flowering, plant growth under snow, plant growth in controlled environments (to provide food and oxygen for astronauts), and plant responses to gravity. He led a project to grow wheat in the Russian space station *Mir*. He spent sabbaticals in Germany, Austria, and Israel (at the Hebrew University of Jerusalem). He also took a leave of absence for a year with the Atomic Energy Commission (now DOE).

Frank retired in 1997, and with his present wife, Mary Thorpe, served in the Ohio Columbus Mission. The couple then returned to live in Salt Lake City, where Frank has since been working on writing projects. He and his former wife, L. Marilyn Olson, are the parents of seven children.